D1141015

THE PLACE OF THE
UNDERGRADUATE CURRICULUM
IN SOCIAL WORK EDUCATION

The Place of the Undergraduate Curriculum in Social Work Education

HERBERT BISNO

VOLUME II

A Project Report of the Curriculum Study
Werner W. Boehm, Director and Coordinator

COUNCIL ON SOCIAL WORK EDUCATION
345 EAST 46TH STREET, NEW YORK 17, N. Y.

Copyright ©, 1959
by the
COUNCIL ON SOCIAL WORK EDUCATION
INCORPORATED
Library of Congress Catalog Number: 59-12413

60
Printed in the United States of America
by H. Wolff Book Manufacturing Co., Inc.

PANEL PARTICIPANTS

The affiliations listed are those of the participants at the time of panel membership.

Chairman

William J. McGlothlin
Southern Regional Education Board
Atlanta, Georgia

Margaret E. Adams
National Association of Social
  Workers
New York, New York

John J. Baldi
University of Scranton
Scranton, Pennsylvania

Sophie T. Cambria
Hunter College
New York, New York

Ernest B. Harper
School of Social Work
Michigan State University
East Lansing, Michigan

Jane G. Judge
Sarah Lawrence College
Bronxville, New York

John J. Keppler
State Department of Social Welfare
New York, New York

Bernice Madison
San Francisco State College
San Francisco, California

Margaret B. Matson
Pennsylvania State University
University Park, Pennsylvania

Coyle E. Moore
Graduate Program in Social Work
School of Social Welfare
Florida State University
Tallahassee, Florida

John J. O. Moore
School of Social Work
McGill University
Montreal, Quebec, Canada

Mereb E. Mossman
Woman's College
University of North Carolina
Greensboro, North Carolina

William G. Nagel
New Jersey State Reformatory
Bordentown, New Jersey

M. Edwin Nuetzman
Division of Social Work
University of North Dakota
Grand Forks, North Dakota

Egon Plager
St. Bernardine of Siena College
Loudonville, New York

Eleanor K. Taylor
School of Social Work
State University of Iowa
Iowa City, Iowa

Esther E. Twente
Graduate Department of Social Work
University of Kansas
Lawrence, Kansas

Harold E. Wetzel
Department of Social Work
University of Kentucky
Lexington, Kentucky

Helen W. Worstell
Ohio University
Athens, Ohio

Project Director

Herbert Bisno, M.S.W.
Department of Sociology
University of Oregon
Eugene, Oregon

PUBLISHER'S NOTE

Board Policy

This project report of the Curriculum Study is published in accordance with the policy adopted by the Board of Directors of the Council at its meeting on October 9–11, 1958. The policy adopted provides that:

The content of Curriculum Study reports are the responsibility of the Curriculum Study staff;

These reports will be published by the Council as submitted to it by the Study staff and given the widest possible distribution;

The Council, through all possible channels, shall encourage thorough consideration and discussion of the findings and recommendations and their implications for social work education and practice.

The Board decided further that:

Publication and distribution of the Curriculum Study reports does not imply Council acceptance of the findings or recommendations;

Implementation of any of the recommendations of the Study can come only after the field has had full opportunity to consider the reports, the appropriate bodies of the Council have considered and recommended action which would modify or change existing policies and standards.

The Board sincerely hopes that the many challenging questions which the Study presents will be given the mature, deliberate and objective consideration they merit and which characterize the true profession.

The Board wishes to register on behalf of the Council its sincere appreciation to the Study staff whose dedicated service brought the Curriculum Study to a successful conclusion.

The thirteen volumes of the Curriculum Study have been numbered to facilitate reference and identification. The comprehensive report has been numbered Volume I, the report on undergraduate education because of its comprehensive nature has been numbered Volume II. The other volumes have been numbered in alphabetical order by title as follows:

VOL.

Acknowledgments

The Board is pleased to make public acknowledgment of its appreciation to the following foundations and organizations whose grants made possible the financing of this Curriculum Study:

FIELD FOUNDATION

ITTLESON FAMILY FOUNDATION

NATIONAL INSTITUTE OF MENTAL HEALTH, DEPARTMENT OF HEALTH, EDUCATION, AND WELFARE

NATIONAL TUBERCULOSIS ASSOCIATION

NEW YORK FUND FOR CHILDREN

OFFICE OF VOCATIONAL REHABILITATION, DEPARTMENT OF HEALTH, EDUCATION, AND WELFARE

ROCKEFELLER BROTHERS FUND

Although all projects of the Curriculum Study were interdependent and each contributed to the others and to the comprehensive report—and the staff worked as a team under one director—certain grants were more particularly earmarked for designated projects. Special appreciation is accordingly expressed to the NEW YORK FUND FOR CHILDREN whose contribution made this report of the Curriculum Study possible.

In addition to grants from these organizations, the Council on Social Work Education made substantial contributions from its own funds.

—Ernest F. Witte

New York, New York   *Executive Director*

May, 1959   *Council on Social Work Education*

Preface

This comprehensive three-year study of curriculum in the education of social workers has been completed under the auspices of the Council on Social Work Education. It has comprised twelve separate projects, one of which is reported in the following pages.

The twelve individual project reports are published separately by the Council to meet the needs of social work educators and practitioners whose interest is especially concentrated in the subject matter of one or more of the projects. No single report, however, can be understood in its proper relation to the whole study without reference to the comprehensive report, *Objectives for the Social Work Curriculum of the Future,* in which the findings and recommendations of the total study are presented. The various project directors worked together as a staff under the over-all guidance of Dr. Werner W. Boehm, Director and Coordinator of the Curriculum Study. Their goal was not only to develop desirable educational objectives for each project's particular area of the curriculum or suggested by particular considerations of practice, but, in addition, to do so in a way that would merge them all into a total educational experience.

Each project was designed to fit into a master plan for the study of the total curriculum. The findings and recommendations of each are relevant to those of the whole Study and have in turn been influenced by all other projects. To be understood, each report must therefore be considered in relation to the comprehensive report, which it supplements by supplying details for the particular area of the social work curriculum.

WHY THE STUDY WAS UNDERTAKEN

Many issues facing social work education were identified in the Hollis-Taylor Report of 1951.[1] It confirmed that the great preponderance of persons engaged in social work activities were still without professional education. It raised such questions as:

Does social work have a well-defined and identified function?

Does it possess a systematic body of knowledge, skills and attitudes in the various areas of social work practice?

Is the content of social work education sufficiently well developed so that it can be transmitted, and is it of such caliber that it can be included properly as a professional discipline within a university?

Progress toward answering these questions was made by the adoption of the Council's Curriculum Policy Statement in 1952, but further study was indicated. Social work education had also to face other issues:

How could it meet the greatly increased need for social work personnel?

How best could it train for a professional practice still in the process of rapid change and development? Can it be broad enough in scope to enable social workers to function in fields just emerging as well as those already established? Will breadth of education to encompass all fields of professional practice result in dilution of competence for specific fields?

How could it inculcate qualities of leadership and statesmanship while at the same time training for competence in specific practice?

Should undergraduate education serve primarily as a basis for graduate training or also prepare personnel for certain social work positions?

The Study considered that materials from which answers to all these questions might emerge would be obtained by focusing upon

[1] Ernest V. Hollis and Alice L. Taylor, *Social Work Education in the United States* (New York: Columbia University Press, 1951).

fundamental questions of curriculum planning and not by piece-meal consideration of the specific questions posed. In education for social work as for other professions, the fundamental considerations in curriculum planning apply, as presented succinctly by Dr. Ralph W. Tyler.[2] Paraphrased for purposes of this study they are:

What are the desirable educational objectives for professional education?

What learning experiences should be selected and devised and how organized, to realize these objectives?

What are the effective means of evaluating whether the objectives have been attained?

Without a clear formulation of the objectives of social work education, that is, the knowledge, skills and attitudes students are expected to acquire, it becomes impossible to plan the learning experiences needed or to evaluate their success. Consequently, the Curriculum Study singled out as its major task identification of the desirable objectives of social work education.

Also, in accordance with Dr. Tyler's definition, each project framed its educational objectives in terms of both the *content* to be covered and the kind and quality of *behavior* to be expected from the student in relation to the content. For example, "familiarity" with a certain area of content becomes distinguishable from behaviors involving more complex manipulations or deeper "understanding" of content at other levels of student learning.

HOW THE STUDY WAS CARRIED ON

The individual projects of the study fell into the following major areas:

1. Specific curriculum areas—projects devised to examine the curriculum in the areas identified by the Curriculum Policy Statement of 1952: Human Growth and Behavior, the Social

2 Ralph W. Tyler, *Basic Principles of Curriculum and Instruction* (Chicago: The University of Chicago Press, 1950).

Services, Social Work Methods (casework, group work, community organization, research, administration).

2. Selected fields of practice—projects devised to study elements of practice in rehabilitation, public social services, and corrections.
3. Undergraduate education for social work.
4. Content on social work values and ethics found throughout the curriculum.

Each project was planned to identify educational objectives in existing curricula; to formulate a series of desirable objectives, the desirability of which was determined by judging their importance, consistency and compatibility with a statement of the nature and function of social work; and to review the objectives in the light of educational theory as to the possibility of their being learned in the time and conditions available. Project directors had consultation and assistance from specially selected panels of educators and practitioners in social work and related disciplines.

WHAT THE STUDY HOPES TO ACCOMPLISH

Responsibility for planning and constructing curriculum belongs basically to the social work schools and departments. As a group they have already come far toward definition of common educational goals for the profession and of content all curricula must have to reach such goals. The Curriculum Study is expected to provide guides for the resolution of the major issues and common questions that it is anticipated will arise in the curriculum planning of all member schools and departments of the Council on Social Work Education.

Author's Foreword

This project received valuable assistance from many people and organizations. It benefited greatly from the stimulation and suggestions offered by Werner W. Boehm, Director and Coordinator of the Curriculum Study, and the other members of the Study staff. The writer is especially grateful to these colleagues for their willingness to give serious consideration to all proposals emanating from the project, even the disconcerting ones, and expresses particular appreciation to Mary R. Baker for her exceptionally knowledgeable editorial assistance. If, however, this monograph lacks clarity, despite unlimited assistance the writer takes full responsibility.

The project director was fortunate in being able to draw upon the thinking of a highly qualified advisory panel, whose members examined the data and recommendations put before them with a high degree of objectivity and in a spirit of exceptional cooperativeness. The chairman, William J. McGlothlin, was of inestimable help throughout the course of the project.

The task of the director was greatly eased by the wealth of experience and understanding brought to the inquiry by his two consultants, Dean Mereb E. Mossman and Professor Harold E. Wetzel. In addition, Dean Mossman generously undertook a research assignment for the project, reported in Appendix A. The director is also deeply indebted to the staff members of the Council on Social Work Education for their general helpfulness and, specifically, for their dedication to the integrity of the Study.

It is hard to see how the project could have been brought to fruition without the creative competence and fidelity of Sylvia Knopp and Lila Leibowitz, research assistants for the Curriculum Study, and Shirley Berkowitz, secretary-in-chief. They served the project capably and devotedly and played a vital part in its completion. The ability and helpfulness of Eve Schoenberger during the period of her participation also made an important contribution.

Among others whose services significantly aided the project were Bernice Dammond, Betty Rodriguez, Dorothy Vestecka, Ruth McCormick, and Adele Mayer. And without the thinking and cooperation of social work educators throughout the country this report would not have come into being. The writer is also indebted to the University of Oregon for having granted him an extended leave of absence.

In view of the likelihood of much sin having crept into this report despite good intentions and excellent advice, the writer must acknowledge that responsibility for all sins of commission and omission is his, and his alone.

Finally, it should be stated that of all the assistance given, none has been more helpful than the cheerful acceptance of a continuing nomadic existence by his wife, Ziona, and his children, Judy and Larry.

Contents

CHAPTER I

Introduction

As one part of the comprehensive Curriculum Study the under-graduate project is a reflection of those same social forces and un-resolved problems responsible for the initiation of the Study as a whole. But there is a central educational question to which the undergraduate project is most specifically related.

This question is: What should be the function, content and organization of undergraduate education in the training of social workers?

The persistent and provocative problems underlying this ques-tion have importantly affected the entire range of social work edu-cation and practice. A series of controversies relating to the subject of undergraduate education have alternately simmered and boiled for over twenty years. Fortunately, this has not been just a period of fruitless "stewing." Progress has been made in identifying the points of contention and exploring some of the suggested resolu-tions. Furthermore, while the debate continued (and because of it) diverse programs of undergradaute education for social work were put into effect. Although most of these developments have not been subjected to a controlled evaluation, the day by day operations of such programs have served to provide data for those engaged in an examination of this facet of social work education.

Implicit in the undertaking of the Undergraduate Project was the belief that the time was ripe for coming to grips with the ques-tion of the desirable function and content of undergraduate edu-cation for social work. This conviction was not based simply on fragmentary reports of experimental programs being tried out in a number of institutions of higher learning. There were other more solid reasons for believing that the time was at hand (or even past due) for a systematic study of the relation of undergraduate education to the entire process of social work education. Produc-tive thinking on the subject had been taking place in groups and conferences throughout the country. Several relatively recent studies, ranging from those with limited purposes to the comprehensive Hollis-Taylor Report had generated much interest and thought.[1] The latter study had stimulated important changes within the social work profession. In a very real sense, all these inquiries helped to provide a readiness within the profession for the present project.

Other influences were also at work. There was a general ferment within social work. One aspect of this was a widespread desire within the profession for a thorough reappraisal of professional education and practice. And the possibilities for such inquiry had been greatly enhanced by the emergence of the National Association of Social Workers and the Council on Social Work Education.[2]

Finally, the desire and support for the Undergraduate Project (and for the entire Curriculum Study) was in large measure a response to developments in our society. Some of the more important of these were:

1. The shortage of trained social workers, and difficulty in recruiting students for graduate study.

2. The increased need for social workers in various programs because of demographic factors and increases in certain types of social problems.

3. Criticism of the efficiency and effectiveness of certain types of social work practice and attacks on certain social work values.

4. The pressure for clarification of social work's place in various new or "underdeveloped" fields of practice and of its function, in order to differentiate social work from other disciplines.

5. The reevaluation of education, both general and professional, with emphasis on use of basic science material and on need for research and development of the body of social work knowledge.

6. The relatively limited use of social workers in the making of high level social policy.

1 Ernest V. Hollis and Alice L. Taylor, *Social Work Education in the United States* (New York: Columbia University Press, 1951); Kenneth W. Kindelsperger, *Approach to the Study of the Public Social Services and Its Relationship to Undergraduate Education for Social Welfare* (New York: CSWE, 1956); Bernice Madison, *The Public Assistance Job and the Undergraduate Social Work Curriculum,* The Rosenberg Foundation (San Francisco: 1954). This does not exhaust the list of such studies, but all three have attracted considerable attention. Of course, the most influential national study of social work education in recent years is the Hollis-Taylor Report.

2 Throughout the remainder of this monograph the initials NASW will be used whenever reference is made to the Association and CSWE whenever mention is made of the Council.

THE HISTORICAL PERSPECTIVE

Allusion to the vigorous differences around the question of the proper function, content, and organization of undergraduate education for social work requires introduction to the issues through a brief discussion of certain aspects of the evolution of social work education in the United States.

Social work education shows some of the same sequential patterning characteristic of other professions. Such similarities merit recognition; however, it is equally important to be sensitive to differences among professions in respect to the development of their educational programs. As we shall see, one way in which the particularity of social work's educational problems and solutions stands out is when its educational programs are considered vis-a-vis the actual practice of social work.

Let us first take note of the transitional stages, characteristic of professions in general, through which social work education has moved: from apprenticeship through a more formalized type of vocational training to an educational program situated within the structure of an institution of higher learning.

One is struck by the relative speed of officially sanctioned movement in the latter stages of this transition. In 1898 the pioneer "school" of social work, a six weeks summer school, was founded by the Charity Organization Society of New York. In 1903–1904 the program was transformed into a one-year course of instruction and by 1910 it had become a two-year program. In 1919, the organization which was to become the American Association of Schools of Social Work (AASSW) came into being, and by 1924 it included among its requirements for membership an organized curriculum, a responsible administrator, a course of study of at least one year (full time) and, for new schools, the added requirement of university affiliation.[3]

Although in 1931 social work education was still divided about half and half between schools with graduate and those with under-

---

[3] Hollis and Taylor, *op cit.,* 19. Also see Ernest B. Harper, "The Significance of the Hollis Study of Social Work Education for the Undergraduate Educational Institutions" (Address delivered at the National Conference of Social Work, Atlantic City, May, 1951), typed.

graduate curricula, this situation was changing in the direction of greater uniformity and more emphasis on study at the graduate level. Then, in 1937, a basic and far reaching policy was promulgated by the AASSW. All professional education for social work was to be at the graduate level effective October, 1939.

Did this policy decision, coming as it did within the context of increased social services and personnel shortages, overshoot its mark? We might speculate, of course, on the extent to which the professional model for trained social workers was (and is) the "classical" professions of law and medicine, particularly the latter, and to what extent this influenced the 1937 AASSW decision. Beside the question of the general appropriateness of this model there are also these factors to be noted: the level of education of most social work practitioners when the new policy was enunciated, and the fact that the graduate curriculum was not built upon a pre-professional base in the same way as medicine nor was entrance into professional school before the attainment of the Bachelor's Degree approved of as in law. Although it is extremely difficult to seek out the causal relationships between a single decision and a host of subsequent events, some cautious judgments are offered as to the impact of the 1937 AASSW policy decision:

1. It probably increased professional self-consciousness and upgraded standards in at least certain types of agencies.

2. Among a portion of the general public, and colleagues in some of the other professions, it probably enhanced the position of the social work profession.

3. It provided a high educational target for the training and selection of personnel.

4. It resulted in further professionalization and increased competence for a relatively small group of elite practitioners.

5. It did not accomplish the overall professionalization of the performance of social work functions.

6. It did not result in the professional preempting of the title "social worker" nor of a sphere of activity considered to be social work's alone.

From the vantage point of hindsight the basic sociological weaknesses of the 1937 policy would appear to have been that the social work profession was not able to provide an adequate supply of persons with the recommended education. A standard was created without a corresponding means for its attainment in a reasonable period of time. A theoretical alternative to ensuring an adequate supply of persons with the desired preparation would have been to restrict the performance of social work functions to those persons properly trained. However, this was not a real alternative since social work had neither the desire nor the power to curtail services in this manner (fortunately!).[4]

A number of factors combined to stimulate an organized challenge to the 1937 position of the AASSW. The more important of these were: (1) the shortage of social workers (and the regional differences in respect to the supply of social workers); (2) the disproportionately small number of social workers with full graduate training who sought employment in the public social services; (3) differences in educational philosophy among various state universities and colleges and private institutions (and related regional differences); (4) the investment of universities and colleges in their already established undergraduate programs of social work training; (5) the desire on the part of universities and colleges for employer and graduate school recognition of the students who had completed their undergraduate programs; and (6) student interest in, and the desire for, education for social work at the undergraduate level.

The AASSW was not oblivious of this challenge: In 1938 a special committee on pre-professional education was set up by the AASSW and in 1939 a one-year graduate program leading to a certificate was created. Nevertheless there was a coalescing of some of the dissident schools and in 1942 they started the National Association of Schools of Social Administration (NASSA). In 1948, Ernest Harper, its third president, gave the following description of the goals and program of this association:

> The NASSA is now six years old. It started life at a meeting of the representatives of eleven institutions in the Southwest and has now more than tripled its membership. Originally it was composed of departments offering undergraduate instruction only; now a dozen or

[4] The educational problems, as distinguished from the sociological ones, involved in this decision to put social work education exclusively at the graduate level will emerge in the later analysis of present social work education.

more member schools provide a graduate major and last year six awarded graduate degrees or certificates in social welfare.

The Association began as a regional organization and was established to encourage the development of at least minimum standards of education for social service. It has now become a national agency concerned with meeting the increasing need for personnel with some preparation for the job in numerous public and private welfare fields. It has stood for a broad social sciences background, flexibility in curriculum building, adaptation to regional requirements and existing university structure, and for cooperation with local public welfare departments. It started as a protest movement against what was felt to be an unrealistic and premature insistence upon graduate training, and an over-emphasis upon professional casework as the major technique in social work. Today the NASSA has a more positive approach to training problems. It advocates a broad program of generic education for numerous marginal fields as well as for social work more narrowly defined.[5]

The period of 1942–1948, during which time negotiations went on between the AASSW and NASSA was "marked by considerable conflict and confusion and often by anxiety." [6] The main questions on which these negotiations centered were those dealing with the development, content, and accreditation of undergraduate education for social work. Despite the fact that important differences between the two groups remained, a very considerable narrowing of the gap between their positions took place as a result of the joint deliberations.[7]

The problem of accreditation was a particularly thorny one. Both AASSW and NASSA recognized the disadvantages of multiple accreditation, within the profession and in its relation to employing groups and national accrediting bodies. The lack of a satisfactory resolution of this problem was instrumental in the formation

[5] Ernest B. Harper, "Accomplishments and Aims of the National Association of Schools of Social Administration" (Address delivered at the National Conference of Social Work, Atlantic City, April 19, 1948), typed.

[6] Hollis and Taylor, op. cit., 38–39.

[7] In 1951 Harper had this to say, "By the summer of 1948 there was a definite trend on the part of both groups away from a belief in either a strictly pre-professional curriculum, based on the social sciences and including only a single 'fields' course, or in a semi-professional or technical one toward a point somewhere between these two extremes," Ernest Harper, "The Significance of the Hollis Study of Social Work Education for the Undergraduate Educational Institution," op. cit., 4.

of the National Council on Social Work Education in 1946 [8] and, later, in the undertaking of the Hollis-Taylor study.

Whatever the disagreement within the profession on certain aspects of that study, there is no gainsaying the fact that it made an extremely important contribution deserving careful consideration by any subsequent analyst of social work education. Certainly many of the questions it faced remain as live issues today. The following conclusions of the Hollis-Taylor Report are particularly relevant to the present study of undergradaute education for social work.[9]

1. The definition of professional education should be broad enough to include those aspects of the arts and sciences that are as basic to social work as the medical sciences are to medicine. This means that the model time span of social work education would then become four years (two undergraduate and two graduate) instead of two years and that the doctorate level would extend it to six years. (p. 177)

   a. The profession should officially recognize that the area of undergraduate concentration (major and minor) offered prospective social workers is an organic part of professional education and should not be characterized by the nondescript term "pre-professional." (p. 175)

2. There should be three separate and articulated responsibilities for the undergraduate college in the total process of social work education:

   a. The responsibility for providing a broad integrated program of general education for prospective social workers and for teaching certain basic social welfare content to all students.

   b. The responsibility for providing, in accordance with direction from the profession, semi-professional preparation for social work technicians when and if job analyses of the field of practice and the availability of qualified personnel make it feasible to formulate such programs of education and training.

---

[8] Not to be confused with the present CSWE, the National Council on Social Work Education was set up as a clearing house, coordinating agency, and administrative body concerned with research, conferences and other such educational activities.
[9] The actual wording used in the Hollis-Taylor Report has been retained wherever feasible. The page numbers in parenthesis refer to the Hollis-Taylor Report, *op. cit.*

   c. The responsibility for organizing and teaching a concentration (equivalent to a broad major) in the arts and sciences
   that would be basic to graduate professional study in social
   work or to the more immediate beginnings of a professional
   career in the field. (p. 156)
   3. The type of general education for social workers should not
differ significantly from that given to any other groups of college
students. (p. 395)
   4. The three social work education functions (general, semi-professional and basic professional education) should be undertaken
by undergraduate colleges only after the rudiments of a mutually
satisfactory plan for cooperative work have been devised and
agreed to between cooperating colleges and the social work profession at the national, state and local levels of operation. (p. 186)
   5. An undergraduate concentration in social work should be
broad enough to include selected relevant concepts of the natural
and social sciences and the humanities.
   a. The type of undergraduate concentration envisioned might
   be promoted through offering courses, such as Human
   Growth and Change, that give professional focus to knowledge and attitudes in related areas of learning. (pp. 181–182)
   6. It is not important how many courses carry social work titles.
Rather the important thing is that the courses that constitute the
undergraduate concentration should include the informational,
philosophical and attitudinal components of the concepts that are
important to further professional growth in social work. (p. 209)
   a. The proposed undergraduate concentration should include
   one or more courses of a specific social work character inas-
   much as it constitutes part of the indispensable foundation
   for more advanced social work education. (p. 209)
   7. The undergraduate concentration should not include concepts and experiences that require the intellectual and social
maturation associated with later stages of graduate professional
development. For example, it should not include the teaching of
professional skills or require students to engage in casework and
other professional practice as a learning experience prior to their
undergoing a series of graduated learning experiences that include
both a knowledge and feeling component. At the other extreme an

undergraduate concentration should not include learning of a technical and vocational nature that can be secured more quickly and effectively as on-the-job training in a social work agency or as outcomes of especially designed semi-professional courses of a terminal character for which credit toward college graduation ordinarily is not given. (p. 182)

8. If the social work profession undertakes a program of semi-professional preparation, it would be most in keeping with the traditions of the profession to encourage junior colleges, community colleges, and the type of four-year college that customarily maintains semi-professional programs to offer the instruction. Primary responsibility for outlining the essentials of acceptable pre-professional programs and for maintaining an approved list of educational institutions to offer them should rest with the social work profession. (p. 173)

9. The person selected to give direction to the undergraduate concentration must be more than an orthodox social scientist since he should also have a background of social work education. However, unusual care must be exercised to avoid employing some nondescript social worker who has neither fundamental scholarship nor a professional understanding of what the social work profession envisions as the objectives of the concentration. What is needed is broad but professionally oriented scholarship. (pp. 185–186 and 209)

10. Colleges, collectively and individually, should be the final judge, within their accrediting standards, of the character and extent of the programs they undertake. The social work profession should not coerce them on what is to be taught nor interfere with their right to determine how a program is to be organized and administered. The profession should recognize that college accreditation applies to all the undergraduate programs and is not subject to review by it. A recognition of the authority of the college does not, however, absolve the social work profession of its responsibility for determining the character and quality of the undergraduate concentration or the semi-professional offering in social work education. Colleges, collectively and individually, should accept the leadership of the social work profession in these matters

just as the profession should accept theirs in matters of general education. (p. 186)

11. Primary responsibility belongs to the individual colleges for incorporating the agreed-upon concepts into courses, for arranging courses into meaningful sequences and for making a workable arrangement by which the concentration is to be administered. (p. 185)

It is clear that the Hollis-Taylor Report envisioned a significant change in the pattern of social work education.

CHAPTER II

Focus and Methodology

In order to deal effectively with the general question of the desirable function, content, and organization of undergraduate education in the preparation of social workers, it became necessary to formulate more specific and manageable sub-questions. As formulated in the study plan for the undergraduate project these questions were:

1. What should be the relationship between undergraduate education and graduate social work education?
   a. What should be the criteria for distribution of educational objectives [1] between the undergraduate and graduate levels?
   b. What objectives are appropriate at the undergraduate level?
      1) What content from the sciences and humanities should be incorporated within the undergraduate program for social work and how should it be organized?
      2) What social work content should be incorporated into the undergraduate program for social work and how should it be organized?
2. What should be the relationship between undergraduate education and the practice of social work?
3. What should be the organization of the total undergraduate program for social work?
4. What types of learning experiences are most appropriate at the undergraduate level?

As the Study progressed it became increasingly evident that it was most fruitful to conceive of the entire period of educational

---

[1] The term, objective, is used in this project in accordance with the definition employed by Dr. Ralph W. Tyler in *Basic Principles of Curriculum and Instruction* (Chicago: University of Chicago Press, 1950). It refers to both the kinds of behavior to be developed in the student and the areas of content in which the behavior is to be applied. An example of this usage is the following statement of an objective "to develop an appreciation of diverse sub-cultural patterns." In this statement "appreciation" constitutes the behavior and "diverse sub-cultural patterns," the content area.

preparation for social work as a totality even though it encompassed a number of educational levels.[2] This raised the question as to whether the phrasing of the study issue concerned with distribution of educational objectives between the undergraduate and graduate levels was as useful and appropriate as it might be. Reexamination led to a reformulation of that question: *What should be the criteria for the distribution of educational objectives between the different stages of the program of social work education?*

The important distinction between this phrasing of the question and the previous wording is that the vertical distribution of objectives is now conceived of as being among all the stages of the program of social work education, rather than emphasizing the division between the undergraduate and graduate years.[3] The merit of the reformulation is that the question no longer assumes a given organizational structure such as the one prevalent today which posits the crucial "break" in the educational experience as being between the fourth and fifth years of higher education.

THE FRAME OF REFERENCE

The undergraduate project was conducted within the pattern and frames of reference established for the Curriculum Study in its entirety as these were set forth in the following documents:

1. The Tyler formulation of *Basic Principles of Curriculum and Instruction* which provided a theoretical approach to curriculum analysis and development;

2. The *Plan for the Social Work Curriculum Study* which provided a general design for all projects for the Curriculum Study;

3. The *Statement on the Nature of Social Work* which provided an orienting framework.

[2] The rationale for this position will be spelled out in a later section of this monograph.

[3] By use of the term, stages, we are implying the notion of the sequential building of objectives throughout continuous phases of the program of social work education. In terms of the existing internal organization of institutions of higher learning these phases may be defined as units within a given period (*e.g.*, quarter, semester, etc.) or as identical with such periods.

PROCEDURES

ORIENTATION

To acquaint himself with the available data and present thinking relevant to the focus of the project, the writer surveyed a relatively wide range of written materials dealing with social work and other professions. These materials included books, articles, theses, conference reports, committee minutes, policy statements, and research findings; the more important published items are listed in the bibliography.

The initial examination of available materials provided the project director with an orientation to the subject matter of the inquiry and served as the basis for a preliminary identification of relevant postulates and issues.

ANALYSIS OF PRESENT PATTERNS

On the assumption that a significant step in the process of arriving at a judgment as to desirable educational objectives would be an examination of present programs, Dean Mereb Mossman undertook a study of existing patterns of undergraduate education for social work among institutions which are members of CSWE. The report of Dean Mossman's Study appears as Appendix A.

REQUEST FOR AND ANALYSIS OF CURRENT TEACHING MATERIALS

All the undergraduate institutions holding membership in the CSWE were asked to provide the project with certain materials used in courses related to social work. The requested materials included course outlines and syllabi, related bibliographies, copies of examinations, assignment sheets, and listings of audio-visual aids. As was expected, availability of such materials varied. Systematically analyzed, they served as a major source of data for the project, particularly in identification of objectives.

In addition, a request for a limited set of materials was sent to selected non-member schools in order to broaden the data base of the inquiry. Altogether 72 universities and colleges submitted some materials.

Two questionnaires, copies of which constitute Appendix B, were developed and sent out to the undergraduate members of the CSWE.[4] The field experience questionnaire was designed to elicit information about programs of student observation or participation in the activities of social agencies which were organized by the academic institution as a definite part of their undergraduate social work-oriented education.

The "special" questionnaire was intended to get data about the vocational identification of students enrolled in courses included within the undergraduate programs of social work. It was also used to get information about what the students in such courses do after completing their undergraduate programs.

Completed field experience questionnaires were turned in by 49 colleges and universities while 47 institutions returned filled in "special" questionnaires. The questionnaires had been sent to approximately 100 institutions.

The procedure employed in the identification of postulates and issues is elaborated on in the next section of this chapter.

Relevant professional literature and the teaching materials secured from the schools were examined and the objectives (both content and behavioral components) thus identified were categorized. An important aspect of analyzing the content dimension of the objectives involved the organization as well as identification of relevant content items.

Since the Study staff was unable to discover a set of ready made criteria that would serve sufficiently well as a basis for the distribu-

---

[4] The term "undergraduate members" as used here always refers to academic institutions.

tion of the educational objectives between the various stages of the program of social work education, it was necessary for this project to take primary responsibility for the development of such criteria, presented and discussed in Appendix C. Suggestions for the criteria were derived from the following sources:

1. The postulates of the undergraduate project.
2. Other findings reported on in this document (including problems of learning commented on in various institutions visited by the project director).
3. Suggestions made by social work and other educators.
4. Reports of and practices in other professions.
5. Recommendations of the Advisory Panel for the Undergraduate Project.
6. Statement on *The Nature of Social Work*.
7. Relevant books, articles, etc.
8. Contributions of the other members of the Curriculum Study staff.

FIELD TRIPS

During several field trips the project director conferred with representatives from 35 to 40 schools, and participated in several statewide or area conferences. In addition to the deliberations of the Advisory Panel the director conferred individually, or participated in group meetings with approximately 120 people.[5]

The primary functions of these individual conferences and group meetings were: (1) to secure a fuller understanding of the programs at various schools; (2) to become more familiar with the indigenous circumstances which condition the character of these programs and which broaden or narrow the range of real alternatives; (3) to delve more deeply into the rationale supporting implicit or explicit objectives identified in the offerings of the schools; (4) to get additional suggestions regarding desirable goals, objectives, organizational patterns and learning experiences; (5) to secure reaction to tentative conclusions and recommendations.

[5] These 120 people were employed in the following states: California, Idaho, Michigan, Minnesota, Montana, New Mexico, New York, Ohio, Pennsylvania, Tennessee, Texas and Utah.

The function of the Curriculum Study document, *The Nature of Social Work,* in this project was to provide a framework of orientation which aided the director in deciding on the importance and appropriateness of the identified objectives.

Considerable use is made of postulates [6] throughout this monograph. They were developed by the writer after the survey of relevant literature. A consideration in the choice of postulates was the degree of acceptance likely to be granted them. In other words, an attempt was made to avoid postulating highly controversial propositions that, for the purposes of the project, legitimately constituted issues rather than premises.

The selected postulates were reviewed by the staff of the Curriculum Study and by the project consultants. In addition, they were considered at a meeting of the Advisory Panel. Although no implication is intended that all those who examined the postulates were in complete agreement with them, there did appear to be a high degree of accord as to their acceptability.

It was hoped that the inclusion of a rather considerable number of postulates would at least partially accomplish the following purposes:

1. To make explicit as many of the significant and relevant postulates as possible so as to lessen the masked impact of important but implicit assumptions.

2. To lessen the number of essentially rhetorical questions which might detract from the real issues.

3. To provide a base for later analysis.

This third point requires elaboration. In a study, such as this one, which is concerned with "what ought to be" (*i.e., desirable* objectives) there are particular difficulties in evaluating conflicting conclusions. It is true, of course, that even in taking up questions of desirability empirical data are relevant, since "ought" statements often contain implicit notions about "what is." Also if one

[6] The term here refers to a statement assumed, without proof, to be true and used as a basis for reasoning.

includes as an aspect of desirability a reasonable possibility of attainment in the foreseeable future, empirical data about the present are helpful and even necessary, since the past and present condition the future and impose limits on the range of alternative possibilities. Nevertheless, in themselves, empirical data are unlikely to be sufficient for the resolution of many of the differences centering around the question of desirability. In these cases the weighing of conflicting proposals may be done in terms of one's own judgment, or on the basis of qualitative (expert) or quantitative (large numbers) agreement, or through the use of logical analysis. In this project we have had occasion to use all of these approaches.[7]

It is in regard to the last method, though, that the explication of a set of postulates is particularly vital. For example, one of the steps in the examination of conflicting recommendations is determination whether the advocates of each view started with similar or different assumptions. If the premises are the same then it is sometimes feasible to analyze the line of reasoning, from postulate to conclusion, offered for each position to see if it conforms to the requirements of logical consistency. On the other hand, if it turns out that the differences as to desirable policy rested on a lack of agreement as to basic postulates, then recognition of this fact may help to lessen confusion and might even, though not necessarily, lead to progress through a reexamination of what had been taken for granted.

The reason for belaboring the value of explicit postulates is that in many discussions centering about differences as to what constitutes a desirable course of action reasoned examination of the alternative views is seriously hampered by the "free floating" and often nebulous quality of crucial assumptions which remain implicit. It is our hope that establishing a "postulate base" at the outset will prove helpful in bringing under a greater degree of rational control the evaluation of conflicting positions as to what is desirable.

---

[7] Of course, the ultimate determination of desirability within the frame of reference of the total Study, rested with the project director.

THE ADVISORY PANEL

A feature of the methodology of the Curriculum Study was the cooperation of an Advisory Panel for each project. These panels, composed of persons of unusual competence in the area of the given project's concern, functioned in an advisory capacity. The panel contributed to this project in the following ways:

1. It offered reactions to the various postulates and assisted in raising, clarifying and establishing a priority among issues;

2. It assisted in identifying appropriate objectives and in evaluating the significance of the selected objectives;

3. It assisted in clarifying conflicts between alternative positions and helped in exploration of alternative resolutions of such conflicts;

4. It assisted in the examination of alternative ways of organizing undergraduate education for social work;

5. It reacted to the findings and proposed recommendations and offered suggestions for changes in them.

RELATIONSHIP TO OTHER PROJECTS

The undergraduate project is intimately related to each of the other projects and the basic questions which provide the *raison d'etre* for the total Study apply to it as well as to the other projects. The very fact that the undergraduate project cuts across the other studies makes the interrelationships between it and the others particularly significant. Procedures set up within the Curriculum Study staff provided for both informal and systematic coordination.

LIMITATIONS

Unfortunately, practical limitations effectively precluded a full scale investigation of each of the problem areas within the purview of the undergraduate project. It is hoped that interested persons will undertake research studies in the future that will help to fill in gaps or build upon this project.

CHAPTER III

The Place of the Undergraduate Program in the Education of Social Workers

A PERSPECTIVE ON PROFESSIONS

There is good evidence for the assertion that the professions occupy a particularly important place in the United States and that their effective functioning is of vital concern to the entire society.[1] While there is general acknowledgment of the significance of the professions, there is less certainty as to that configuration of characteristics which sets the professions apart from other types of vocational activities. The consensus seems to indicate that the following are the essential criteria of any profession: (1) it requires an organized body of specialized knowledge; (2) it necessitates special and sometimes protracted study and training of an intellectual and technical nature, capable of being transmitted through a required educational discipline; (3) it demands a high degree of individual responsibility and competence; (4) it has the provision of a necessary and skilled service as its basic purpose; (5) it represents an organized activity involving a plurality of persons performing a similar function according to shared norms; (6) it tends toward self-organization for the promotion of standards of professional competence and the advancement of professional self-interest; and (7) it is expected to demonstrate, as a primary obligation, a responsiveness to the public interest and welfare.[2]

[1] Talcott Parsons, "The Professions and the Social Structure," *Essays in Sociological Theory—Pure and Applied* (Glencoe, Illinois: The Free Press, 1945), 185. While the professions may be treated as a unitary analytical category for some purposes, as in this instance, in other cases this may represent too high a level of generalization and the differences between professions may have to be focused upon.

[2] For a more complete discussion of the characteristic attributes of a profession the reader is referred to Morris L. Cogan, "Toward a Definition of a Profession," *The Harvard Educational Review*, XXIII, 1 (Winter, 1953); A. M. Carr-Saunders and P. A. Wilson, *The Professions* (Oxford: Clarendon Press, 1933); E. T. Hiller, *Social Relations and Structures* (New York: Harper and Brothers, 1947); Parsons, *op. cit.;* and Abraham Flexner, "Is Social Work a Profession?" *Proceedings of the National Conference of Social Work, 1915.*

Although enhancement of the social good and promotion of professional self-interest are characteristics of organized professions, they are not necessarily compatible at all points. One of the crucial points at which considerations of public responsibility and professional self interest *may* come into conflict is in determination of educational standards. The dynamics of the concern of the professions with educational standards are by no means uncomplicated. On the one hand we see clearly the genuine desire for protecting the interests of the society as a whole and, specifically, those of the user of service by an ever-increasing level of competence. On the other hand, we cannot, in good conscience, avert our eyes and fail to notice another set of tendencies at work, tendencies that seem to be most heavily weighted in the direction of professional self-aggrandizement.

In a mood of pseudo-profundity, but with serious intent, we have attempted to express these tendencies in the form of two "laws" (with apologies to Professor Parkinson). The first of these we have named the law of professional velocity:

> The internal dynamics of the process of professionalization result in an upward and onward motion of the profession which is expressed in a continuous pressure toward extending the educational requirements for desired professional statuses irrespective of the absence of public clamor for such professional velocity.

Of course, this is not a law at all but it does convey the sense of a phenomenon that often appears to characterize the developmental process of professions. For example, it is striking that even in periods during which there is extension of programs and shortage of personnel, professions often appear to be more preoccupied with extending educational requirements than with providing greater numbers of workers to man the expanded programs. (This does not, however, keep the professions from seeking expansion of programs utilizing their services.)

The second of our "laws" is the law of professional disassociation:

> As the process of professionalization goes on the professionals proceed to disassociate themselves from the uninitiated, respectfully re-

ferred to as sub-professionals, technicians, aides, the untrained and laymen.

Here again is a tendency that appears in the development of professions. Insofar as this process is a concomitant of that differentiation of functions that occurs with the maturation of a profession it is a useful and socially responsible development. However, this is probably not the only explanation for the disassociative process. In part it appears to be the result of deliberate policies, adopted by various professions, designed to enhance their prestige and public acceptance by means of invidious comparisons with related technician and "sub-professional" groups, and even with other professions. This may be accomplished through the use of symbols such as titles, wearing apparel, and similar devices. Thus, the lines of demarcation between those with the prestige status and those in lesser positions is made clear for all to see. Certainly the emphasis on that which is divisive has at times been socially harmful.

These remarks are not intended to be an iconoclastic assault on, or a churlish depreciation of, the importance and integrity of professions in general and social work in particular. The concern for putting the professions within a realistic perspective is precisely the conviction that they do play an extremely significant part in contemporary society and that they do attempt to be responsive to the public interest. It is relatively harmless to overlook romantic overidealization of things of little moment, but it can be extremely serious when matters of real importance are involved. It is in this sense that our belief in the need for a detached look at social work education can be traced to a passionate conviction as to the vitality of social work and greatness of its potential contribution.

At least one other possible misinterpretation might arise. The writer has pointed out that one cannot necessarily assume complete harmony of interests between the policies of a profession and the general welfare. However, there is no intention to imply the contrary; that everything that promotes the self-interest of the professional is anti-social and indecent. The professional has every justification for pursuing his legitimate interests, including the desire for recognition and approval. Indeed, in many instances there may well be a compatibility between such concern with professional self-interest and social responsibility. We have already stated our belief that in numerous cases the desire for improved educational standards and for differentiation of functions is in the best interests of both the profession and society. The point is that, while the pursuit of professional self-interest, singly or collectively, *may* promote the common good, it does not *necessarily* do so. And it is in just those situations in which a conflict of interest arises that the professional, subject though he may be to the usual human frailties, is called upon to respond with professional self-discipline. In so doing, he adds luster to the meaning of professional.

A MATTER OF EDUCATIONAL PHILOSOPHY AND EDUCATIONAL REALITIES

A study of engineering education begins with these words:

> The most abstract and theoretical of the problems confronting the humanities and social sciences in engineering education is also the most practical. This is the problem . . . of specifying a philosophy upon which programs may be built . . . The conflicts and misunderstandings which bedevil many campuses depend ultimately for their resolution on the working out of an educational philosophy that is mutually acceptable to the engineering and liberal arts faculties and to which both can give their wholehearted support.[3]

So, too, in this study of social work education we find ourselves first confronted by persistent problems of educational philosophy. The postulates which underlie our analysis of these problems are:

1. One of the major responsibilities of higher education is to prepare a body of people ready and competent to perform the tasks which the society needs to get done; hence, the curriculum must bear some general relation to the occupational demands and division of labor in society.

2. It is incompatible with the past and present philosophy of

3 *General Education in Engineering: A Report of the Humanistic Social Research Project* (Urbana, Illinois: The American Society for Engineering Education, 1956), 1.

liberal arts education to have an undergraduate program that is basically oriented along the lines of narrow vocationalism.[4]

3. Education in all industrialized countries with a highly developed division of labor is faced with the problem of the interrelated, but sometimes conflicting, requirements of specialization and integration (*i.e.,* relating specialized parts to each other and to the whole).

QUESTIONS AND CONCLUSIONS

However it might be phrased, a question that a faculty considering the advisability of starting an undergraduate social work program would almost certainly face at the outset would be: Would an undergraduate program that includes specific social work content, and that is viewed as part of the continuous and total process of preparation for social work, appropriately fit within the framework of a liberal arts college?

It is readily apparent that the real difficulty in replying to this question resides in the ambiguity of the concept, liberal arts. Not that it has been left undefined. On the contrary, we suffer from a superabundance of conflicting definitions.[5] Although one suspects that many of the disputants could be disarmed if the vagueness of the concept could be dissipated, yet the question of whether an undergraduate social work program could fit within a liberal arts framework cannot be bypassed simply by pointing out the semantic difficulties. There is an issue of real significance in the question.

The traditional approach to liberal education that has run coun-

---

[4] By *narrow vocationalism* we mean a course or an academic program characterized by a *predominant concentration* upon such as the following: (a) the development of skill in the use of techniques directed toward application in specific job situations, (b) the accumulation of technical information relevant to the future job, (c) description of the nature of the vocation rather than analytically studying the vocation and relating it to other parts of the social order.

[5] Liberal education has been variously defined, often in conflicting terms: "generous, rather than restricted; universal rather than provincial; befitting free men; fit to make men free; an education suitable to men; an education which men and women should share alike; a discipline of the mental faculties; a harmonious development of mind and body; a cultural education; knowledge for its own sake; classical rather than scientific learning; reading a few Great Books rather than many modern ones; education in the arts and sciences; 'liberal' arts rather than 'illiberal'; education for leisure rather than for occupations; general rather than specialized, professional education. And yet, certain professions have been called liberal." Thomas Woody, *Liberal Education for Free Men* (Philadelphia: University of Pennsylvania Press, 1951), 1-2.

ter to the development of undergraduate programs of social work education stresses the importance of education producing "cultured" human beings who love beauty, knowledge and antiquity. Education oriented toward the world of work tends to be considered outside the pale. A modified traditional position may recognize "new" subject areas (such as sociology) and may temper the goal of "universal man" with acceptance of some degree of specialization at the undergraduate level. But the key idea is one of a real distinction between liberal education and education with a professional orientation.

This position has to be examined from both sides. First, is the case for excluding professionally oriented work from the liberal arts college a sound one? Second, are the arguments convincing for treating liberal education and professional education as dichotomous?

The traditional notion of a liberal education fit within a social pattern characterized by a leisured elite and by restriction of the prerogatives of citizenship, and even of freedom, to the relative few. An educational goal of preparing the "universal man" is comprehensible only in terms of the past, of a world without a tremendous accumulation of specialized knowledge and without a highly developed technology.

Despite the changes in society, we have kept away many of the educational trappings of yesteryear and have attempted to preserve the substance of the past as well. Many of us find it hard to accept this commonplace fact of life: that although the Middle Ages spawned the modern university and liberal arts college, the parent failed to survive the progeny.[6]

6 For an amusing and instructive pursuit of this subject, see Howard Mumford Jones, "Education for One World" in *Goals for American Education*, ed. Lyman Bryson, Louis Finkelstein, and R. M. MacIver (New York: Harper and Brothers, 1950), 213–215. After a passage which pointedly and with good humor describes the origins of some of our present academic practices, Professor Jones, himself a professor of English at Harvard, continues:

"A striking fact about medieval education is that it was put together by and for men without women, without families, without individual economic necessities and without any personal responsibility for the welfare of society as we understand the phrase today . . . the individual teacher . . . was under no obligation to prepare anybody to get a job in a fiercely competitive society; to this day the more ancient, respectable, and economically useless departments in American colleges . . . will not admit the obvious fact that colleges prepare students for jobs. For older and more conservative members

Not only is the traditional notion of liberal arts an inappropriate guide to thinking about contemporary educational problems and programs; what is actually taking place in the liberal arts programs of American colleges and universities differs from our idea of it.

1. At the present time only a small minority of college students experience a four-year undergraduate program which is dominated by the purposes and "climate" of a traditional liberal arts education.

2. Many liberal arts colleges and universities provide, as liberal arts offerings, both general education and specialized courses.[7]

3. The specialized offerings of liberal arts departments are increasingly acquiring a vocational orientation, most often of a preprofessional or professional character.[8]

4. Most college students and their parents view undergraduate education as at least a part of their overall preparation for a vocation.[9]

The range of specialized offerings is really rather remarkable. There are important variations among schools but the following course titles, drawn from the catalogs of liberal arts departments in several major universities, may be viewed as illustrative: Archaeological, Advanced Drawing and Painting, Practical Astronomy,

---

of our faculties a liberal education is still a mysterious something that takes place in a timeless and spaceless world of pure intelligence, without boom or bust, without rising prices or falling income, without salaries or taxes, sex or family, illness or retirement, political parties or global warfare."

[7] By *general education courses* are meant courses focused on knowledge, attitudes, values, and abilities which all "liberally" educated college students are expected to possess as essential for the achievement of self-realization and for an understanding of, and ability to cope with, the world about them. By *specialized courses* are meant courses in which the main emphasis is put on content and abilities intended for the person with a particular interest or for the potential specialist.

[8] By *liberal arts departments* are meant those subject matter fields (sometimes referred to as disciplines), which usually have, or share, a departmental identification and which have been customarily, or are now located within the liberal arts college of a university (*e.g.*, chemistry, philosophy, sociology). The typical pattern in the United States is for such departments to offer a "major" and sometimes a "minor" leading to an academic degree (B.A. or B.S., M.A. or M.S., Ph.D.) rather than to a professional or technical degree. It might be noted that liberal arts colleges are losing students, and even departments, to specialized schools within the universities. For a discussion of various of these trends see *Liberal Education*, summary of a discussion by the Trustees of the Carnegie Foundation for the Advancement of Teaching, reprinted from the 1955–1956 Annual Report.

[9] See Wilbur B. Brookover, *A Sociology of Education* (New York: American Book Company, 1955), 46–49.

Immunology, Laboratory in Virology, Microchemical Analysis, Algology, Physical Chemistry, Thermodynamics, Textile Analysis, Dynamic Economics and Business Fluctuations, French Advanced Literary Composition, Petroleum Geology, Theory of Functions, Mathematical Logic, Comparative Physiology, Personality Assessment, Social Psychology of the Interview, Advanced Quantitative Methods in Sociology, Population and Migration, and Nomadic Societies.

Recognition of the present extent of specialization at the undergraduate level is implicit in the setting up of "adapted" or "service" courses, given primarily as a service for students who are majoring in a subject area other than that in which the course is taught. Such a course is specifically oriented toward the interests, knowledge level and purposes of those for whom it is given. Actual examples are: Mathematics for Liberal Arts Students, a Short Survey of Organic Chemistry ("primarily for students not majoring in chemistry") and Survey of Algebra and Analysis ("for upper division and graduate students in social sciences without college training in mathematics").

It should be emphasized that these are courses taken at the undergraduate level within the structure of liberal arts majors. Nor can there be any question but that many of these courses have a vocational orientation, either in the sense of preparing students for employment immediately after the first degree or in the sense of specific preparation for additional training prior to employment.

Ironic contradictions appear in some of the institutions that pride themselves on being liberal arts colleges. We were informed by one school that it no longer offered any social work courses because of the belief that *training* should be in the professional schools rather than in liberal arts colleges. However, perusal of its catalog showed that the student could select any one of the following as a major course of study (this is not an all-inclusive list): Laboratory Technique; Medical Record Library Science; Painting, Drawing, Printmaking, and Sculpture; Merchandising; Personnel Work; Secretarial Studies; Health, Physical Education, and Recreation with Emphasis in Therapeutics; Occupational Therapy (approved by the A. O. T. A. and accredited by the Council on Medical Education and Hospitals of the A.M.A.). In addition, one of the functions of the English major was defined as follows: "Pre-professional training for teaching, journalism, editing, script writing, librarianship, and research." Vocational uses are also cited for other conventional liberal arts majors. Among the undergraduate courses taught in the psychology department of this college are: Tests and Measurements and Child Guidance Clinic.

This is by no means an isolated instance. It is rather an example of the confusion in philosophy and practice in colleges and universities throughout the country; it is also an indication of the gap between the verbal adherence to the traditional concept of a liberal arts education and the realities of present practice.

In summary then, what we see is that despite energetic efforts to perpetuate the traditional conception of a liberal arts education, it has not proved possible for higher education to resist the logic of events.

Vocationally-oriented subject matter (that is, having special and intended pertinence to a particular profession or other occupation) is now incorporated in much of the liberal arts education in this country. We see further that, at least in the case of many institutions, it would be naive to recommend that, *in order to avoid specialization and a vocational orientation,* a student take a regular liberal arts major rather than, let us say, an undergraduate social work program.

We must conclude that the traditional meaning of a liberal education has eroded and is out of harmony with present realities and trends. This in itself would not justify supporting such realities or reinforcing these trends. There is no virtue in change for its own sake or in lightly dismissing traditional beliefs and practices. One can appreciate the concern of Santayana when he wrote, "Ideas are abandoned by virtue of a mere change of feeling without any evidence or new arguments. We do not now refute our predecessors, we pleasantly bid them goodbye."

With real appreciation for the validity of this comment, we take the position that the arguments and evidence do support the following conclusion: *the long-enduring dichotomy between liberal arts and professional education is unwise and should be modified.*

What are some of the undesirable consequences that stem from attempts to maintain the dichotomy?

A lack of harmony between appearance and substance in higher education. As we have already seen, appearances are often deceiving in contemporary higher education. The fiction that a liberal arts education has nothing directly to do with professional preparation can scarcely disguise the widespread existence of the vocational component.

There is clearly no basis for anticipating a return to a medieval world, in education or in any other realm. We must face the fact of no return and confront the realities head on.

A destructive gulf exists between liberal arts and professional education, to the detriment of both. A creative rapprochement will result in gains for each.

> The most persistent and troublesome of all the problems is the deep chasm that separates the academic community from the professional educators in many of our universities. This problem is accentuated by the reluctance on both sides to admit that it exists and that it will not be solved until it is faced squarely and traced to its origins.[10]

A lessening of the reciprocal contribution between the liberal arts and professional education. One of the conspicuous ironies in erecting high walls between the liberal arts and professional education is the self-defeating consequences of such action. Policies based on the perception of professional education as an interloper tend to result in the relative isolation of professional education. This usually eventuates in a more technical approach in the professional schools, bereft as they are of the direct impact of the liberal arts. (Striking cases in point are the hospital schools of nursing and the typical teachers' college. The trend is clearly away from this pattern in both of these professions.)

The most important error is the failure to see that, like a self-fulfilling prophecy, the separating of such schools virtually *insures* that they will stress method and technique at the expense of understanding. Obviously, the most effective way to prevent this is to create a structural and functional relationship through which the

10 Paul Woodring, *New Directions in Teacher Education* (New York: The Fund for the Advancement of Education, 1957), 78.

liberal arts disciplines can assist in liberalizing professional (and other types of vocational) education. The development of an intellectual tradition and emphasis occurs over a period of time and this process is hastened as apprenticeship and trade schools give way to university-centered training. The liberal arts also suffer by isolation from the professions. They do not have the influence they should have on professional education, and some of the basic disciplines miss the useful "feedback" that would be more readily available to them if they had a closer relationship with the professional consumers of their theories and findings. The liberal arts disciplines, particularly the humanities, tend to develop an unfortunate and undeserved reputation for being "useless," of little "practical" value, and of refusing to face the "real world." This adds to the strong anti-intellectual bias in our culture which isolates theory from practice, and values the latter more. Finally, attempts to maintain impermeable barriers between liberal and professional education contribute to an extremely dangerous distinction between thinkers and actors. Obviously, contemporary civilization is in desperate need of thinkers who act and actors who think. In the words of John Dewey:

> A truly liberal and liberating education would refuse to isolate vocational training on any of its levels from a continuous education in the social, moral, and scientific contexts within which wisely administered callings and professions must function.[11]

A possible lack of focus and motivation in the students. It is the writer's impression, based both on his talks with other educators and on his own experiences in teaching and advising, that relatively few students delay their vocational choices because of a commitment to a classical type of liberal education. Rather the student (particularly the upper division student) who is taking a wide range of elective courses without organizing them in terms of an educational or vocational goal is usually "shopping around," and lacks clarity about his life goals.[12] Furthermore, as Howard Mum-

11 Quoted in Woody, *op. cit.,* 266.
12 This is probably not equally the case in those atypical institutions, usually private schools with relatively small but financially well off student bodies (often mainly or entirely composed of women students).

ford Jones suggests, the years devoted to taking a large variety of general education courses may be characterized by a breadth of exposure but this does not mean they are "broadening." He goes on to say "it is wonderful how, when the individual establishes such a goal, [professional or vocational] education comes into focus." [13]

Several schools reported that the students who seemed to get the least out of their schooling were those without a determined vocational goal. One of our largest and most prominent universities is now considering a proposal following a faculty study that students be allowed to select a major as early as the freshman year. This was prompted by the finding that students often find themselves at sea when not identified with a particular program served by a special advisor. The writer was told at several schools (including some sectarian institutions for women) that "the happiest students are those who know rather early in their college experience what they want to major in." It was also reported that decisions as to a major during the freshman year are becoming increasingly common.

To quote Professor Jones again:

> The imputation of inferior intellectual status to vocational or professional training is astonishing, in view of the patent fact that medical students, law students, engineering students and other students who know their own minds, work about twice as hard as students in the liberal arts courses.
> The instinct of the veterans now in colleges, most of whom demand vocational or professional training, is sounder than the theory of academic humanists. *"Making a life" is a fine phrase. But you cannot in most cases "make a life" without first making a living.* (Italics the writer's.) [14]

So speaks one humanist.

A lack of preparation for effective job competition. While there has been considerable discussion recently about the market place value of students who did not take a vocationally-oriented program of study, the fact remains that such graduates are often at serious

13 Howard Mumford Jones, *Education and World Tragedy* (Cambridge: Harvard University Press, 1946), 92 and 95.
14 Howard Mumford Jones, *Education and World Tragedy, op. cit.,* 91–92.

disadvantage when seeking employment. This is less serious, of course, during a period in which labor is in short supply. Obviously these potential employes cannot secure positions for which technical training is necessary unless trained personnel is not available. If they are hired in lieu of persons with the desired training, they may well find themselves employed at a less favorable wage. Furthermore, without specialized preparation, they may be compelled to accept positions which do not really interest them. The situation is particularly acute for older women who return to the labor market, either because of a desire to do so or because circumstances necessitate it. In view of the fact that "in our society there is no single situation which is potentially so capable of giving some satisfaction at all levels of basic needs as is the occupation" the lack of vocationally-oriented education is a serious matter for many persons.[15]

We also know that many of the job seekers are in no position either to return to school for advanced work or to go on immediately for graduate study. Finally, we should keep in mind the ambiguous place of adolescents and younger adults in our society. The period of "preparation for life" has become so extended that these young people often have a sense of being "fifth wheels." This lack of a meaningful, functionally necessary place in the workings of society, when added to the relative absence of societal goals in American life, creates much frustration and unhappiness.[16]

The newer professions are put at a disadvantage. When vocationally oriented programs are not available at the undergraduate level, there will be a tendency to gravitate toward the older and better known professions. After all, if there is no personal knowledge of professions that are not high in the prestige hierarchy the

[15] Anne Roe, *The Psychology of Occupation* (New York: John Wiley and Sons, Inc., 1956), 31.
[16] The comments by Dean Donham of the Harvard School of Business Administration, quoted by Professor Jones, are also worth noting: "In my observation, the liberal arts graduate who stops with the A.B. and enters active life in many cases faces pathetic problems. Somehow he feels his training ought to prepare him to do a better job in life but, judging by the difficulties of making a real start and the drifting process through which he goes, it does not. Some colleges seem to glory in this fact. It is frequently stated that liberal arts training gives cultural values, trains men for life; not to make a living. But cultural values fly out the window when men can't get and hold jobs and little self-respect remains if they can't make a living." Quoted in Howard Mumford Jones, *Education and World Tragedy, op. cit.,* 93–94.

student will have little reason to select them. A profession like social work, which is relatively unthought of *as a professional choice* by the public at large and the general student body, is likely to be at a severe disadvantage unless it is perceived as an *interesting vocational alternative*. In other words, the traditional liberal arts approach, rather than having an equal impact on all occupational groups, discriminates against those with less visibility and recognition while conversely it benefits the traditional professions.

Another factor that puts the newer professions at a disadvantage from the point of view of recruiting students in a traditionally oriented liberal arts college is that most of the faculty will be relatively uninformed about social work and may often be somewhat negative in their attitudes toward it. Without a social work-oriented program (and a social work-oriented faculty member) neither the students nor the "traditional" faculty members are likely to have their misconceptions modified. This then will work against recruitment of students both for graduate training and for the field of practice.

The case against the continuation of the liberal arts—professional education dichotomy is a strong one, but it is not free of problems by any means. To get at the major difficulty, the position we support had best be formulated in affirmative terms. It can be stated simply. *We believe in an interweaving of liberal and professional education.*

By this phrasing we do not mean that liberal and professional education are identical. There remains a difference, but this does not imply the need for a barrier. Professor Charles Frankel makes this point in an interesting manner:

> The latter [professional education] is aimed at promoting an individual's ability to deal with specialized problems that others bring him. This is what is meant, I take it, when it is said that professional education is education for practice. Education in the arts and sciences, on the other hand, is primarily an education aimed at developing an individual's ability to ask his own questions and to make his own demands upon his experience. This, I take it, is essentially what is meant by calling it "liberal" education. But though there is a distinction, it is a distinction only in degree and in emphasis. Far from there being a justification for a sharp separation between the programs of the pro-

fessional and non-professional divisions of a university, the tendency of educational policy in professional schools, I would timidly suggest, should be in the other direction.

The reasons are fairly plain. Professional service involves the ability to make complex practical judgments and to weigh conflicting interests and values.

And since most of the key positions in modern society are occupied by members of the professions such judgments frequently carry far-reaching social implications . . . that a properly conceived professional education should have an essentially liberal character is also plain when we reflect on what is involved in saying that the skills of a given profession are embedded in a developing body of knowledge whose roots are in the fundamental arts and sciences.[17]

Even with Professor Frankel's caution as to the difference being one of degree and emphasis, his words might make the distinction appear to be clearer than it is in practice. For example, to what extent is research in the basic sciences influenced by questions posed by society, governmental agencies, or business organizations? Isn't the Ph.D. fundamentally a professional degree, insofar as its function is to prepare the candidate to be a teacher or professional researcher? In this respect, too, are not undergraduate majors in the basic sciences often part of the students' total professional preparation? These questions are raised to emphasize even more the extent to which professional education and liberal education blend into one another.

Acceptance of some difference between professional education and liberal arts education immediately raises a pointed and important question: If the recommendation for interweaving liberal and professional education were put into effect, might not the traditional liberal arts disciplines be harmed? Rather than resulting in a liberalizing of professional education, might the consequence of this intermingling be the undermining of the traditional liberal arts disciplines by making them subservient to the vocationally oriented programs? This is clearly a danger, particularly because of the cultural impulses toward "practicality" and immediate usefulness. However, let us view it in just that way—as a danger rather

[17] Charles Frankel, "Professional Education as University Education," *Education for Social Work*, *Proceedings* of Sixth Annual Program Meeting, Council on Social Work Education (New York: Council on Social Work Education, 1958), 16.

than as an inevitable consequence. Phrased in this way, the problem is how to prevent this threat from becoming a reality.

Two ways to lessen the danger that professional education may corrupt the traditional disciplines are: (1) frank recognition of their different functions within the college of liberal arts and a mutually helpful division of functions, and (2) developing vocationally oriented programs of *a liberalizing character*. As we shall use the term liberalizing in this project, it implies something about both the nature of the content and, more crucially, the manner of treating the content. The liberalizing elements of professional education involve an approach that emphasizes the student's achievement of the following objectives:

1. Understanding the broad purposes of professional activities and relating them to an understanding of man and societies of men;

2. Understanding the relationships between the profession and the social, political, economic and intellectual aspects of life;

3. Understanding the principles and values underlying the profession's ways of knowing and doing;

4. Development of professional convictions compatible with social and individual well-being;

5. Development of an awareness of, and ability to scrutinize critically one's own professionally relevant preconvictions;

6. Integration of the intellectual and emotional components of professional learning;

7. Heightening of the imaginative, creative, and independent use of professional content;

8. Development of a disciplined and creative approach to professional problem-solving;

9. Stimulation of responsible and courageous action on behalf of professional goals;

10. Stimulation of an interest in explanatory analysis of a theoretical and abstract character.

Without necessarily being an all inclusive list, these qualities convey a sense of the general orientation of a professional education that liberalizes and is thus compatible with a liberal arts framework.

There is a positive answer to the question: *Can an undergraduate program which specifically focuses on social work and is viewed as part of the total process of preparation for social work fit within the framework of a liberal arts college?* Note, however, that we say *can* rather than *will*. This is because such a program, to be compatible with the function of a liberal arts college, must meet the requirement of being "liberalizing." In other words, the character of the social work program is all decisive. The conclusion we have come to is that there should be an interweaving of liberal and professional education and that there is no inherent reason why a liberalizing professional education should not be accommodated within the structure of the present day liberal arts college. The recommendations presented in later sections of this report have been formulated, in part, on the basis of this conclusion. They will demonstrate in concrete terms a possible constructive interweaving of liberal and professional education.

CHAPTER IV

The Content and Characteristics
of Current Undergraduate Offerings

The findings in this chapter, on the content of existing undergraduate social work programs and the interrelationship among
their various segments, are based on analysis of materials submitted
by 72 universities and colleges.[1] A majority of these institutions
provided course outlines and, in some cases, reading lists, copies of
examinations and related materials. These sources of data were
augmented by replies from about fifty institutions to the two questionnaires sent to them by the project (Appendix B); commonly
employed texts and supplementary readings were examined, and
the project director conferred individually or participated in group
meetings with approximately 120 people, most of them social work
educators, from colleges and universities in twelve states.

Two important reservations as to these source materials need to
be made. First, the real "heart" of a course is often the lecture or
class discussion. We did not have access in this study to lecture
notes or transcripts of class discussions. Second, there was no comprehensive "sample" of student reaction to their undergraduate
social work courses on which to draw, although we did make use
of several relatively limited studies of this type. In evaluating the
findings, both these limitations of the data should be kept in mind.

The characteristics of undergraduate social work programs re-
vealed by this analysis will be stated as fourteen generalizations,
each with more or less extended explanation and discussion.

[1] For a discussion of the types and structure of current undergraduate social work
offerings, based on an examination of college catalogs, see the report by Dean Mereb
Mossman in Appendix A.

FINDINGS AND COMMENTARY[2]

1. *Undergraduate social work content courses appear to stress a descriptive-informational approach, with relatively little conceptualization and analysis.*

Many of the courses appear to be oriented around a rather detailed specification of a variety of social welfare programs.[3] This is frequently true, for example, of courses in public welfare which often combine description of program specifics with materials on agency procedures. They are characterized by relatively little theoretical content. This information-giving approach was also quite common in those courses (*e.g.*, child welfare) that were planned as a survey of services for special groups of people.

Courses designed to introduce the student to social work, whatever their titles, typically included a *description* of the historical development of social welfare programs, particularly those served by social workers.[4] This was usually followed by a cataloging of existent programs (and the different settings), coupled with a description of the profession of social work and its methods.

The implications of this information-giving and enumerative approach are highlighted by what is usually *not* found in the present courses. By way of illustration, the treatment of historical materials shows an attempt is usually made to put the historical origins of modern social work within the framework of a changing Western civilization. However, these changes are frequently handled in a stereotyped fashion and, of most importance, the recital of changes is not accompanied by an analysis of the processes of change.

Little use is made of conceptual tools (theories or concepts, and so on), and there is a corresponding lack of stress on understanding the dynamics and patterns of social changes.[5] Conspicuously absent

2 In these generalizations there is no implication that every course conforms exactly to them. The fact that there are striking exceptions to almost all the findings does not, of course, invalidate the generalizations.

3 For other data pertaining to the content of social work content courses, see Appendix A (particularly pp. 220–226).

4 See p. 221 in Appendix A. Only infrequently does one find a special course in the history of social work.

5 It should be noted that American social science itself has done relatively little by

is a concern for explaining the significance of a confluence of institutional forces at a given moment of history. (For example, why was the reform movement in the U.S. at the turn of the century able to muster support from "respectable" segments of the population?) There is little indication of historical data and theories being consciously used as sources of hypotheses; nor does one find explicit emphasis on the relationships of values and idea systems to the sociocultural matrix.

The treatment of contemporary social work is similarly short on analysis. Topics, such as social work as a profession, do not usually include a critical examination of the nature of professions, differences between types of professions (*e.g.*, "entrepreneurial" and "employe"), the role of professions in society, and related questions. The organization and administration of social welfare programs is not examined from the perspective of organizational theory or from the point of view of the policy-making process.

Factors suggested from the source materials that may have contributed to the favoring of a descriptive, information-giving approach over a more conceptual treatment are:

    a. The conception of the undergraduate college's functions as being to "teach about" social work and to prepare for citizenship, along with the lack of guidance from professional organizations and graduate schools;

    b. The lack of a theoretical preparation on the part of some instructors;

    c. The lack of teaching materials of an analytical nature;

    d. Student pressure for an emphasis on the concrete and "practical," with practical often defined as non-analytic and non-theoretical, and pressure for "practical" training from some social work practitioners.[6]

---

way of systematic analysis of social change. This, of course, increases the difficulties for social work education in this area. However, it may well be that social work has a contribution to make to the social sciences that would assist in advancing the knowledge about the processes of social change.

6 Dr. Bernice Madison reported the following in her California study: ". . . in addition to considering it important for workers to possess the knowledge and skill required for interviewing, providing a professional relationship, referring and case recording, the majority [of supervisors] thought it important for them [public assistance workers] to know about the current welfare programs and public assistance laws in California and budgeting in relation to clients' needs . . . In contrast, few supervisors considered

e. Political factors within the educational institutions (*e.g.,* competition for students between departments, or even colleges).

f. The absence of adequate in-service training programs in many agencies and the assumption by some colleges and universities of what are really the functions of in-service training.

g. The relatively low level of conceptualization in social work in general and the limited amount of social work knowledge of a systematic character.

2. *The content and organization of undergraduate social work offerings reflect the lack of a consistent underlying rationale.*

Dean Mossman points out in her analysis a considerable diversity in the range of current course offerings. It is often difficult to identify the criteria used to decide whether or not to offer a given course. For example, why is a course in child welfare offered rather than a course in services for the aged? Is there convincing justification for either?

A related problem concerns the selection of content to be included in a given course. Some child welfare courses include a good deal of "human growth and behavior" material. Is this an appropriate place for such material? It would appear that the content and structure of some of the courses now being taught developed as the result of fortuitous circumstances, historical "drift," or the demands of expediency.

There is also question as to how much emphasis has been given to considerations of integration and continuity. Indications are that many programs are lacking in both.[7]

The confusion as to what content should be included in undergraduate social work offerings and how these offerings should be organized may reflect, in part, the prevailing uncertainty as to the proper functions of undergraduate social work programs. The discontinuity between educational levels has also made it difficult for undergraduate faculties to develop a coherent program of social work education.

---

knowledge of historical development and of current welfare programs important." Bernice Madison, *The Public Assistance Job and The Undergraduate Social Work Curriculum* (San Francisco: The Rosenberg Foundation, 1957), 67.

[7] In this connection it is interesting to note that the data gathered by the Public Social Services Project showed that a considerable number of students take "isolated" social work content courses without completing an organized sequence.

3. *Difficulty is often encountered by students in relating content from the basic disciplines to social work content.*

A frequently heard complaint is that the student does not show the benefit of his work in the basic disciplines when dealing with related materials in social work content courses. Instructors in both undergraduate and graduate social work courses made this observation repeatedly. It needs to be recognized that, with the present degree of specialization, even introductory courses in the basic disciplines are taught without much reference to one another and they are learned by the student in an equally discrete manner. Furthermore, the instructors in these basic disciplines frequently fail to point up the possible "applications" of such content.

Illustrative of the problem are the following comments: "Students who take courses in the sociology of groups don't seem to have any advantage in courses in social group work over students without such preparation" and "Students who take economics don't seem to be able to relate what they have learned in those courses to political science, sociology, or to social work." From a student came this puzzled and puzzling comment: "I enjoyed both my sociology and social work courses but, frankly, I just can't see any relationship between them. For example, what is the relevance of the concept of ethnocentrism to social work? None that I can see!" Although one might attribute this remark to a lack of intellectual sophistication, the recurrence of the sentiment expressed, if not of the specifics, suggests the existence of a genuine problem.

The adverse consequences of the present difficulty in relating content from the basic disciplines effectively to social work are important. Two of them are inefficiency in the learning process, with a loss both to the student and the instructor of the social work course; and reinforcement of the negative attitudes of many social workers, including some social work educators, toward the social sciences. As Grace Coyle has observed, ". . . it is clear that there is within the profession considerable mistrust and skepticism as to whether the social sciences have anything to offer which might be of practical use to social workers or in social work education." [8]

[8] Grace L. Coyle, *Social Science in the Professional Education of Social Workers* (New York: Council on Social Work Education, 1958), 6.

4. *In many instances social work content courses do not draw upon the relevant theoretical contributions of the basic disciplines. One partial exception is the incorporation of rather advanced psychological (particularly psychoanalytic) concepts and theories in certain of the courses.*

Although there appears to be considerable support among educators for the idea that an important function of undergraduate social work content courses is that of integrating content from the basic disciplines within a social work framework, this has been effectively accomplished in relatively few cases.[9]

The reasons are varied; among them are the difficult problem of how to "translate" concepts and theories from the basic disciplines into social work so that they are directly usable in dealing with social work phenomena, and the lack of comfort on the part of some social work educators in making use of such content. Also, those who teach the basic sciences have not always been maximally helpful.

The borrowing and adapting of concepts and principles from the basic sciences by social work educators should be selective enough to allow for theoretical coherence. The major dangers in the utilization of such materials are: (1) the tendency toward a premature and "blind" commitment to a particular set of concepts or a general theory and (2) the opposite propensity to borrow and adapt in so eclectic and indiscriminate a manner that the instructor will be flexible to the "point of being positively invertebrate." The former tendency is most likely to appear in undergraduate social work content courses in the use of psychological, particularly psychoanalytic, materials. The latter tendency which has been called both "intellectual beachcombing" and an "academic smorgasbord" is most characteristic of the way materials from anthropology, economics, political science, and sociology have been treated. A profession, in attempting to use content from the basic disciplines, is truly between Scylla and Charybdis.

Of course, the integration of content from the basic sciences

---

9 In his New York State study Professor Kenneth Kindelsperger found the same problem. "Most of the courses were given in an isolated fashion with little effort being made to integrate the social welfare content with the basic social sciences." Kindelsperger, *op. cit.,* 6.

within a social work framework necessitates, in the first place, possession of this knowledge by the teacher and the student. The data gathered in this project indicate that students frequently come into their social work content courses with inadequate knowledge of certain subjects. The inadequacies mentioned frequently are in economics, political science and, to a somewhat lesser extent, human development. There appears to be a tendency on the part of social work students to avoid courses in these areas unless they are specifically required to take them. Even when these subjects are required, the designated courses are often those that emphasize content such as public administration, state and local government, and "practical" economics courses. There is a definite lack of attention to courses in political and economic theory.

The same imbalance is reflected in the comparatively little use that is made of materials from economics and political science in social work content courses. Even within the fields of sociology and psychology, from which prerequisite courses are more often selected, there is indication that social work students avoid the more theoretically oriented courses.

5. *An increasing effort is being made to utilize data and concepts from the basic disciplines in social work content courses.*

The writer was struck by the widespread interest in and readiness to experiment with the synthesizing of research findings, concepts, and generalizations from the basic disciplines in the teaching of social work content courses. There appeared to be a very definite recognition of the desirability of broadening the framework within which social work content is presented, and an appreciation of the value of treating such content more analytically than has been the case heretofore. In a number of schools efforts to create a more fruitful union of the basic sciences, humanities and social work are already well underway.

There is, at the present time, a sharp increase in books and other teaching materials that relate content from the basic disciplines to social work and other professions. The appearance of this literature reflects a "movement" already underway. The availability of such literature will, in turn, aid and abet the trend. It is important, of course, that the use made of materials from the social sciences be critically selective since, as social work has reason to know so well, "intellectual marriages" are not without peril.

6. *One of the intended purposes of undergraduate social work content courses appears to be the teaching of the ideology of social work.*[10]

Although the phrasing of this purpose varied, the essential idea behind it was widely expressed. Some instructors indicated that they *introduced* the student to the values of social work. Others put it in terms of providing the student with an *appreciation* of social work, including its values. There was evident a rather widespread concern about the fact that many students come into social work content courses with an ideology alien to that of social work. One instructor commented, with a good deal of feeling, that: "Many of our students come from the town of ———. As you may know it's a wealthy community. A substantial number of these students come into my courses with the notion that the only legitimate activity of government is fighting wars. I do my best to change this view of the nature and responsibilities of government."

Particular mention was made, too, of the rather punitive and harshly moralistic attitudes of some students. The idea that there are *reasons* for behavior was reported as not "really believed" by many students. Other faculty members mentioned the persistence of "survival of the fittest" attitudes toward the indigent. It was also stated that ideologies alien to that of social work were expounded in certain of the courses (specific mention was made of economics and political science courses) that are required of, or recommended for, social work students.

7. *In many of the social work content courses there appears to be an uncritically "idealistic" bias in the treatment of certain types of the content.*

There appears to be a rather superficial and uncritical use made of terms such as democratic, professional, and similar highly-valued concepts and phrases. This also seems to be the case in the discus-

[10] Since the concept of ideology may be employed in a variety of ways, in this project it will be defined as a system of assumptions, ideas, beliefs, values, and modes of thinking characteristic of some collectivity, such as a group, class, sect, profession, religious order, or nation.

sion of social work values. On occasion, too, social work values are confused with assumed or hypothetical knowledge.

It is interesting that concepts such as conflict, social control, power (though the concept, power structure, is used), class, self-interest, and coercion are seldom employed in the analysis of events and policies. Related to this tendency is the approach taken toward social problems. It appears that social problems (social disorganization is a common term) are often attributed to other conditions that are themselves considered pathological ("evil is caused by evil" assumption), as well as to social change. Similarly much of the analysis of contemporary American society has an unreal or outdated quality about it.

It might also be noted that there seems to be acceptance without much critical analysis of the present organization of the social services though not of specific programs, including the wide diversity in auspices.

8. *A major gap in undergraduate social work programs is the lack of study of the legal institution, and its relationship to other social institutions.*

The problem in this respect is that in most universities or colleges no broad law course with an institutional focus is available to social work students. Sociology courses, such as criminology, often contain some material of this sort but it is usually quite limited. Courses labeled "social institutions" seldom devote much attention to the legal institution.

Undergraduate courses in law and social work (and there are only a few of these) as well as other social work content courses appear to emphasize the legal aspects of social work practice, without much analysis of the fundamental nature of the legal institution and its relationship to other social institutions.

9. *The terms "social work" and "social welfare" are often used interchangeably and sometimes in a rather confusing manner.*

The most usual reasons for employing the term "social welfare," rather than "social work," in courses or program descriptions are: (1) to give less of a vocational implication; (2) to stress a broad institutional framework; (3) to imply as a purpose familiarity with an area of subject matter rather than preparation on a professional level; and (4) for purposes of community or college relations.

While there are certainly good reasons for using the term "social welfare" (when the content justifies such usage), it would seem undesirable to use it to "mask" a social work program or to perpetuate the belief that a sharp discontinuity between the undergraduate and graduate social work programs is essential in order to justify the former.

10. *There appears to be considerable variation and confusion reflected in the teaching of social work methods courses.*

The variation and confusion is manifested in respect to: (1) purpose; (2) degree of specification; (3) extent of emphasis on technical content; (4) teaching materials; (5) range of methods covered; (6) breadth of treatment; and (7) the students for whom the course is designed.

There are several explanations for the diversity of focus and treatment of materials in the methods courses, the most important of which is probably the confusion as to what is the legitimate function of methods courses at the undergraduate level. As Dean Mossman pointed out in her report, the schools offering methods courses describe them as pre-professional. Yet the course outlines often suggest that they are technical in their focus and oriented toward preparing the students for at least "partial competence" if they should go directly into practice after graduation. Some of the methods courses include units of work on techniques of practice, such as case recording. One gets a strong sense that these courses are "restrained professional courses," reflecting uncomfortable attempts to achieve a compromise among various pressures and purposes. It is worth noting that few of the courses are taught from a generalized problem-solving perspective.

Among the texts assigned in undergraduate casework courses are those by Gordon Hamilton, Florence Hollis, Helen H. Perlman, Herbert Aptekar, Annette Garrett, Anne Fenlason, and Cora Kasius. In group work courses, the texts by Gertrude Wilson and Gladys Ryland, Harleigh B. Trecker, Grace Coyle, and Alan Klein appear to be most used. It should be noted that there are very few methods texts, if any, written expressly for the undergraduate level.

Among the rather unusual aspects of the teaching of methods courses is the fact that occasionally they are planned primarily for students being prepared for other vocations than social work, such as nurses or recreation personnel. Also, there is some confusion in titles. Sometimes courses called interviewing seem to be very similar to courses in social casework. In other cases there is a clearer distinction. However, few of the courses in interviewing included topics such as interviewing in research. In other words, they were primarily focused on interviewing applied to social work, or to social work and a few of the related helping professions.

It is also difficult to determine why courses in certain methods are given rather than others. Upon inquiring at one school why a course in group work was given rather than a course in casework, the writer was told "We thought we weren't supposed to give a course in casework at the undergraduate level. If it's all right to do so we would like to, since some of our students do field work in a public assistance agency."

This comment brings out in bold relief one of the basic problems influencing both the written descriptions as well as the character of undergraduate methods courses: that is, confusion as to function. This same problem is reflected in the fact that, although courses entitled "social work methods" sometimes cover a range of methods, more often they focus primarily on one method.

Related to the fundamental question of appropriate function is the apparent recognition that undergraduate methods courses are not in "professional good standing." This fact probably helps to explain the reluctance one finds to list "limited preparation for practice" as an explicit purpose of such courses. In actuality, though, this appears to be one goal for a number of such courses.

11. *There seems to be considerable dissatisfaction with the academic equipment of the students enrolled in undergraduate social work programs.*

The following list of reported academic weak spots in students enrolled in undergraduate programs, or those just entering graduate school, was reported primarily by undergraduate educators, but among the informants were also administrators and teachers in graduate schools and a few practitioners.

a. Lack of overall intellectual capacity or interest, particularly in dealing with theoretical materials.

b. Limited general problem-solving abilities.

c. Lack of independent and creative thinking.

d. Lack of intellectual discipline and understanding of need for it.

e. Possession of "lady bountiful" and rigidly moralistic attitudes.

f. Overemphasis on the "practical" and concrete.

g. Lack of interest and personal involvement in matters of social policy.

h. Inability to relate content from the basic disciplines to social work content courses.

i. Lack of adequate knowledge of certain social sciences, particularly economics, political science, and social psychology.

j. Lack of adequate knowledge of statistical principles and insufficient skill in use.

k. Lack of skills in speaking and writing.

It should be understood that the above reactions, secured during the writer's field trip, were not intended as balanced evaluations of either the capacities or the performance records of the students. Nor do they constitute a reliable basis for judging the relative quality of students in comparison with those in other disciplines. They are simply reported weaknesses in the academic equipment of students who are or have been enrolled in undergraduate social work programs.

12. *The question of the desirability of undergraduate field experience remains highly controversial and in a state of massive confusion.*[11]

The following data were secured from replies to the field questionnaire to which 47 undergraduate members of CSWE responded:

a. Field experience was available in the preceding school year to

---

11 Field experience was defined in the questionnaire as regular, assigned student observation and/or participation in the activities of a social agency or institution, as a planned part of the undergraduate social work-oriented educational program of a college or university.

students with an expressed interest in social work in 38 schools, and not available in 9 schools.

b. Of the 38 having a field experience program, 23 made the experience available to all students with an expressed interest in social work who desired it, and 14 only to some (one failed to answer this question); 17 gave field experience to students with an expressed interest in other fields than social work, while 20 did not; 30 offered a type of field experience involving both observation and participation, 4 offered only observation, and 4 only participation.

Responses to other questions indicated that a wide variety of activities are subsumed under the heading of observation and participation, as the list in Appendix D shows. The nature of the diversity suggests either the absence of consistent and well thought-out criteria for setting up field experience programs or that expediency takes priority over such criteria. Most of the respondent schools have set up some type of arrangement for the supervision of students in the field experience programs. They also indicated that provision was made for integration of field and class experiences. Personal interviews with faculty members at a number of these schools suggest, though, that really adequate integration and supervision was relatively uncommon.

There can be little question but that the problem of undergraduate field experience has been unresolved not only because of thoughtful differences of opinion but also because of confusions in analysis—confusions which have become almost impenetrable due to dogmatic assertions and assumptions. The obfuscation surrounding the entire issue has been compounded by the fact that some professional social work practitioners and graduate school faculty members have treated field participation as a sacrosanct part of the graduate curriculum, hence, inappropriate for serious analysis at any but the graduate level.

Partially as a result of this attitude, the field experience aspect of social work education is particularly discontinuous between the different levels of social work education. This also accounts, in part, for the fact that undergraduate field experience programs exhibit a good deal of that incoherence, crudeness, and excessive expediency characteristic of a "bootlegged" activity operating on a "shoestring." Often, too, undergraduate social work educators have treated field experience in an inappropriately cavalier manner, thus alienating members of the profession who might have been willing to re-examine their own positions on the question. What are some of the prevalent confusions?

First, discussions of an undergraduate field experience program often become tangled up around the question of whether its purpose is to achieve a certain type of practice competence, or whether it is conceived primarily as a learning experience through which various objectives of "classroom courses" might be more readily achieved. Or does it have both purposes?

Second, there has not been an adequate differentiation of function in the practice of social work and this obviously hampers decisions as to appropriate functions for undergraduate field students.

Third, there appears to be real question as to whether interviews between caseworkers and their clients have to be as inaccessible a student experience as has been the case until now.

Fourth, it somtimes appears that field experience and agency experience are synonymous terms. The failure to distinguish between the two has undoubtedly contributed to the difficulties surrounding the question.

Fifth, great confusion exists as to the differentiation between the educational objectives of undergraduate field experiences, of volunteer work, and of summer work experiences. Inconsistencies in this respect are not unusual even within the same educational institution. For example, in one school students are encouraged to apply for membership in the summer institutional programs of the American Friends Service Committee or to accept positions as dormitory counselors. However, they are not permitted to participate in a regular undergraduate field experience program. In other cases, volunteer programs necessitating considerable skill in interpersonal relations are encouraged by the same schools that would not consider instituting an undergraduate field experience program. In at least one such case, the volunteer program is not under the auspices of the graduate school of social work even though there is one on campus. (There is no undergraduate social work concentration at that institution.) The writer must admit to being baffled in his attempt to discover a consistent set of rational principles that would justify the current melange of programs.

Sixth, the use of "lack of maturity" as grounds for *categorically* rejecting the desirability of undergraduate field experience is so untenable, and so often contradicted in practice and argument, that it only contributes to the already prevalent obscuration. For a school to recommend students to public welfare agencies, while insisting that only three to six months earlier none of them was mature enough to participate in carefully supervised field experiences, scarcely stands the test of reasonableness. Or to recommend students for away-from-home summer internships or encourage them to be dormitory counselors, while maintaining that they are *categorically* too immature for field experience in an agency, is hardly a consistent position.

Several other factors need to be noted in regard to this question of field experience. One is the recruitment use made of field experience programs by many schools. Such experiences often capture or solidify the student's career interest in social work. Many instructors claim that the reverse is also true and equally important: that the undergraduate experience provides an opportunity for both the student and the faculty to discover if a student is not suited for social work.

A second consideration to be kept in mind is that, under present circumstances, there is a real danger that the student's activities in the agency will be dictated by agency needs rather than being determined by sound educational objectives.

Finally, we come to the question of what effect undergraduate field experiences have on the student's performance in graduate school. It has been said (and was said to the writer by the dean of a graduate school) that undergraduate field experience often has an adverse effect on the student and results in a need for relearning at the graduate level. However, it is interesting that professionally trained practitioners and educators who commented to the writer upon *their own* undergraduate field experiences expressed favorable reactions toward this phase of their training, even when the field experiences were given under conditions far from ideal. The number of such informants was limited, though, and not a valid indicator without systematic study of the reactions of persons who completed graduate work to their undergraduate field experiences. Another questionable point about the graduate schools' attitude toward undergraduate field work is the willingness or desire of some schools to have potential students work in an agency before entering upon graduate study, though the agency may well be one which lacks adequate supervision.

It is indeed striking that many time-honored arguments against field experience on the undergraduate level seem to be caught in a web of logical contradictions and inconsistent practices, and fare badly when subjected to probing.

13. *There is a need for more specified and required content from the basic disciplines in undergraduate social work programs.*

We have previously listed some of the reported academic deficiencies of students who take undergraduate social work content courses. It has also been mentioned that social work students seem to avoid taking courses in economics and political science. Furthermore, it is difficult to understand the logic behind the practice of giving the student a choice, let us say, of two out of six courses, when these courses are in different subject areas and are by no means equivalents as to content. While it is sometimes argued that the student gets a sense of what the social sciences are like, and what their methodology is, by taking work in any of them, the extent of similarity is often very limited. Actually the social sciences do not possess a unified body of theory or a unified methodology. It would appear, then, that if there is justification for requiring work in the basic disciplines as part of the undergraduate social work program, a differentiation as to more and less important content needs to be made, thus permitting an increased specificity in requirements. (One rather unusual practical objection to this finding was raised by a faculty member who argued that those departments excluded, or relatively so, from the list of required courses might retaliate against his department.)

14. *The question is still unsettled as to what is the most desirable "academic home" for undergraduate social work programs.*

As Dean Mossman's report showed, the most usual administrative arrangement is for undergraduate social work programs to be located within sociology departments. However, there are problems associated with this organizational pattern. In institutions (usually universities) in which the sociology department has, as a definite goal, the preparation of professional sociologists, one sometimes finds a lack of enthusiasm or even hostility on the part of the "pure" sociologists toward the social work program that may be housed within the department. Often, however, there is an ambivalence in this respect.

On the one hand, the preparation of social workers may appear as an intrusion on the energies and resources of the department in achieving its goal of turning out professional sociologists. Also, some sociologists may have the attitude that social workers are a less desirable product than sociologists, and that assuming the function of turning out social workers hurts the department's prestige. In addition there may be a fear that as an applied discipline, social work may attract more students because it is "practical," with such a consequent expansion of this aspect of the department's program that the "tail wags the dog." This has sometimes been a well founded fear. On the other hand, of students enrolled in the sociology departments, more come because of their interest in social work than in being professional sociologists, and these students often play an important role in justifying the department's budget, including expansion in "straight sociology." Also, members of the sociology staff may well accept the responsibility of a university for preparing persons to staff social work positions. At any rate, the basis of the ambivalence not uncommonly found in sociology departments is quite evident. In some institutions though, a very satisfactory working arrangement based on mutual respect and a balancing of departmental goals has been developed.

The location of a social work program within a sociology department raises other problems as well. If students are not allowed to enroll in the social work program *as such* unless they are sociology majors (though they may take individual courses), there is danger of limiting unduly the enrollment that might come from other departments. This is the case in some schools. Also, the requirements for a sociology major may overload the social work student with sociology courses, while making it difficult for him to take as much work as he should in other departments. Another problem is that the number of social work offerings may be sufficiently limited so that a full time faculty member, even though hired primarily to teach the social work courses, would be expected to be able to carry his weight in teaching certain sociology courses. This means he should be competent in sociology as well as in social work, and it is often difficult to find such a person.

The difficulties enumerated have led some schools to create special undergraduate social work majors and even departments. Such an arrangement, while avoiding some of the problems associated with placement in a sociology department, has serious drawbacks of its own. One of these is that as it represents a competitive major it may be informally "boycotted" by other departments in the sense of social work not being discussed in introductory courses. This can be serious, since many students first become acquainted with social work as a result of hearing it discussed in courses such as introductory sociology. Also, the budget of a social work department may be too limited. More serious than either of these problems is that the social work teaching staff may lose touch with the basic social sciences. This is more likely to happen if they are not members of another department in which they have teaching responsibilities. An equally important danger is that there will be an extensive proliferation of social work content courses, thus raising the possibility of a too specialized and narrowly vocational program.

There does seem to be a relationship between the administrative organization of the undergraduate social work program and the extent and characteristics of its offerings. Comparison of the offerings provided under three different organizational patterns resulted in the following tabulation. All of the schools charted are undergraduate members of the CSWE. Indications are that nonmember schools tend to have less developed social work programs, in general, than the member schools.

Another administrative arrangement sometimes employed is that of an interdepartmental social work program. Such an organizational pattern is obviously free of some defects noted in the other structural arrangements, but also has its own problems. If it is not the direct responsibility of a graduate school it may well acquire a free-floating character which presents budgetary as well

Patterns of Departmental Organization

	Type I	Type II	Type III
	Social work courses located in a sociology department but with no social work concentration.	A delineated social work concentration (curriculum) within a sociology department.	A social work major located either in a social work department or a social science division.
Average number of social work content courses per school	3.4	4.2	7.2
Percentage of schools with a course(s) in social casework	24%	46%	77%
Percentage of schools with course(s) in social group work	25%	33%	69%
Percentage of schools with general methods courses	17%	13%	23%
Percentage of schools with field experience programs	66%	60%	92%
Percentage of schools with field experience programs in which the field experience is open to non-social work students	58%	22%	17%
Percentage of students in social work courses whose major occupational interests not social work	60%	60%	46%

as other difficulties. Furthermore, this plan does not answer the question of the home of the instructional staff and the relationship of that staff to the basic sciences. Such a program can be a discordant medley, sacrificing depth for a not really integrated breadth.

A variety of organizational arrangements are being tried out.

None is free of disadvantages and each has desirable features. However, although difficulties are commonly associated with the various types of administrative structure and need to be guarded against, they do not appear to be inevitable concomitants of any given arrangement.

CHAPTER V

The Relationship Between the Undergraduate Phase of Social Work Education and the Practice of Social Work

POSTULATES

1. Positions defined as being within social work (and probably different functions within such positions) vary as to the demands they impose on the worker as to exercise of judgment, kinds and levels of skills, and scope and depth of knowledge and understanding.

2. Persons who hold social work positions, without possessing the requisite professional education for membership in NASW (and such persons numerically predominate in social work practice), tend to find themselves in an occupational "no man's land"; that is, without a clear, cohesive and satisfying occupational identification. The probability is that such persons will either become a recognized and "legitimate" category of social worker or develop other definite occupational identities.

3. The rationale for staff development programs is improvement in the services rendered by a particular agency through increasing the effectiveness of the workers in the implementation of its program.

The relationship between undergraduate education and social work practice will be dealt with by raising three crucial questions, discussing and drawing conclusions about each, and finally stating some general conclusions on the subject.

Question 1:

Should the shortage of social workers with graduate training be treated as a legitimate consideration in the determination of whether to provide social work education at the undergraduate level?

DISCUSSION

The following comment by Professor Robert Merton provides a useful departure for our discussion:

> What is considered occupational choice from the standpoint of the individual becomes the process of recruitment from the standpoint of the profession and the allocation of personnel in various occupational statuses from the standpoint of the society. What the individual defines as a promising opportunity afforded by the labor market, the profession defines as an 'acute shortage,' and the society defines as an imbalance of occupational distribution. These all patently refer to the same facts from the different perspectives of the individual, the occupational group and the society. The functional problem of articulating these three systems so that the flow and distribution of occupational choices are such as to meet the aspirations of individuals, the requirements of the profession, and an optimum balance among the occupations is one which is still poorly understood.[1]

In this chapter attempt will be made to interrelate these three perspectives. The initial vantage point will be that of society. Here the imbalance between the societal need and the supply of trained social workers comes sharply into focus.

If the United States is to become increasingly a society of users of the services offered by social workers, it must also become increasingly a society of social workers. Yet, as of this time, the need for service (and the requirements of existing programs of service) has outrun the supply of trained personnel. The problem of the shortage of social workers is as dismal as it is familiar. In 1950 only 20 percent of the persons holding social work positions in public assistance programs in the United States had any graduate social work training, and only 4 percent had two or more years of such training. It was said that at least 3000 budgeted social work positions were vacant. The number of social work positions in public assistance held by persons without even a bachelor's degree has

---

[1] Robert K. Merton, "Some Preliminaries to a Sociology of Medical Education," in *The Student-Physician*, ed. by Robert K. Merton, George G. Reader, and Patricia L. Kendall (Cambridge: Harvard University Press, 1957), 68.

been calculated to be about 20 percent. It is important to recognize, too, that a disproportionately large number of the trained social workers work in certain types of voluntary agencies.[2]

Some more recent studies indicate an equally depressing reality situation. As of October 1, 1955, there were, in the Greater New York area alone, at least:

> 489 vacancies in the casework category in the public agencies,
> 165 vacancies for fully trained caseworkers in the voluntary agencies,
> 27 vacancies for case aides in the voluntary agencies.[3]

The report in which these figures appeared also contained the following comments:

> The percentage of vacancies in these important departments (public) ranged from 4 percent to 38 percent of total staff. Many of them report the quantity and quality of service rendered adversely affected by these staff shortages . . . it may be estimated from the partial data reported, that 175 to 250 trained group workers could be absorbed immediately . . . In group work the needs were so great that a good estimate of the actual figure could not be reached. A large majority of the agencies reporting stated that they did not have fully qualified practitoners on the staff and have had to use part-time "session" workers instead, with consequent effects on the quality of their work.
>
> Thirty-four (34) agencies in all categories, except group work, were found to use aides or other pre-professional workers.[4]

A study in Texas conducted by Charles Laughton showed that 31.2 percent of all the social welfare workers in Texas did not have a college degree. The percentage of workers in the public assistance programs without at least a bachelor's degree was even higher, 51.5 percent.[5]

---

[2] For a fuller discussion of these points see Hollis-Taylor, *op. cit.*, 77–98, and Fedele F. Fauri, "The Shortage of Social Workers—A Challenge to Social Work Education," *Proceedings*, Third Annual Program Meeting, 1955, Council on Social Work Education (New York: CSWE, 1955).

[3] Social Work Recruiting Committee of Greater New York, *Personnel Shortages in Social Work in Greater New York* (New York: SWRC, 1955), mimeographed, 1. These are incomplete figures supplied by only 50%–80% of the agencies in the various classifications. Also the classification of social worker reported by agencies was used. It may or may not have denoted a requirement for professional education.

[4] *Ibid.*, 1–2.

[5] Charles W. Laughton, *Staffing Social Services in Texas: The Problem and the Challenge* (Austin, Texas: The School of Social Work, the University of Texas, 1957), 33.

It has recently been asserted by Ernest Witte, Executive Director, CSWE, that although 12,000 new recruits are needed annually to fill positions in public and private social agencies, only 1,800 were turned out by the graduate schools of social work in the preceding year.[6] And the prospects are that increasing numbers of social workers will be needed in the future.[7] Thus, there is no likelihood that there will be, in the foreseeable future, a sufficient supply of persons with full or partial graduate education to staff most or all of the positions defined as social work by the social work profession. We can anticipate continued employment of persons without training and even greater pressure for undergraduate programs that are specifically focused on the preparation of social workers.

The really drastic shortage of trained social workers is an established fact. And let us acknowledge that among the claims society has a right to make upon the professions and occupations is the claim for competent personnel in sufficient numbers.[8] For the training of these persons the profession must necessarily look to its educational arm. In identifying and comparing the aims of ten professions William McGlothlin found that two aims, common to almost all of the professions, were:

> Professional education has one aim of providing professionally educated entrants to the professions in adequate numbers to satisfy society's needs . . .
>
> Professional education has a second aim of maintaining or increasing the quality of professionally educated entrants to the professions to satisfy society's need.[9]

[6] Quoted in *The New York Times*, May 23, 1958, 22.

[7] Philip M. Hauser, "Demography and Human Ecology in Relation to Social Work," *The Social Welfare Forum*, 1956 (New York: Columbia University Press, 1956), 175–201; Hollis-Taylor, *op. cit.*, Chapter III; and Charles Laughton, *op. cit.*, 12–13. Professor Laughton projects an increase of 1000 more positions to fill in 1960 over the 3000 existent in 1955.

[8] Although this is seemingly an obvious fact it sometimes appears to be overlooked. One can see it more clearly (although it is operative in all societies) perhaps in a "new" nation in which the claim made upon education is very direct and obvious. For example, the following statement appears in the catalog of the Hebrew University of Jerusalem (a private institution). "These events immediately gave rise to a serious dearth of trained personnel in the country and *the duty of Hebrew University lay clear*. The training of physicians and scientists, of lawyers and jurists, of teachers, economists, sociologists, agronomists and civil servants had to become one of its chief concerns." *Bulletin of the Hebrew University of Jerusalem*, 1958, 6.

[9] William J. McGlothlin, "The Aims of Professional Education," *Education for Social Work, Proceedings*, Sixth Annual Program Meeting (New York: CSWE, 1958), 21–22.

Thus, the professions' responsibility to society for providing the trained personnel required to perform the tasks that need to be done is recognized by them at least in statements of aims, although it seems less honored in practice. One justification given for not training sufficient numbers of entrants to professions is that this would mean the sacrifice of another of their responsibilities—the concern for quality. Two points need to be made in respect to this argument. First, the criteria used to determine qualitatively adequate preparation are always relative to the time and place. An implicit element in establishing educational requirements is always the reality ingredient. For example, it would probably be a good thing if psychiatrists possessed a competent understanding of sociology and social-psychology. Yet, such understanding is not a usual educational requirement. It would obviously be unrealistic to require such an extensive range of advanced study, at least at this time. Requirements for a profession are set with a view to "what the traffic will bear." Hence, the qualitative and quantitative are not totally discrete.

Secondly, this is true in another sense also. The extension of services, because additional, reasonably adequate personnel had become available, to persons who would not have otherwise received them, might well represent a *qualitative* gain for the users of these services even if the competence of such personnel left something to be desired. Should this not be kept in mind when policy decisions have to be made as to whether intake should be restricted because social workers with two years of graduate training are not available; when decisions have to be made as to the function of undergraduate training? Often such policy questions are framed simply in terms of quality *vs.* quantity, and often the response is the stereotyped one.

CONCLUSION

In view of the need and the social responsibility of the profession our conclusion is that the shortage of social workers with graduate training should be treated as a legitimate consideration in deciding whether to provide social work education at the undergraduate level: this does not imply, however, that this social need should be allowed to outweigh all other considerations or to turn colleges and universities into technical schools turning out narrowly trained technicians.[10]

Question 2:

Should the decision whether to provide social work education at the undergraduate level be determined in part by the competitive position of social work as a vocational alternative for the student?

DISCUSSION

The use of the term "competitive" may be disturbing to some. Should social work compete for personnel with other occupations that also perform important social functions? Does this kind of competition lead to an irresponsible pirating of manpower? There is no denying the fact that such competition may work out badly. But our social system is predicated on the assumption that the free competition of civilian occupations for manpower within certain ground rules will, in the long run, prove to be in the best interests of society.

Of course, there are times (usually in a crisis situation) when the government steps in to improve the competitive position of a particular occupational group(s). Even in this case, though, occupations compete for governmental intervention on their behalf. In general it may be said that the existing rules of the game require each occupational group to compete for personnel as effectively as it can (within the norms governing such competition), since this is the basic process on which our society relies for the allocation of manpower. Thus the question of the competitive position of social work as a vocational alternative is both legitimate and important. The facts of the case suggest strongly that social work will indeed be in a difficult competitive position if it continues to insist that professional preparation for practice must be exclusively at the graduate level. What are these facts?

1. It is possible for students to go into other occupations competitive with social work and to complete their professional train-

10 An exaggerated response to the demand for personnel or job preparation can, of course, be very damaging to educational programs. The writer was thus concerned by the following statement which was made to him during the course of his investigation: "Our undergraduate social work program is essentially geared to the market. Its characteristics are primarily a reflection of this and student demand rather than of intra-university policy or conditions."

ing in less time than is now the case in social work. Education and nursing are two such fields.[11]

> The significance of the length of time required by present programs of social work education for the profession's competitive position becomes even more apparent when it is related to the fact that social work depends largely upon the available supply of women for its recruits . . . Matters of real concern for a field employing women predominantly include: (1) the fact that 60 percent of college graduates are men; (2) the knowledge that fewer women than men proceed beyond the bachelor's degree into graduate education; (3) the observation that only about one-half of the women college graduates in this country currently are in the labor market; and (4) the fact that the two largest professional fields of employment for women—nursing and education—currently are in short supply with both engaged in high priority, nationwide recruitment campaigns. The recruitment of educated women is, and undoubtedly will be for some time to come, highly competitive. The social welfare field will have to move fast and aggressively even to hold its own in this race for woman power.[12]

Even for a profession with higher status and better pay, such as law, the average required period of professional training is somewhat less than in social work.[13]

2. Another fact of life that places social work at a competitive disadvantage is this: programs of study offered by other disciplines have, as at least one purpose, the preparation of undergraduate students for immediate employment in positions which social work assumes to be within its legitimate area of functioning. Illustrative of this are the training of "group workers" by the recreation, physical education, or education departments of universities; the preparation of personnel for work in correctional institutions and

[11] The following statement regarding the process of career selection appeared in a recent study of student nurses: "The evidence of this chapter suggests that nursing, as an occupation, is seen by students to be one alternative in a 'pool' of occupational choices which have in common suitability for women, the requirement of skill and education, *but not extended education* (italics the writer's), and moderate rather than large or marginal incomes." Thomas S. McPartland, "Formal Education and the Process of Professionalization," *A Study of the Registered Nurse in a Metropolitan Community*, Part V (Kansas City, Missouri: Community Studies, Inc., 1957), 45.
[12] Charles W. Laughton, *op. cit.*, 24–25. The lowering of the average age at which marriage takes place should also be kept in mind.
[13] Fauri, *op. cit.*

courts by sociology and psychology departments, and the preparation for personnel counseling by schools of business administration. The number of illustrations could be added to generously.

3. A significant consideration in the competitive position of social work is that of the socio-economic background of the undergraduate student oriented toward social work. A recent study of
undergraduates in a number of American universities produced
this finding:

> Seventy-one percent of the wealthiest students planned to enter
> some branch of business or law or medicine, compared with only 38
> percent of the poorest students. On the other hand, the less well-to-
> do student tends to gravitate toward such salaried professions as
> engineering, teaching, *social work* (italics the writer's), and science
> . . . nearly half the students considering themselves working class
> selected one of the salaried professions of engineering, teaching, social
> work, or science, compared with about one-third of the middle class
> members and one-sixth of the upper class . . .
>
> It is clear that as family wealth increases the tendency to choose
> "business" occupations, medicine, or law increases as well, even among
> those who identify with the same social classes.[14]

Other studies give us approximately the same picture, and a study
of graduate students in schools of social work by Dr. Milton Wittman reinforces the findings of other studies.[15] Although Dr. Wittman found that there was a "high incidence of graduate students
with fathers' occupations listed in the professional classes" the income of the parents of 40 percent of the students was under $4000
and 70 percent of the parents had incomes under $6000. Clearly,
these students came from a lower socio-economic position than
students in many other professions. The income data also suggests
that the occupational category of professional and managerial
classes needs to be broken down further into sub-categories. It is
also consistent with other data on the characteristics of social workers that a majority of the graduate students in schools of social
work have had intervening work experience between the comple-

14 Morris Rosenberg, *et al., Occupations and Values* (Glencoe, Illinois: The Free Press,
1957), 54 and 57.
15 Milton Wittman, *Scholarship Aid in Social Work Education* (New York: Council
on Social Work Education, 1956), 26–28.

tion of the undergraduate program and entrance in the graduate school.[16]

The pattern is clear: the student who goes into social work is less adequately prepared, financially, for extended graduate study than students going into professions such as medicine and law. This calls into question once more the realism of the present length of the training period for social work, particularly when viewed in regard to competing occupational alternatives.

Though scholarships can help somewhat there is little chance that they can sufficiently compensate for the differential income. For example, there is extensive help available to graduate students in the physical and social sciences. This means that as long as competing disciplines get such aid it is highly unlikely that the amount of assistance available to social work students would radically change its competitive position.

4. Social work is also at a disadvantage in recruiting men into the profession.

Some of the factors that make it particularly difficult for social work to compete with other professions and business for male students are:

    a. The image of social work as a woman's field
    b. The societal emphasis on technology and defense-related science
    c. Values and attitudinal factors

Social work is a "people-oriented" field which puts a relatively high premium on humanitariansm and a comparatively limited stress on profit-making. Our society tends to promote the acquisition of different values and attitudes in men and women and it is the latter whose values and attitudes are most compatible with the function and ideology of social work. The following report of a study on occupations and values brings this out very clearly.

> Relatively speaking, the women are people-oriented, the men extrinsic-reward oriented. These data suggest that society, through the inculcation of role prescriptions, encourages men and women to want different things from their work. . . Men and women thus tend to

[16] *Ibid.,* 24–25.

select distinctly different occupations. Further evidence of the sexual division of labor appears when we ask students what type of organization they expect to work in. Women are much more likely than men to choose a humanitarian, educational, non-profit organization. Compared with the male students, only a small minority of women expect to achieve occupational independence in the sense of becoming independent entrepreneurs or professionals. Almost all of them will be subject to some sort of occupational supervision or domination.[17]

5. Social work's modest prestige and financial rewards are a handicap in competition with other professions.

A number of studies have indicated that the public does not rank social work as one of the high prestige professions.[18] This may be partly the result of the negative images of social workers held by various "publics." It is interesting in this connection to note that students who are planning to enter the high status professions, such as medicine or law, are less likely to take undergraduate social work courses than students who are identified with occupations of lesser prestige.[19]

A second problem in interesting students in social work is their probable earning power in relation to the comparatively long training required. "The public school teacher, for instance, earns the basic professional education degree in four years of college, and goes into jobs with a pay range like that in social work." [20] Together, the limited prestige and earnings are a barrier to recruitment for the social work profession.[21]

6. The low visibility of social work as an occupational alternative also places it at a competitive disadvantage.

As we have previously noted, social work has a problem of being understood—of having its contemporary functions known and being seen as a vocational alternative of a professional character. The importance of this factor in the choice of a career is evident in

---

[17] Rosenberg, *op. cit.,* 49–50.
[18] Harold L. Wilensky and Charles N. Lebeaux, *Industrial Society and Social Welfare* (New York: Russell Sage Foundation, 1958), 309–311.
[19] See Appendix E.
[20] Wilensky and Lebeaux, *op. cit.,* 311.
[21] Differential prestige and income even influence recruiting as between the established high prestige professions, to the advantage of medicine as compared with law. Merton, Reader, and Kendall, *op. cit.,* 137.

the case of other professions as well. One writer, in discussing the fact that prospective law students decide on their professions at a later age and somewhat more tentatively than do medical students, relates this to several differences between the two professions, one of which is "the greater difficulty people have in forming a clear idea of what a lawyer does." [22]

A finding which has bearing on the matter of the low visibility of social work as an occupational alternative was reported in a study of registered nurses. The main vocational possibilities that had been considered by the nurses prior to their decision in favor of a nursing career were (in order of frequency): teaching, office jobs of various sorts, creative and performing arts, and medical specialties such as physical therapist and laboratory technician. While there is a miscellaneous category that may or may not have included social work, the interesting result is that social work was not rejected as an occupational possibility by many (if any) of the nurses. Apparently they did not even see it as an alternative.[23] This finding is particularly meaningful since nursing is a competitor (friendly, of course) of social work in respect to recruitment, as well as being within the range of occupations in which one might expect to find some interchangeability as to career choices.

It is strikingly evident that social work is at a competitive disadvantage in the search for recruits. There is good reason for believing that the length of the required period of educational preparation and the "official" policy of putting professional social work training at the graduate level and treating it as discrete from undergraduate study are unrealistic in terms of this problem. The potential value to the profession of having an undergraduate program clearly identifiable as a professional alternative is indicated in the reports of two recent studies. In one, the investigator concluded that a factor which contributed to the earlier commitment to professional school by medical students (as compared with law students) was the more extensive premedical course requirements.[24] The second study is perhaps even more illuminating for our prob-

[22] This hypothesis, advanced by Wagner Thielens, Jr., is reported on in Merton, Reader, and Kendall, *op. cit.*, 106.
[23] McPartland, *op. cit.*, 35-36.
[24] Wagner Thielens, Jr., "Some Comparisons of Entrants to Medical and Law School," in Merton, Reader, and Kendall, *op. cit.*, 132-133.

lem. In his analysis of stability and lability of occupational choice among college students, Morris Rosenberg reports as follows:

> With the exception of the College of Arts and Sciences, therefore, students entering any of the other colleges [within Cornell University] as undergraduates begin to receive training in the fields of specialization of their respective colleges. It is in these fields of specialization that the lowest degree of change occurs. Students in the colleges of Engineering, Home Economics, Hotel Administration, and Architecture are the most stable in their occupational choices. These are followed by Medicine, Law, and Teaching. It will be noted that these latter fields require specialized training; in law and medicine, however, students have not officially started such training but are usually taking some courses in preparation for such advanced work . . . In general, then, it appears possible to make the following statement: in those fields requiring extensive specialized training, *in which training is started at the undergraduate level* (italics the writer's) we find the smallest amount of occupational turnover; in those fields requiring specialized training in which the official formal training has not started at the undergraduate level but in which some preparation may be underway, the amount of turnover is somewhat higher; and in those fields requiring relatively little specialized training the amount of turnover is highest.[25]

Thus, it is interesting that "with the exception of social work, none of the seven most changeable occupations involved specialized and long-term training for occupational practice." [26]

The conclusion, then, is that *early* specialization is an important factor in the crystallization of occupational choice.

What is the explanation for this finding? Rosenberg offers this suggestion:

> The psychological reasons can probably be accounted for in terms of a theory of *involvement and investment.* Our expectation would be that people might feel just as tentative in their selection of a stable as of a changeable occupation at the outset. However, as they begin to take courses in their fields, even if these be pre-medical or pre-law courses, they develop a certain involvement in the problems and content of the field which tends to anchor their choices. This interest is

[25] Rosenberg, *et al., op. cit.,* 64–65.
[26] *Ibid.,* 63.

probably reinforced by regular interaction with other people who are becoming technical specialists.[27]

The absence of specialized work that is clearly related to social work as a professional alternative at the undergraduate level undoubtedly deepens the hole in which social work finds itself competitively. Of course, it may be argued that the early hardening of career choices is not desirable from the point of view of allowing the student an opportunity to explore a variety of choices; that it prematurely freezes his career pattern before he has attained emotional maturity, and the knowledge on which to base a reasoned decision. There is merit in this contention. However, from the viewpoint of the societal allocation of manpower and recruitment into the profession, it would appear that social work must be concerned with achieving a more favorable competitive position in respect to the process of career selection by undergraduate students.[28]

CONCLUSION

The present competitive situation would appear to warrant serious professional consideration of social work education at the undergraduate level as one important means by which the profession can be seen and considered as a vocational choice.

Question 3:

Should social work education at the undergraduate level have as ONE goal preparation of students for employment upon graduation? [29]

DISCUSSION

Important as are considerations of personnel shortage and the competitive recruitment position of social work, one cannot mini-

---

27 *Ibid.,* 65.
28 The writer has been told that some of the recruitment literature for one of the competing disciplines is aimed at eighth-graders.
29 As was pointed out both in Dean Mossman's report and in our findings many existing undergraduate programs do in fact prepare students for employment in social work. However, uncertainty as to the appropriateness of this function, and confusion as to how it should be implemented, have had an adverse impact on the undergraduate programs. See Appendix A, and Chapter IV.

mize the crucial question of what training is necessary for performance of a given social work function. (It is in discussing this question that we link up society's concern with allocation of personnel, the profession's interest in recruitment, and the student's selection of an occupation.) In social work, as in any other field, planned employment of personnel with varying amounts or kinds of professional preparation will require careful differentiation of the professional functions they are to perform.

It would appear almost axiomatic that, under present circumstances, the most advantageous use of social workers with graduate training requires a differentiation of social work functions so that social workers with such training will be used most appropriately. Yet, despite the seemingly simple and obvious quality of this statement, it leads us down a difficult road. The first roadblock is the question: Is such differentiation of function feasible in social work? Before one can catch his breath he is confronted with a second massive "stopper": What would be the nature of this differentiation of functions? *Let us in all honesty say that we cannot answer either of these questions on the basis of this investigation. Definitive answers will be available only after the social work profession does a comprehensive national study of practice.*[30] *However, there are suggestive clues which, while a long way from firmly based conclusions, provide grounds for experimentation and interim working arrangements.*

THE SITUATION IN OTHER PROFESSIONS

By looking to other professions for clues to what might be appropriate, social work runs the danger of the false analogy. But an equally serious danger that may prevent our learning from others is to assume that analogy must be false because of social work's extreme uniqueness. We shall attempt here to maintain a balance without developing too serious a case of invertebracy. There appears to be a pattern in the development of professions. As they mature (assuming a shortage rather than a surplus of personnel), they tend to analyze their functions and gradually functional dif-

---

[30] The public social services project of the Curriculum Study has analyzed the job of the social worker in certain programs, but its design did not provide for securing answers to the problem of functional differentiation *within* the category of caseworker.

ferentiation takes place. This is often accompanied by the emergence of new professional or technician groups or by the creation of different "levels" within the profession.[31] Although this is a process many professions have gone through, it has seldom come about without a certain amount of "blood, sweat and tears." In her well-known report for the National Nursing Council, Esther Lucile Brown wrote:

> What then is a possible solution of this very difficult problem of obtaining a supply of nursing care that is quantitatively and qualitatively sufficient? Along with many other persons, we believe that the answer is inherent in the questions: What kinds of nursing functions need to be performed? Can persons be found and prepared to fulfill these functions effectively, whether they be graduate nurses or not?
>
> One basic error, common to some other professions as well, has been primarily responsible for the difficulties currently encountered Emphasis has been centered upon the "nurse" or at best "nurses." The term as employed by the nursing profession and the laity responsible for making policy, moreover, has almost always meant the graduate nurse, the R.N. . . . So long as attention is centered on the graduate nurse, no other avenue is open except that of the present frantic and probably futile effort to recruit more prospective R.N.'s. . . . Once emphasis is shifted to nursing, however, several roads seem to point to potentially larger supplies of service and to possibly increased efficiency both on the nonprofessional and the professional levels.
>
> Pressure of circumstances has been leading steadily toward those roads. Unfortunately the experience gained has not been sufficiently examined, assimilated, and fashioned into a philosophy for planned future action. For a long time two systems of nursing care have existed side by side. So fixedly, however, have eyes been focused on one of these systems—that of graduate nurses—that the other, if recognized at all, has merely received the designation of "auxiliary." Only recently and in a relatively small number of places have any profound efforts been made to fuse members of these two systems into *coordinated teams* in which each person, according to background, training, and experience, performs certain functions essential to total nursing care.[32]

31 See *Education for the Professions,* ed. and organized by Lloyd E. Blauch, Department of Health, Education, and Welfare. (Washington, D.C.: U.S. Government Printing Office, 1955), 1.

32 Esther Lucile Brown, *Nursing for the Future* (New York: Russell Sage Foundation, 1948), 57–58. The present development of the two- and four-year nursing programs represents an interesting step in the direction suggested by Dr. Brown.

It is of no little significance that Dr. Brown, who is a student of the professions, received the following mandate from the nursing organization that sponsored her study:

> To view nursing service and nursing education in terms of what is best for society—not what is best for the profession of nursing as a possible "vested interest." If it was found that the larger interest of society conflicted at any point with the interests of nurses, the director would be expected to represent the social welfare.[33]

A recent study in the realm of another profession raises some of the same questions we are facing in social work. (The very recurrence of problems from profession to profession is itself of import.)

> There are not enough psychiatrists to perform adequately the work our society is demanding from the profession. To be sure, nobody knows how many psychiatrists are needed; some well-informed sources suggest twice or three times the present number but this is only a guess . . . From a social and economic viewpoint we are obliged to think of training a less expensive therapist. . . . Do we need more therapists? If we do we ought to train more. If we cannot train a sufficient number of psychiatrists, we ought to train other therapists in the mental health field. . . . As long as these counselors, and with some courage we might call them therapists, are well trained and do not dabble in fields beyond their training, there should be no meaningful objection to such a venture. To be sure, therapy, at least since the days of pure magic, has been the prerogative of the medical profession, but why should a nonmedical problem, such as emotional reeducation in work and family life, remain in the domain pre-empted by the medical profession? Why should we not train a new professional specialist? . . . Therapies which demand basic medical knowledge should remain the prerogative of the medical profession, but outside of this medical orbit, psychiatrists and medical analysts have little right to block attempts to train an adequate number of therapists to do the job our society needs. The public would get used to such a profession, and the profession, in due time, would develop the sense of responsibility and regard for human welfare and dignity which have rewarded the medical profession with such high prestige in our society.[34]

[33] *Ibid.,* 11.
[34] August B. Hollingshead and Frederick C. Redlich, *Social Class and Mental Illness* (New York: John Wiley and Sons, Inc., 1958), 375, 377–378.

It is evident that there is a similarity in the problems facing nursing and psychiatry although in one case the suggested solution is "integrated differentiation" within the profession while in the other the emphasis is on the development of a new professional group. In both approaches, a differentiation of function is called for.

THE PRESENT SITUATION IN SOCIAL WORK

The pertinent characteristics of the present situation in social work are as follows:

1. Much of the actual practice of social work, particularly in public agencies, is carried on by persons without specific social work education of a formal sort.

2. There is a considerable amount of *expedient* differentiation of functions or tasks in many agencies. In some places "levels" of social worker have been developed and related to various levels of social work education. However, this has not been done on a nation-wide basis. Also, from the point of view of membership in the professional association, the *social worker is the graduate trained social worker* (except for those blanketed in at the start).

3. Many undergraduate colleges report active recruiting of their students by public social agencies.

4. In some agencies the college graduate whose undergraduate major or concentration has been in social work (or in some cases sociology or psychology) is favored over the graduate whose course of study was in another area. This "favoring" may be manifested in eligibility for certain positions not otherwise open to students without graduate study, in pay differentials, in skipping over the traineeship category, and so on.

5. A certain amount of experimentation with "case aides" and "social work technicians" who have not had graduate study is now underway. There has in the past been considerable discussion as to the feasibility of using this level of social worker, and some are presently employed; indications are that consideration of the functions of such aides and the actual use of them are both increasing. The Family Service Association of America, for example, reports that there was a 13 percent increase in the use of case aides in 1957.

Various agencies using aides (or technicians) report that such personnel may be of real help in increasing the effectiveness of the agency's programs.[35] However, it should again be pointed out that extensive and systematic study of functional differentiation in social work is necessary before any firm conclusions can be arrived at on this score. It is the writer's belief that with further job analysis and experimentation it will be found feasible, in many agencies, to employ persons with different levels of education to perform different social work functions.[36]

6. Two aspects of functional differentiation in social work need further clarification. The first concerns the occupational identification and status of the social worker with less than two years of graduate training. Should he be identified as a social worker or should a new technician or a new "subprofessional" occupational group be formed? In view of the shortage of graduate trained social workers it would appear most unwise to encourage the formation of a separate occupational group since we would then have a majority of the persons performing social work functions not classified as social workers. Furthermore, since such a high proportion of the workers in certain of the public social services (such as public assistance or child welfare or corrections) might be incorporated within the new occupational group, the divergence between public and private services might be sharpened and social work increasingly identified with the latter exclusively.

It would seem much more desirable to have "levels" within social work. This would present problems, of course, such as the tensions produced by a hierarchical arrangement within a profession and the question of promotion from one "level" to another. Though these are significant and troublesome problems they appear to be much outweighed by the positive consequences of keep-

---

35 National Social Welfare Assembly, *The Use of Case Aides in Casework Agencies* (New York: NSWA, 1958). Among the interesting papers in this pamphlet are: Anna Budd Ware, "The Case Aide in a Single Function Agency;" Ruth B. Robinson, "The Case Aide in a Multi-Function Agency;" and Fergus T. Monahan, "The Case Aide in a Military Setting." Another reference on the subject is Ellery C. Russell, "Case Aides Free Casework Time," *Child Welfare*, XXXVII (April, 1958).

36 Some interesting suggestions of criteria for classifying occupations by level of function, involving degree of responsibility, capacity and skill, are presented in Roe, *op. cit.*, 149–152.

ing all the functions proper to social work inside the profession.

A second aspect is that of titles. The writer finds the terms "aide" and "technician" inappropriate from the point of view of a meaningful description. Even the term "assistant in social work" would not be sufficiently explanatory or accurate in terms of the function performed, at least in many public agencies. Although not a perfect solution, it would seem that a title such as "social work associate" might combine the purposes of indicating it is a lower "level" (which could then be differentiated specifically from the more highly trained "social worker") without unduly emphasizing the invidious status differential.

It is ironic that social work, as a profession, has looked more kindly upon the volunteer and untrained worker than upon the "partially trained" social worker. While this is not incomprehensible in light of what we know about the prestige preoccupations of professions, it is hardly a justifiable position when subjected to analysis. In his field trip the writer found considerable support from social work educators, at both the graduate and undergraduate levels, for the contention that a differentiation in the functions of social workers is feasible and that different levels of educational preparation might be suitable for different "levels" of social work practice.

CONCLUSION

Until further research provides a validated basis for a systematic differentiation of function which can be widely related to different educational levels we must remain tentative in our conclusions on this point. What can be said without any hesitation is that, at the very least, the student who takes the proposed undergraduate program of social work education should be much better prepared than a student without such preparation to be employed in social work.[37]

---

[37] Two considerations, in addition to those already discussed, might be kept in mind. Are the "publics" and policy makers willing *to pay* to have all social work functions performed by workers with full professional preparation? *As presently constituted,* are not many social work positions (particularly at the beginning level) insufficiently interesting and challenging in respect to exercise of judgment, responsibility, use of skills in interpersonal relations, to attract professional social workers?

GENERAL CONCLUSIONS

On the basis of assumptions we postulated and the preceding analyses of the shortage of social workers, the difficult competitive position of social work in regard to recruitment, and the possibilities of effective differentiation among social work functions, we conclude as follows:

1. Social work education at the undergraduate level should have as one goal the preparation of students for employment in social work upon graduation.

2. Such undergraduate education might appropriately aim at the preparation of "social work associates." It should not and need not fail to prepare students simultaneously for advanced training and full professional standing.

3. "Legitimatizing" a category of "social work associates" would necessitate, as a minimum, specification of relatively attainable, definite, but limited educational requirements, and appropriate recognition of this occupational status by the professional association.

Inclusion of educational preparation for an occupation within a college or university goes a long way toward legitimatizing it. For social work associates, it would imply that they are being prepared in at least a minimally adequate manner for the positions they will hold, in contrast with the present view of them as less than adequately prepared substitutes for presently unattainable professional social workers. Of course, professions are not static and it is possible that in the future other levels may be developed. With such further differentiations, social work associate and "social worker" might be upgraded, or even merged.

4. The probability is that legitimatizing the social work associate category would result in an overall upgrading of social work standards, greater adequacy of service, and improved personnel morale, as well as raising the societal evaluation of social work, provided the following minimum conditions were met: (1) clear recognition (by employers, board members, legislature, and so on, that certain social work positions, because of their defined functional characteristics, need to be filled by professional social work-

ers with completed graduate education; (2) the availability of a reasonably adequate number of social workers to fill such positions; (3) establishing of salary and other status differentials commensurate with the various levels of preparation; (4) a quality of job performance by social workers and social work associates that reflects the differential value of their training in comparison with persons with less or no special education.

5. A conclusion that follows logically from the preceding one is that students who qualify, upon graduation, for the status of social work associate, should be granted employment preference for appropriate types of social work positions over those without such training.

6. While the development and expansion of agency in-service training programs is highly desirable, such programs constitute an inappropriate method, in principle, of meeting the need for more social workers. Such programs should be used to complement formal social work education rather than to substitute for it at any level.[38] Conversely, specific training for performance in particular settings *is* appropriately included in in-service training programs but is not a legitimate function of an undergraduate college.

[38] The view was expressed to the writer by a prominent social work educator that she would rather see the shortage of social workers dealt with by in-service training programs than by developing undergraduate programs. It is the writer's view that this position is unsound educationally, and would not result in liberally educated social workers.

CHAPTER VI

The Relationship Between the Undergraduate and Graduate Phases of Social Work Education

POSTULATES

1. There should be a high degree of continuity between the undergraduate program for social work and graduate social work education.

2. The strict allocation of "liberal" education to undergraduate education and specialized professional education to graduate schools tends to result in undesirable discontinuity between these stages in the educative process.

THREE QUESTIONS DISCUSSED

We can get right to the heart of this chapter by asking three questions so inextricably related that they will be discussed at the same time.

Should the undergraduate and graduate programs (and the levels within them) be conceived of as stages in a single program of social work education?

Should more specific content than is now the case be required for admission to graduate schools of social work?

Should students who have completed a sound undergraduate social work concentration or major receive preference from the admissions committees of graduate schools of social work?

DISCUSSION

In seeking answers to these three questions, we need initially to see what the present situation is; then turn to how well the existing arrangements work (that is, what are the consequences); and finally, examine the data available, from both social work and other disciplines, that might have a bearing.

What is the present relationship between undergraduate education and graduate education for social work? The picture is confused, but a general pattern seems to be identifiable. Let us turn first to the admission requirements pertaining to academic qualifications laid down by the graduate schools. Although the range is from the rather specific to nothing more than a bachelor's degree, the typical statement found in the graduate school catalog specifies a certain number of hours in the social and biological sciences; some may also list the major science areas in which these credits should be taken, and a lesser number enumerate such courses as statistics, biology, abnormal psychology and the like.[1]

The really significant fact about the requirements is their relative lack of specificity and, most importantly, the absence of any demand for prior social work content.[2]

In view of the above facts it is not surprising that our study indicates, in practice, little planned continuity between undergraduate education and graduate social work training.[3] Among the effects of this discontinuity on undergraduate schools are: (1) uncertainty about what the graduate schools and the profession want them to do; (2) confusion as to the process of student selection; (3) annoyance at the apparent lack of understanding of, or hostility toward, their programs by the graduate schools; and (4) uncertainty as to the function of their programs, if any, in social work education.

This discontinuity poses some serious difficulties for the graduate schools also. First, the students entering graduate schools of

[1] See Katherine D. Lower, "Undergraduate Preparation Prerequisite to Admission to Graduate Schools of Social Work: From the Graduate Point of View," *Selected Papers Re: Undergraduate Education,* Sixth Annual Program Meeting, Council on Social Work Education, 1958 (New York: CSWE, 1958), mimeographed; and "A Summary of 37 Contacts with Graduate Schools of Social Work which Indicated their Reactions to Certain Basic Questions on Social Work Education" (Processed, Goshen, Indiana: Goshen College, 1956), 5–6.

[2] The writer was told by a student that the dean of a school of social work in a large university told her to avoid any social work courses on the undergraduate level, even though there was a so-called concentration offered in that university on the undergraduate level.

[3] A similar conclusion was arrived at by Margery Ross in her Michigan study, "Influences Affecting the Development of Undergraduate Social Work Education in Seven Michigan Colleges from 1920–1955" (Unpublished doctoral dissertation, University of Michigan, 1956), 242.

social work do not possess a shared body of prerequisite learning. There are serious gaps in their background as well as unexpected familiarity with some of the graduate content.[4] This, in turn, has these negative consequences: (1) much unprofitable duplication between undergraduate and graduate courses, particularly during the first year of graduate school; (2) a considerable part of the graduate curriculum is not of graduate caliber since it necessarily has to "introduce" the student to many areas for which there is no foundation of specific prerequisite knowledge on which to build; [5] (3) many students appear to have difficulty in relating relevant content in the basic disciplines learned during their undergraduate years to courses in graduate schools.[6] As a result, students often find the first year of graduate school unduly frustrating and the instructor finds his teaching assignment difficult. It is common to have students write to their former teachers in the undergraduate college complaining about the "low level" of work in graduate school, the lack of challenge, and the amount of "deadly" duplication. At the same time they often express considerable enthusiasm for undergraduate social work courses.[7] The writer got these reactions literally from coast to coast. Specific examples were given, such as re-using in graduate schools papers originally prepared for undergraduate courses (and getting "A's" on them).

One must sympathize though, with the teacher in the graduate school. Under present circumstances he will necessarily have a problem in determining in what key to pitch his course and what the appropriate focus should be. The following gentle comment in a study of legal education is much to the point. "I venture the thesis that law teachers are unable to get an adequate perspective on their immediate assignments unless they have an insight into what use their students have made of their time before entering law

---

[4] This finding is also supported by data from other projects of the Study.

[5] This elementary quality is expressed in two general areas: basic science material (*e.g.,* basic anatomical content) which is normally taught in undergraduate departments, and in being responsible for "introductory" social work content. See the findings reported on in Chapter IV.

[6] See Chapter IV.

[7] See, for example, Alfred Kadushin, "A Study of Suggestions Made by New York School of Social Work Graduates for Changes in the School." Unpublished masters thesis, New York School of Social Work, 1958; Margaret B. Matson, "Undergraduate Preparation Prerequisite to Admission to Graduate Schools of Social Work: From the Undergraduate Point of View." *Selected Papers Re: Undergraduate Education, op. cit.*

school." [8] Apparently, faculty members in graduate schools of social work often know relatively little about the actual content of their students' undergraduate education, although in at least one graduate school visited by the writer an exploratory attempt is being made at systematic probing of the knowledge and attitudinal resources and limitations of the entering student.

A second major problem created for graduate schools by the existent discontinuity between the undergraduate and graduate years is the difficulty in recruiting students for graduate school. We have already referred to the conclusion by Morris Rosenberg that specialization at the undergraduae level is related to the stability of occupational choices through the processes of involvement and investment. Another recent study points in the same direction.

> For the model student, then, the definite career choice is keyed to the institutional requirements of the educational system. He does not prolong his choice much *beyond* the point when he must select courses appropriate to medical school prerequisites nor does he arrive at the decision before the socially prescribed time . . . Law students make their career decision an average of two years later than medical students . . . The discrepancy can more readily be explained by the more specialized educational prerequisite of medical schools.[9]

Hence, despite the barriers imposed by prerequisites, it is very likely that their absence actually hurts recruitment by graduate schools. It seems to be a fair guess that social work will be outdistanced if it fails to interest and involve students in social work in the undergraduate college.[10]

Other problems for graduate schools of social work created or aggravated by the discontinuity between "levels" include:

1. The crowding of the graduate curriculum by "basic" knowledge and other content that might be appropriately taught at the undergraduate level.

[8] Albert J. Harno, *Legal Education in the United States* (San Francisco: Bancroft-Whitney Co., 1953), 127.
[9] Natalie Rogoff, "The Decision to Study Medicine," in Merton, Reader and Kendall, *op. cit.,* 115–116.
[10] It seems likely that social work concentrations and/or separate offerings tend to increase the number of students going on to graduate school rather than lessen it. The data secured by Professor Laughton are of real interest in this connection. They indicate that undergraduate introductory courses in social work and social work majors are related to securing a professional education. Laughton, *op. cit.,* 30–31.

2. Increased isolation of the school of social work and its faculty from the rest of the university, particularly from the basic sciences and the humanities.

3. Inadequate lines of communication with, and impaired influence upon, undergraduate schools, reflected in a lack of familiarity with the nature of undergraduate education.

4. Delaying the process of socialization of the neophyte into the profession, with an additional burden thus imposed on the graduate school for accomplishing this in short order. What is involved here is a delay in what Robert Merton has called *anticipatory socialization*.

> Having chosen the field, he [the student] is likely to incorporate into his present self-image aspects of his future occupational status . . . This image of his future occupational status is likely to influence the student's *present* attitudes, values, and behavior; he may start to think and behave in a way which he believes will be appropriate when he actually enters occupational practice.[11]

Social work is at a disadvantage in this respect when compared with other professions having less discontinuity between the undergraduate and graduate school years. This is particularly important since social work is an occupation in which value and attitudinal considerations are highly relevant. Furthermore, there is a sound basis for arguing that social work's ideology is sufficiently different from that of important sections of the community, and in some cases from that of the prospective social worker's family and friends, to make desirable an early and continuing "initiation" into social work.[12]

5. Adding to the student's problems in adjusting to graduate school and making it difficult for him to decide whether he should be a caseworker, group worker and so on, since he lacks the proper basis for such a decision.[13]

[11] Rosenberg, *op. cit.*, 24. See also the report of the Curriculum Study's project on values and ethics.
[12] Empirical support for this contention appears in Norman Polansky, William Bowen, Lucille Gordon and Conrad Nathan, "Social Workers in Society: Results of a Sampling Study," *Social Work Journal*, XXXIV (April 1953); Rosenberg, *op. cit.* An analysis of social work ideology in a societal context appears in Herbert Bisno, *The Philosophy of Social Work* (Washington, D.C.: Public Affairs Press, 1952).
[13] Although many factors are involved, it is interesting to note that when one compares the transition of medical and law students from the undergraduate college to

In spite of the serious difficulties associated with the present discontinuity between undergraduate education and the graduate school program, there are those who believe that articulating the various "levels" into a single coherent program of social work education would be a most unfortunate development. Some of the arguments put forth by those who oppose an integrated undergraduate-graduate social work program are stated in the following propositions, with the author's replies:

It would destroy the autonomy of the liberal arts college and undermine liberal arts education.

Part of the answer to this contention was provided in Chapter III when the writer took issue with the liberal arts professional education dichotomy. But there are additional considerations involved.

First, as we envision it the total program would not have to be under the administration of a graduate school. Rather, the undergraduate phases of the program might well remain under the jurisdiction and administration of the liberal arts college.

Second, in accordance with the position already enunciated, the social work objectives recommended for the undergraduate stages and discussed in detail in Chapters VII–XI, would be of a liberalizing character. Indeed, the results of the program suggested herein would be, we believe, a more liberal total educational experience than most students now get.

Third, it would not be necessary to have specific accrediting of the undergraduate stages by the social work profession. Some ways to enhance the quality of the undergraduate programs and achieve a measure of uniformity without this type of formal accreditation are: recommendations and consultative service by the CSWE; support from NASW and employer associations such as the American Public Welfare Association; preferential admission policies by graduate schools, as well as preferential hiring of graduates by employing agencies.

---

professional school, the law student who has had less of an organized undergraduate program directly linked to professional school than the medical student, faces a more competitive first year (the "flunkouts" are much higher than in the medical school) and views the transition as a sharper break with the past. Thielens, *op. cit.,* 145–151.

Fourth, there would be no necessity for subordinating courses taught in the basic disciplines to professional purposes.

Fifth, with the present discontinuity eliminated, the notion that the undergraduate college should teach "about social work" rather than teach social work would be allowed to die a natural and well-deserved death. As seen in Chapter IV, this last idea has been one of the main causes of the existing emphasis on informational-descriptive social work courses, at the expense of conceptual learning. Interestingly enough, these are the courses that most violate the spirit of liberal arts and most closely approximate "narrow vocationalism."

It is our position, then, that the integrity of the liberal arts college would be preserved and that the impact of the overall program would be to turn out more rather than less liberally educated social workers.

An articulated undergraduate-graduate program is not feasible regardless of its desirability.

It is perfectly true that there would be many problems in implementing the program. It will be necessary to identify educational objectives for the different levels and show their continuity. Requirements for graduate school will have to be spelled out and adhered to within reasonable limits. This should (and could) be done in such a manner that, while requirements could be fulfilled on the undergraduate level, applicants coming directly from practice and from other undergraduate fields would not be excluded; provision could be made for such students to make up any deficiencies.

Many of these problems should be worked on jointly by both undergraduate and graduate schools. The procedures set up to establish a foundation for graduate study would have to blend, as well as possible, with procedures to allow competent people to enter graduate school at different periods in their professional life. (Qualifying examinations might be employed in this connection.) Actually, this is done now in many "academic" graduate departments in which the student has to make up background deficiencies but is not precluded from entering the department.

Setting up specific requirements for graduate school would hamper recruitment for graduate schools at a time when the need is to encourage the maximum number of students to enter.

We do not think that setting up specific requirements would aggravate personnel shortages. Although some students might be deterred from going on, the overall effect could be expected to be an increasing supply of students both for graduate schools and for immediate employment. The evidence previously cited indicates that the development of social work as a definite undergraduate vocational choice, intimately tied in with graduate school and practice, is likely to attract and hold more students than has been the case heretofore. Both "investment" and "involvement" would be working for social work. Also, the setting up of requirements may help to interest good students who have steered away from social work on the grounds that it did not represent enough of an intellectual challenge.

A program which has vocational possibilities at the end of four years is likely to increase greatly the flow of students into it. The additional time beyond the bachelor's degree is likely to seem less discouraging to a senior who knows he could stop at that point than to a freshman who is told he has to go to school for six years before he can legitimately break into the social work labor market.

Nor should one overlook the effect upon the entire university of having a defined social work program. This provides an opportunity for interpretation as well as recruitment. Also one would not anticipate agencies cutting down on scholarship funds for graduate study since, even with social work associates, the demand for social workers with graduate education would continue to exceed the supply.

A few cautions are in order. The requirements should not be so numerous that making up deficiencies would appear to be well nigh hopeless. Also, the graduate schools should build systematic procedures by which unmet requirements could be made up. Finally, it is possible that, with the greatly increased efficiency of an articulated program, the length of the total social work program could be reduced. The possibility of a single program consisting of four years of undergraduate work and one year in graduate school will be discussed in a following chapter. If such a reduction in the overall period of preparation for a professional social worker were achieved in the future, it would, of course, greatly increase the number of students going on for graduate training.

These then are the arguments and our replies. There are those who point to legal education and say that it would be a desirable model for social work. (Few undergraduate requirements, but the student would be permitted to enter professional school earlier.) Our response would be that it is questionable whether the combination of "loose" undergraduate requirements and early entrance into graduate school has worked out well for law.[14] Various studies of lawyers tend to suggest that legal education has not solved the problem of liberalizing professional education. Another suggestion that has been made is that there be two years of general education followed by four years of professional training. Our objections to this and other proposals that would allow the student to have a rather free "general education" for a number of years, followed by admission to graduate school prior to conclusion of the fourth year, is that it intensifies the liberal arts-professional educational dichotomy and increases the already artificial compartmentalization of the students' intellectual experiences. We believe that there is a greater danger of narrow vocationalism when the student goes into graduate school prior to securing his bachelor's degree than in an interweaving of liberal and professional education throughout the undergraduate and graduate years. Also from one practical point of view these proposals fail to exploit the possibility of numerous undergraduate colleges preparing social work associates and at the same time increasing the supply of recruits to graduate school. Thus, such plans would not realistically come to grips with the important problem of recruitment.

Some may ask though: isn't the proposed articulated undergraduate-graduate social work program a step backwards? Are not other disciplines moving in the other direction? What about under-

---

[14] This system is also being tried in teacher education now. The late Judge Vanderbilt, a student of legal education, was very critical of prelegal education. He argued that there was no time for teaching the fundamentals of the social sciences in law school—they should be taught on the prelegal level. Despite the crucial nature of such knowledge for lawyers, he felt they weren't coming into law school well prepared. Arthur T. Vanderbilt, *Men and Measures in the Law* (New York: Alfred A. Knopf, 1949), 54–61.

graduate medical education? It is true that there have been attempts to broaden and liberalize the training in several of the professions. But these steps have to be viewed in terms of the realities involved. For example, the elimination of a major and the use of the term pre-professional does not mean that a discipline has no specialized requirements which are an organic part of the total program of education for that profession. No matter what they major in, most "pre-meds" have to take a large number of specialized courses. "With rare exceptions, entrants to the University of Pennsylvania School of Medicine are required as undergraduates to take at least 52 semester hours of specified courses in biology, chemistry, physics, mathematics and English." [15] And in many cases students recognize the desirability of taking "recommended" courses in order to improve their chances of being accepted into medical schools.

An interesting comment, compatible with our thinking, was made recently by the President of Smith College who argued for cutting down on the time it takes to get a Ph.D.

> The Doctor of Philosophy "bottleneck" is in part responsible for the present teacher shortage, Dr. Benjamin F. Wright, President of Smith College, says in his annual report . . . Frequently, the Smith College president claims, it takes longer to get a Ph.D. than an M.D. He adds that *if a student devoted most of his time during the junior and senior years to a special field two years of additional study in graduate work should be sufficient.* (Italics the writer's.) [16]

In our judgment a single program of social work education, undergraduate-graduate, would be both more efficient and more "liberalizing" than the present arrangement; and it would improve the quality of undergraduate social work offerings while, at the same time, putting graduate social work education at a truly graduate level.

15 Thielens, *op. cit.,* 133.
16 *The New York Times,* Sunday, February 9, 1958, Section E, 9.

CONCLUSIONS

1. The undergraduate and graduate programs (and the levels within them) should be conceived of as stages within a single program of social work education.

2. Specific content should be required as prerequisite for admission to graduate schools of social work.

3. Students who have completed a sound undergraduate social work concentration or major should receive preference from the admissions committees of graduate schools of social work.

We will conclude this chapter by saying that we believe the goal of preparation for employment in social work as a social work associate and the goal of preparation for graduate study in social work are both legitimate goals of the undergraduate phase of the program of social work education. Furthermore, we believe that it is desirable and feasible for both goals to be achieved by one undergraduate program. This latter point will be developed in Chapter VII.

Organization of Content
in the Undergraduate Phase
of Social Work Education:
The Development and Nature of the Objectives

POSTULATES[1]

1. In accomplishing the purposes of undergraduate education it is more important to help the student develop the ability to acquire and utilize knowledge in an appropriate, meaningful and creative fashion than to attempt the impossible task of teaching him all he needs to know. Hence, course emphasis should be on the cultivation of disciplined intellectual powers, rather than on information accumulation, although such powers are developed, of course, through working with specific content.

There should be more emphasis on underlying principles and goals than on the teaching of technical skills, and, when technical skills are taught, they should be associated with the development of understanding of principles and purposes.

2. The student should be helped to develop a broad "world view" rather than a narrow outlook limited to his own immediate vocational interests.

3. The student should have some opportunity to pursue his own interests, no matter how broad or esoteric they may be, by means of elective courses.

4. The student should be helped to develop interest in matters of social policy and to participate constructively and selectively in the process of social change.

5. "Social work content courses" are not inherently antagonistic to the purposes of a liberal arts education. They may be taught

1 There is no implication intended that these postulates are applicable only to undergraduate education.

from a broad conceptual and analytic point of view quite devoid of "narrow vocationalism." [2]

6. Integration of related and important content should not be left to chance. It should be "built into" the undergraduate social work program.

7. The question of the number of specific credit hours devoted to social work content courses is not as significant as the nature of the content, how the courses are taught, including behavioral objectives, and the proportion of the students' total undergraduate study devoted to such content.

8. An academic department, in which the dominant purpose and attitudes are at variance with or antagonistic to social work is an undesirable "home" for social work content courses as well as for the coordination of an undergraduate program for social work. Such antagonism is likely also to affect adversely both the learning experience and recruitment for graduate schools of social work or for positions in the field.

QUESTIONS

In this and the following chapters we will confront several clusters of questions. The first set is as follows:

1. What objectives are appropriate for the undergraduate phase of the program of social work education?

   a. What content drawn from the basic sciences and humanities should be incorporated within social work content areas in this phase of the program of social work education?

   b. What social work content should be incorporated within the social work content areas in this phase of the program of social work education?

2. How should the content from the basic disciplines be employed in, and distributed ("vertically" and "horizontally") among the social work content areas in this phase of the program of social work education?

3. How should the social work content be organized within, and

---

[2] The question of what should be included within "social work content courses" will be taken up in detail later in this chapter. It should be noted at this time, though, that we do make a distinction between such courses and "social work relevant courses" given as a part of the traditional discipline.

distributed among the social work content areas in this phase of the program of social work education?

A PROBLEM AND A
STRUCTURAL-FUNCTIONAL MODEL

As we explored the dimensions of the above questions a problem kept getting in our way. It was raised by the finding, reported on in Chapter IV, that students had serious difficulty in relating content effectively from courses in the basic disciplines to undergraduate and graduate social work courses. The problem was that of explaining this finding and suggesting how this situation might be most effectively dealt with. In seeking a solution we questioned fellow educators, examined course materials, consulted studies of other professions, perused relevant literature, and drew upon personal experience.

On the basis of this inquiry, and drawing upon previously formulated guiding principles for the distribution of educational objectives,[3] we constructed a structural-functional model for the organizational relationship between basic knowledge areas and social work content areas.

UNDERLYING PROPOSITIONS OF THE MODEL

This structural-functional model was based on the following propositions:

1. *The fundamental content in each relevant basic discipline should be learned within its own frame of reference.*
There are two important facets of this proposition. The first is that since the various disciplines have their own frames of reference it is important, for the student's own understanding, to be able to fit content from any discipline into its appropriate frame of reference, especially if he wishes to take advanced courses in these disciplines. The second is that attempts to integrate content from the different relevant disciplines around a particular profes-

[3] The criteria developed for distribution of educational objectives are general guides rather than a set of rules or a precise instrument. They are listed and discussed in Appendix C.

sional focus (in this case, social work) before the student has had at least the fundamentals in these areas leads to superficiality and extremely inefficient teaching and learning. What we are suggesting is that it would usually be unwise to rely on specially adapted courses in the basic disciplines that are very strongly oriented toward social work for the introduction of the fundamental content from a basic discipline, and that it would be equally undesirable to introduce the student to the fundamental content of the basic disciplines for the first time in social work content courses. The latter situation is not uncommon in social work at present.

2. *"Spiraling repetition" is desirable and should be distinguished from unprofitable duplication.*
Planned repetition at a "deeper" level, or emphasizing a new set of relationships, is a requirement for effective learning. It is certainly essential if continuity and sequence are to be achieved. Concretely, this means that the use of content from the basic disciplines in social work content courses would be desirable after at least the fundamentals have been acquired by study in those disciplines. It might be added parenthetically that without such use the content learned in the basic disciplines is likely to become "intellectually inoperative" if not completely forgotten. To a considerable extent this is what happens at present.

3. *Content from the basic disciplines should be integrated and employed within a social work framework at a point in time when it is still relatively fresh in the student's mind.*
The implication of this proposition is clear. It is highly unrealistic to expect that effective use can be made of content from the basic disciplines in social work content courses after a lapse of several years, if there were no "reinforcement" during the intervening period. However, this is precisely what occurs very frequently in present programs.

4. *There is no general analytic frame of reference, at present, that adequately unifies the institutional, small group, and individual levels of analysis.*
Basic to understanding why there is, as yet, no unified theory of man and society, not even an integrated "science of social man," is

recognition of the fact that different levels of analysis do exist; For example, principles explaining the behavior of the individual organism do not provide an adequate explanation of human collectivities. Similarly, theoretical formulations dealing with the nature of small groups may not prove explanatory at the societal level. Furthermore, even at the same level of analysis one often looks in vain for a "common framework of understandings."

A considerable amount of attention and effort is currently being directed toward the establishment of a unified theory of behavior (*e.g.,* general systems theory). Also constructs such as *social role* are proving useful in interrelating certain aspects of the different analytical levels. Nevertheless, no satisfying comprehensive theory has yet emerged and, in the writer's judgment, none is in the immediate offing. There would appear to be prior steps that have to be taken before there is much likelihood of an adequate unified framework being developed. The following statement by Theodore Newcomb is much to the point:

> The present requirement for a unified science of man is not fusion of the different levels of inquiry, but recognition and understanding of what is identical and what is distinctive. From such recognition and understanding theoretical integration may yet emerge.[4]

5. *The expectation that the student can effectively make the abrupt shift from learning content in the basic disciplines within their own frames of reference to the creative use of such content in practice-focused social work courses is probably unrealistic.*

There has been much recognition of the technical difficulties of "translating" content from the basic disciplines so that they would be meaningful and useful within a social work framework. Strangely enough, though, there has not been much systematic discussion of the structural preconditions within a total educational program for achieving such translation and integration (nor what is really meant by integration).

Let us look at a situation facing the social work student in many schools. The intellectual gymnastics required of him by the com-

4 Theodore M. Newcomb, "Sociology and Psychology," *For A Science of Social Man,* ed. John Gillin (New York: The Macmillan Company, 1954), 256.

monly existing organizational patterns are indeed formidable. Note the following facts:

  a. In a number of professions there are intermediate courses that "mediate" between the basic disciplines and the practice-focused courses. For example, in medical schools a distinction is made between the *basic sciences* and the *medical basic sciences.*

> Departments of a medical school . . . fall into two general categories—medical basic science (or preclinical) departments and clinical departments . . . The medical basic science departments are generally the departments of anatomy, biochemistry, physiology, pharmacology, bacteriology (microbiology), and pathology.
>
> These departments, although frequently known as basic science departments, do *not cover the fields of the truly basic sciences,* but have as their roots the basic sciences of biology, chemistry, physics, and mathematics. *They really represent those portions of the true basic sciences from which have developed certain organized bodies of knowledge of definite value to medicine, and they might be called "medical science departments."* (Italics the writer's.) [5]

  These medical science courses, as well as their functional equivalents in other professions, serve as intermediate courses in several respects. First, they are in-between from the point of view of the stage (location in time) of the educational program in which they occur. Second, they mediate between the basic sciences and practice-focused courses (in medicine referred to as clinical) in the sense of bringing basic science content into a new synthesis which provides a usable knowledge base for practice. Third, they bring together content from more than one discipline and incorporate it within the "synthetic" medical science course. This appears to be a crucial aspect of their mediating function. In other words, they provide a transitional step both in terms of sequence and integration.

  b. In examining Chart I, which depicts a not unusual structuring of the present program of social work education, note that with one exception there are no transitional basic knowl-

[5] John E. Deitrick and Robert C. Benson, *Medical Schools in the United States at Mid-Century* (New York: McGraw-Hill Book Company, Inc., 1953), 157–158.

CHART I

A Typical Picture of the Organizational Relationship Between Basic Knowledge Areas and Social Work Content Courses

BASIC KNOWLEDGE (Area "A")	BASIC KNOWLEDGE (Area "B")	BASIC KNOWLEDGE (Area "C")
Focus: *Institutions and larger pluralities.*	Focus: *Groups and groups in relation to persons in the group (the small group primarily).*	Focus: *The person himself and in interaction with his immediate environment and with other persons.*
e.g., economics, geography, law, pol. sci., soc. psych., sociology	*e.g.,* social psych., and relevant aspects from other disciplines.	*e.g.,* biol., child devel., ed., med. (incl. psychiatry), psych., social psych.

PRACTICE

Might or might not have typical undergraduate courses such as Introduction to Social Work, Methods of Social Work, etc.

GRADUATE

GRADUATE

SOCIAL SERVICES	HUMAN GROWTH AND BEHAVIOR

Other typical
Graduate Courses

edge courses that serve the function of being integrative "mediators." The one exception is the course in human growth and behavior. However, for a number of reasons this course has not served too effectively in this type of intermediate capacity. In the first place, it has usually been given concurrently with, rather than prior to, the practice-focused courses. Second, there has been a tendency for it to be taught either from the viewpoint of another discipline or as a multidisciplinary potpourri. In either instance it did not provide a coherent social work knowledge base. Finally, the human growth and behavior course has seldom done much in the way of integrating content from the social psychological and "institutional" (basic knowledge areas "A" and "B" on the chart) areas.

This brings out a problem that is more acute in social wok than in a profession such as medicine. The basic *medical* sciences bring together and synthesize content from various disciplines but these disciplines are usually within the same level of analysis (at least in terms of the "levels" we have specified). However, in social work two "mediating" steps have to occur. First, content from the different disciplines *within* a level of analysis (*e.g.*, anthropology, economics, political science, sociology, and so on) has to be integrated within a social work framework. Second, this same process of bringing together into a new configuration has to occur in respect to the content from the *different* levels of analysis (*e.g.*, sociology and physiology). There is serious question as to whether both of these integrating functions can be effectively accomplished in one stage.

It is apparent that the present "typical" patterning of the social work student's learning experience from the undergraduate through the graduate phases makes little provision for the transitional steps in integrating and synthesizing content from the basic disciplines within a social work frame of reference. Thus, a severe and probably unrealistically heavy burden is imposed on the student.

This problem has not gone unrecognized. Various approaches designed to compensate for an inadequate grounding in the basic sciences and for the lack of "intermediate" knowledge courses have been tried. One such approach is teaching courses in "social process" or "socio-cultural understandings" within graduate schools of social work. Another development is the seminar or course at the undergraduate level which seeks to accomplish the integration of various content from the basic sciences within a social work framework. However, most of these attempts, while clearly recognizing the crucial problem, are not yet structurally patterned over a number of years in such a way as to be consistent with all the propositions underlying our model.[6] For example, courses at the graduate level which are designed to perform this integrative function usually meet neither the "requirement of sequence" nor the problem of too much lapsed time. Further, these courses usually emphasize integration of content from disciplines within only one, or at the most, two of the levels of analysis.

In concluding these comments, it ought to be noted that the most usual types of undergraduate social work courses (*e.g.,* Introduction to Social Work, Social Work Methods, and so on) do not function as "mediating basic knowledge courses." Nor is such a claim ordinarily made for them.

THE STRUCTURAL-FUNCTIONAL MODEL

In developing our structural-functional model we built upon the conclusions arrived at in earlier chapters of this monograph, the Curriculum Study document, *The Nature of Social Work,* and, of course, the specific propositions just discussed.

The structural-functional model itself is pictured in Chart II. Layer 2 on this chart provides for three basic *social work knowledge areas* which are fundamental to the methods and similarly practice-focused sequences. It assumes that each of these areas would integrate content from basic disciplines *within* a given level of analysis. Area D would do this for those disciplines concerned with the study of larger collectivities; Area E for those disciplines that treat groups and other forms of social interaction from a social psychological perspective (including both those that put more emphasis on the social and those that stress more the psychologi-

---

[6] Although the problem has been recognized it usually has not been approached in terms of our formulation.

The Structural-Functional Model

THE RELATIONSHIP AMONG THE BASIC KNOWLEDGE AREAS, HUMANITIES, TOOL SUBJECTS, THE BASIC SOCIAL WORK KNOWLEDGE AREAS, AND SOCIAL WORK PRACTICE—PREPARATORY CONTENT AREA

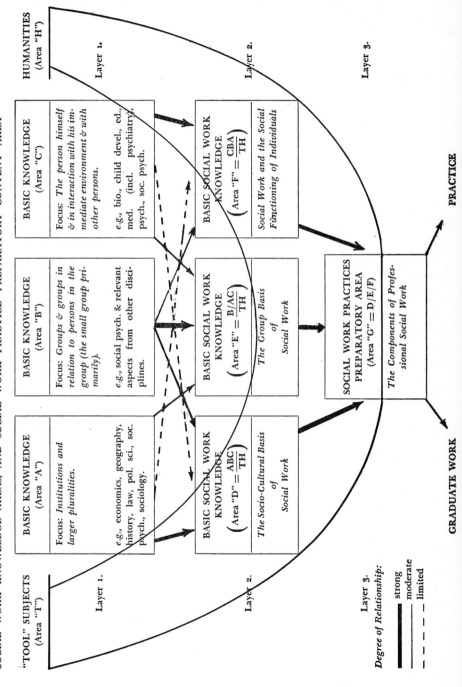

cal); Area F for those disciplines that focus on the person, both as organism and as a participant in interaction.

However, it should be noted that each of these basic *social work knowledge areas* draws upon each of the three basic knowledge areas, although with different degrees of emphasis. This is shown on the Chart by the vertical and diagonal lines indicating degrees of relationship. The short horizontal lines connecting the three basic social work knowledge areas (D, E, and F) suggest that there would be interplay (*e.g.,* cross reference) between them. Content from the humanities (*e.g.,* philosophy, literature) and tool subject (*e.g.,* statistics, formal logic, communications) would cut through each of the areas. This is shown by the large curved lines. The humanities would assist in providing a philosophical perspective as well as an enriched understanding of human experiences; the tool subjects would provide, as the term suggests, the skill resources to perform certain necessary operations.

Content Area G, on the third layer, would draw upon the three basic *social work knowledge areas* (D, E and F). It thus synthesizes knowledge derived from three levels of analysis into a systematic examination of the totality of social work practice. The content in this area is also designed to provide a preparatory base for those students who would secure employment in social work upon completion of their undergraduate studies (social work associates). This, then, represents a second stage in the transition from the basic knowledge areas to the specific study of the actual doing of social work.

Also implicit in the model is the interrelationship between the *function of the parts and the purposes of the entire program* that is depicted. In other words, while each area has its own function, all of the areas pictured are related to the goals of preparation for more advanced training on the graduate level and for employment in social work immediately after completing the undergraduate program. This means, of course, that the model is predicated on the assumption that these purposes can be realized with a single educational program. The *crucial importance of this approach is that it permits those who may enter employment after securing the Bachelor's Degree to continue their advanced training* with a basis from their previous study. (Of course, some "refresher work" may be necessary.)

The model is not all inclusive since *it does not include the specific work in the various basic disciplines that the students will be expected to take throughout the entire four years of under-graduate schooling.*[7] Despite limitations, we believe that the structural-functional model presented here meets the requirements set for it. Its theoretical rationale is that the clarification of structure and function is a necessary condition for the determination of appropriate educational objectives.

A SECOND PROBLEM

The wages of problem-solving is more problems. Our structural-functional model has left us with the academic version of the problem of "togetherness," how to achieve integration of content. The teaching and learning problems associated with the integration of content from different basic disciplines within the framework of a professionally oriented course or sequence of courses are difficult as well as numerous. There is a discouraging lack of evaluated data on which to base a judgment as to how best to accomplish such integration. However, it would appear that we can safely assume, as a starting point, the correctness of the following statement:

> In talking about integration . . . we constantly ran into the argument that integration was all right but after all it must take place in the mind of the student. This is such an obvious platitude that we would not mention it if we did not believe that it is actually being used to the detriment of necessary developments in some programs in the humanities and social sciences. Of course integration must take place in the mind of the student if it is to be effective. So must all learning . . . Integration must, nevertheless, be prepared for, and arrangements must be found which will encourage it to take place.

[7] It should be clearly understood that the objectives discussed later in this chapter are only for the social work content areas. These areas, it is anticipated, would constitute only a limited portion of the undergraduate program. Hence, *throughout* his undergraduate years, the student would take a heavy load of work in the basic sciences and the humanities.

The mere placing of two related facts within the same consciousness does not, strangely enough, insure that that consciousness will in fact relate them.[8] (Italics the writer's.)

Accepting as valid the principle that integration needs to be planned for and structured within the educational program, the question remains as to how this should be done. We might begin by surveying some of the possibilities. These include vertical integration, horizontal integration, integration of purpose, and interdisciplinary integration. The first refers to the "correlation of consecutive courses in such a way that one course builds on the facts, concepts, or methods developed in previous courses; the second refers to the interrelating "of work in one course with the work in another course which is being taken concurrently with it"; the third refers to the "use of one course to accomplish several basic objectives"; and the fourth refers to the "drawing together into a single course or series of courses of the principles and data from several fields of knowledge." [9]

Structural provision has been made in the first three types of integration. The assumption of, and necessity for, the fourth type is also built into the model. However, there was no more than a hint as to how this might obtain. The problem involved is suggested by the meaning of the term, integrate to *bring parts together into a whole.* For us the immediate question is how best to bring together content from the basic disciplines into a coherent whole within social work content courses. The method adopted is necessarily related to function and content.

Let us focus then on basic social work knowledge areas D, E and F, that is, Layer 2 of our structural-functional model. At the present time perhaps the most usual type of systematic procedure employed in integrating content from the "institutional level" (basic knowledge area A) into a social work framework is to introduce selected concepts from various disciplines, explore their dimensions and show how they apply to social work. This is sometimes done by means of a specific course, although the instructors in the other social work content courses are also encouraged to use

[8] *General Education in Engineering: A Report of the Humanistic-Social Research Project, op. cit.,* 26.
[9] *Ibid.,* 22–23.

such concepts in their own teaching whenever feasible. It appears that such courses normally do not expect the student to enter with much usable content from the basic disciplines. In view of the present prevalent discontinuity between undergraduate and graduate education in social work, this is a not unreasonable expectation.

Despite its appreciable values the above approach strikes the writer as having two very serious drawbacks. The first is that concepts and principles from the basic disciplines are likely to be perceived by the student as being rather discrete. Since they are not synthesized into a coherent whole, they tend to be described rather than utilized—with the latter occurring, when it does, mainly via illustrations. The concepts are also likely to be seen by the student as simply having application for social work, rather than becoming a part of the student's own social work perspective and intellectual framework. Another way in which content from various disciplines may be integrated is by having representatives from a number of disciplines discuss their respective fields in terms of similarities, differences, and their potential or actual applications to social work. Such *multidisciplinary courses or seminars* possess the advantage of having each of the disciplines represented by its own spokesman, thus reducing the likelihood of a distorted use of materials from these fields. The major weakness in this approach is that the student is even less likely than in the first instance to be able to incorporate the content within a coherent framework.

A third approach is to employ the content (*e.g.,* concepts, methods, principles) from the basic disciplines *as part of the analysis* that seeks to explain or illuminate some aspect of social work and its data.[10] Although this method is difficult, it appears to the writer to be the most promising from the point of view of developing a coherent conceptual framework which encompasses content from the basic disciplines.[11] Hence, this is the integrative procedure adopted in the formulation of objectives.

[10] Some interesting attempts to relate several basic disciplines to each other in a manner somewhat like the third approach appear in *Common Frontiers of the Social Sciences,* ed. Mirra Komarovsky (Glencoe, Illinois: The Free Press, 1957).

[11] By a coherent conceptual framework we mean a configuration of consistently linked concepts, principles, etc., drawn from various disciplines. We distinguished between a coherent conceptual framework and a unified *theoretical system* achieved via a set

EDUCATIONAL OBJECTIVES

PROCEDURES

With the two preliminary problems out of the way (even if not thoroughly resolved), we finally turn to the question par excellence of this project: What are desirable objectives for the undergraduate phase of the program of social work education? The social work content areas for which objectives will be recommended are named in Chart II.

How did we arrive at these objectives? Some ideas came from persons conferred with on the field trip. The literature of social work also was helpful. But in this aspect of the study the most important resource was the course materials received from schools. The mode of operation in examining them was as follows:

1. The writer looked over the materials and made notes about aspects to be reexamined later.

2. A set of procedures for systematic analysis of the materials was worked out. These included abstracting statements of purpose, topical headings, concepts, generalizations, the most important bibliographical information and similar data. All of this information was put on cards and classified under appropriate headings. In addition, after other materials such as course examinations and assignments were studied, general impression and "highlight" cards were filled out. These were used to "flag" certain characteristics of the materials at the time that the course data was again reviewed.

Of course, all of the procedures had to be carried out within time and money limitations. As it turned out, materials from 45 schools were systematically treated in accordance with the stated procedures. Much of the actual abstraction of data was done by Sylvia Knopp, who was associated with this and other projects as a research assistant. The abstracted data was then studied by the writer, and selected course materials again examined by him. This was followed by a categorization of the data and by preliminary

---

of perfectly complementary master concepts applicable to all the subject matter of all the disciplines—thus providing a new science of man. As we have pointed out before, we do not consider the latter presently feasible.

decisions as to appropriateness and importance. These decisions were based on *The Nature of Social Work* (functioning as a "philosophy screen") [12] and the postulates and previous conclusions of this project.

The next step was an organizing of the content data into areas. This was done in accordance with several sets of principles. One of these was the "criteria for the distribution of objectives." (See Appendix C.) Another instrument employed was the structural-functional model. Content which the writer believed is, or could be, most appropriately taught in non-social work content areas was excluded from the objectives developed for the social work content areas. This did not mean that concepts and data used in courses in the basic disciplines were automatically excluded from these areas. On the contrary, the content for the social work content areas was developed on the assumption that certain prerequisites in the basic disciplines would be established. However, it was believed that content from the basic disciplines that was incorporated in the social work content areas should meet the requirement of "spiraling repetition" and should be employed within a social work framework. Certain content, which, on the basis of his entire study, seemed to the writer to be desirable for inclusion, was incorporated in the objectives even though it was not found (or at least not much emphasized) in the course materials of the schools.

The objectives presented here are by no means the only ones that could justifiably have been formulated. However, we do believe that they are very important objectives; that they are consistent with the principles of continuity and integration; and that they are in harmony with what we consider a sound "construct," (developed from an educational vantage point) of the nature and characteristics of social work practice and its place in the scheme of things (*i.e., The Nature of Social Work*).

THE NATURE OF THE OBJECTIVES

It needs to be emphasized and reemphasized that the objectives are for an *area of content* and that the charts of objectives (presented

[12] This document provided an orientation for all the projects. It was an adaptation, rather than an equivalent, of a "philosophy screen," which is an integral part of the system of analysis developed by Dr. Tyler.

at the end of each content area discussed) *do not constitute course outlines.* Neither are they "blueprints" of prescribed teaching content. The development of specific courses is, and remains, the responsibility of the individual institutions.

What, then, is the purpose of the recommended objectives? We hope that they may accomplish the following:

1. To suggest and put within a coherent social work frame of reference, conceptually formulated content (and related appropriate behaviors) for inclusion in the program of social work education, particularly in the undergraduate phase.

2. To suggest lines of experimentation in the conceptualization and organization of social work content within the program of social work education, particularly in the undergraduate phase.

3. To suggest conceptual content taught *in* the basic disciplines that might be particularly useful to provide a foundation for or to complement the social work content areas.

4. To offer clues as to what conceptual content should be required of incoming students by the graduate schools of social work.

The same *behavioral terms* are employed in all the objectives specified in this monograph. They are "familiarity with," "understanding," "performing," "advocating," "valuing," and "identifying with." Since these terms are used within a particular scheme and for a specific purpose, the meanings given them need to be spelled out.

Familiarity with—to be well acquainted with something, be it a fact, a concept, a principle, or sources of information.

Understanding—the following complex of operations and attributes: (a) knowledge; (b) recognition of the dimensions and implications of the content; and (c) the abilities to analyze, to relate, and to evaluate. The previous behavior, "familiarity with," is subsumed under the behavior of understanding. Understanding applies to whatever content it may be related to, whether this be facts, concepts, generalizations or theories.

Performing—to carry out; to participate in. This may apply to any type of operation or activity, from the formulating of research hypotheses to the observing of an interview.

Advocating—espousing; supporting; defending.

Valuing—to regard highly.

Identifying with—to associate oneself with in feeling, belief, interest or action.

It is apparent that all of the above behaviors subsume sub-behaviors which might well have been isolated and used as primary behavioral headings. However, it was thought that such a degree of refinement of the behaviors at the present time would be premature and of questionable usefulness. We were also of the opinion that the gain that might inhere in the use of "narrower," and consequently more numerous, behavioral headings would probably be more than offset by the difficulty in using such headings as guides to the development of appropriate learning experiences. Finally, we wanted to avoid the risk of seeming to make "distinctions without a difference."

With the content of undergraduate social work education organized into four areas, three on Layer 2 and one on Layer 3 of the structural-functional model (Chart II), the educational objectives recommended as desirable for each of the four content areas will be discussed in the next four chapters. The narrative discussion in each is concluded by a chart which designates and links graphically the behavioral and content aspects of the objectives. Each chapter contains a selected bibliography of references which the author has found helpful for the understanding and presentation of content referred to in that chapter. The final chapter deals with teaching and organization of this content in the undergraduate curriculum.

CHAPTER VIII

Desirable Objectives for Content Area D—The Sociocultural Basis of Social Work

This area of content has the social welfare institution as its primary focus. It draws heavily upon disciplines that are oriented toward larger collectivities. The framework is provided by the interrelationship of those major components which comprise the content aspect of the objectives.

An overview of all the objectives in this content area, charted as to their major content items and their behavioral aspects, may be useful in reading the discussion of each objective. The chart will be found on page 147.

Objective I:

*Understanding of Social Welfare as
the Primary Institutional Context of Social Work.*

TERMINOLOGY

Certain of the concepts central to this objective are variously defined, both in social work and in the social sciences. While this fact complicates their use it does not make them valueless.

> Precise words are to be preferred to vague ones, but the ultimate proof of precision is given by what people do with the word or by what it makes them do, and not by its tightness of fit into any previously conceived theory.[1]

Despite important theoretical differences in interpretation, a concept such as "social institution" does convey an idea of importance and the social phenomena it denotes are widely recog-

[1] John Madge, *The Tools of Social Science* (London: Longmans, Green and Co., 1953), 57.

nized. For this reason this and similar terms will be used; the meanings given them will be dictated by existing usage and by our purposes and expectations as to the potential utility of such usage. No extended discussion of the dimensions of meaning nor exploration of the substantive questions involved will be made except as necessary for the task at hand.

Our definitions of the key concepts of this objective are as follows:

Social welfare—a social institution, the primary activities of which center about the maintenance and enhancement of the emotional, intellectual, physical and social aspects of human functioning.

Social institution—patterned relationships arising from the activities of groups of people in the performance of certain social functions.[2]

In a progress report on another project of the Curriculum Study, Irving Weissman made the following comment:

> By and large, however, there appears to be a high measure of agreement that in essence a social institution is (1) a fairly stabilized form of behavior (organizational behavior element); (2) of human beings grouped together (group formation element); (3) for a common purpose (conceptual element); (4) sanctioned and regulated by society (normative element); (5) and made operative through materials, tools, or equipment (physical element). By virtue thereof (6) a distinctive culture is likely to develop (culture component).

It should be noted that while Professor Weissman focuses on the "institution-building" function of social work, the writer's emphasis is on the social welfare institution as "context."

In the frame of reference of this project social welfare is viewed as the primary institutional field in which and through which social work, along with other professions and occupational groups, discharges its functions. Social work, then, as a profession within this institutional context, may be considered an institutional association.[3] As defined in *The Nature of Social Work*, its goal is,

2 This definition is an adaptation of that employed in Raymond Firth in *Human Types* (Rev. ed.), Mentor Books (New York: New American Library, 1958), 82.
3 Our use of the term institutional association is in harmony with the position taken

the enhancement of social functioning wherever the need for such enhancement is either socially or individually perceived. Its primary focus is on social interaction. The patterns, directions, quality, and outcomes of man's social relationships (social interaction) in the performance of his various roles (social functioning) become the professional concern of social work.[4]

Our use of the concept, social welfare, is more inclusive than is usually the case. It encompasses the functions of what are sometimes called the "helping professions."[5] We have included them within the institutional rubric, social welfare, on the grounds that they share high priority concern with the functioning of the individual. This, in turn, provides them with a common social purpose. In a recent study five major traits, when taken together, were identified as distinguishing what the authors called the "social welfare structure in America." They are: (1) formal organization; (2) social sponsorship and accountability; (3) absence of profit motive as dominant program purpose; (4) functional generalization, integrative rather than segmental, view of human need; and (5) direct focus on human consumption needs.[6] Obviously not all of what we have considered to be the helping professions, in all facets of their functioning, meet all of the criteria. For example, the entrepreneurial (private practice) aspects of medicine, clinical psychology, and social work would seem incompatible with the second and third criteria. On the other hand, public education,

---

by E. T. Hiller, *op. cit.*, 219–226. The problem in usage arises in part from the fact that although there is a real distinction between institutions and associations as Professor MacIver has analytically demonstrated, "institutions, in short, are impossible without associations, and most associations operate in institutionalized ways . . ." Robert Bierstedt, *The Social Order* (New York: McGraw-Hill Book Company, 1957), 302.

[4] The document defines social functioning more fully in these terms, "Social functioning in this context designates those activities considered essential for performance of the several roles which each individual, by virtue of his membership in social groups, is called upon to carry out. . . . All role performance requires reciprocal activity, or social interaction, between individual and individual, individual and group, and individual and community."

[5] Clinical psychology, medicine, nursing, social work, teaching, and related occupational groupings. Although law is sometimes so classified it is excluded here since it is basically rooted in another well-recognized institutional framework which has a different focus than that of the other helping professions. This is true of the clergy as well.

[6] Wilensky and Lebeaux, *op. cit.*, 146. Except as otherwise noted, the remaining citations in discussion of Objective I are also from this source, pp. 138 and 147.

while meeting all of the suggested criteria, is not usually considered as part of "social welfare" in the United States. This is understandable in terms of history and culture, rather than reflecting a rational classification system.

In the U.S. there is apparently a tendency to exclude from the welfare category any service, no matter how identified with welfare it may have been in origin, which becomes highly developed, widespread in its incidence among the population, and professionally staffed by persons other than social workers.

This tendency is seen by Wilensky and Lebeaux as reflecting the residual conception of social welfare—that social welfare institutions should become operative only when the functioning of the "basic" institutions breaks down.

It is evident that many difficulties stand in the way of developing a thoroughly consistent and satisfying definition of social welfare. Furthermore, it is important to recognize that the present specialization and relative autonomy of institutional functions is not universal in time or space.

No doubt many persons will wish we had adopted a narrower conception of social welfare.[7] Our rationale for the more encompassing definition is that it highlights certain similarities in overall purpose and is economical. There is no inherent reason, of course, why a more limited conception of social welfare should not be adhered to. However, the first educational objective under discussion would be substantially modified by any contraction in the meaning of social welfare unless the institutional areas eliminated from the definition were included in the content under this objective, even though differently designated. *Our conception of social welfare is that its services are "normal 'first line' functions of modern industrial society." The substitution of the "residual" view of social welfare services would do violence to our formulation of the objective.* Wilensky and Lebeaux nicely relate the question of definition to changes in our society:

[7] Helen L. Witmer, in treating social work as a social institution, delimited its institutional functions rather severely. Her view is essentially the "residual" approach. *Social Work: An Analysis of a Social Institution* (New York: Farrar and Rinehart, 1942).

As the residual conception becomes weaker, as we believe it will, and the institutional conception increasingly dominant, it seems likely that distinctions between welfare and other types of social institutions will become more and more blurred. Under continuing industrialization all institutions will be oriented toward and evaluated in terms of social welfare aims. The "welfare state" will become the "welfare society," and both will be more reality than epithet.

Significance of Objective I

An understanding of social welfare as the primary institutional context of social work is of importance to the prospective social worker in at least the following respects:

1. It points up the significance of institutionalization (as structure and process) for the practice of social work.

2. It provides a context for questions of policy and the process of policy-making.

3. It helps to provide a perspective for viewing social work in terms of its social functions and in relationship to other professions (in terms of both similarities and differences).

4. It helps to clarify the concepts of social welfare and social work.

Objective II:

Understanding of the Interrelationship Between the Social Welfare Institution and the Social Structure and Culture.

TERMINOLOGY

The conception of *social structure* which we have found most useful is that described in the following statement:

> Life in a community means organization of the interests of individuals, regulation of their behavior toward one another, and grouping them together for common action. The relationships thus created between them can be seen to have some kind of plan or system, which may be called the social structure.[8]

A social institution, as we have defined it, is one of the basic units of a social structure.

8 Firth, *op. cit.,* 82.

There is more to a social structure than the interrelations of its institutions but these institutions . . . do make up its basic framework.[9]

In addition to the institutions one must also include the stratification and cellular systems as crucial components of a social structure. By a cellular system we mean the groupings of people into associations (*e.g.,* professional associations, trade associations and unions, social clubs) and into geographical units (*e.g.,* neighborhoods, communities, villages, cities).[10]

Social stratification is an extremely important type of social differentiation. We shall use the concept of *social stratification* to refer to the differential allocation of power, privilege, and prestige among hierarchically ordered collectivities of people who occupy the same strata. These "collectivities" are estates, castes, classes, and status groupings.[11]

We shall use the concept of *culture* in accordance with Edward Tylor's widely quoted definition:

Culture taken in its wide ethnographic sense, is that complex whole which includes knowledge, belief, art, morals, laws, custom, and any other capabilities and habits acquired by man as a member of society.[12]

The breadth of this view is both its virtue and its vice. In view of the continuing technical controversies about the meaning of culture a loose definition has real advantages; however, the lack of precision, while making the concept of culture easier to handle,

9 Gerth and Mills, *op. cit.,* 23.

10 The concept of "cellular system" is used by W. J. H. Sprott, *Science and Social Action* (Glencoe, Illinois: The Free Press, 1954), 29–31.

11 Max Weber's valuable distinction between class and status groupings is, unfortunately, too often disregarded or dismissed at the present time. See *From Max Weber: Essays in Sociology,* translated and edited by H. H. Gerth and C. Wright Mills (New York: Oxford University Press, 1946), Chapter VII. The following formulation by Weber has a remarkably contemporaneous ring to it (with the exception of the term honor): "In content status honor is normally expressed by the fact that above all else a specific style of life can be expected from all those who wish to belong to the circle. Linked with this expectation are restrictions on social intercourse." (187)

Oliver C. Cox makes an interesting distinction between political class and social class in his provocative analysis, *Caste, Class and Race* (New York: Doubleday and Company, Inc., 1948).

12 Edward B. Tylor, "The Science of Culture" in Logan Wilson and William L. Kolb, *Sociological Analysis* (New York: Harcourt, Brace and Company, 1949), 61.

makes it less useful as an analytic tool. The following statement helps to sharpen up its meaning.

> "Culture" in the abstract is a generalization from "cultures," while *a* culture is itself an abstract concept ascribed to some identified social group. The important components of current usage would seem to include (a) a conception of shared ways of behaving, predispositions to behavior, and (perhaps) products of behavior, and (b) the restriction that if something is a part of culture, it is learned-transmitted socially rather than biologically. Trouble enters primarily with the identification of what is shared. . . . In practice, the extent of uniformity or of patterning appears to be broad enough to make it convenient to talk about cultures, without dismissing the probable need for more differentiated concepts.[13]

Finally, we should recognize that while "culture is a concept not a theory" it contains the basic theoretical notion that "a very wide range of human phenomena is cultural in nature." [14]

Social Welfare in The Social Structure and Culture

An understanding of the social welfare institution within a societal and cultural context presupposes understanding of a basic principle of social organization and culture. This principle is that the parts of a society and culture are interrelated and interact in a complex and often subtle manner.

Most particularly we are interested in the way in which these components are themselves shaped in organization and function by the totality of which they are a part. This aspect of the system of internal coordination deserves serious attention. For example, in what ways are the economic, political, religious and social welfare institutions interrelated? In what ways are these institutions functionally complementary? Or in what respects are they non-symmetrical and relatively autonomus? In seeking answers to questions such as these it is important to keep in mind theoretical formu-

13 M. Brewster Smith, "Anthropology and Psychology" in *For a Science of Social Man,* ed. John Gillin, *op. cit.,* 40. For a rich though concise discussion of culture see Clyde Kluckhohn, "The Study of Culture" in *Sociological Theory,* ed. Lewis A. Coser and Bernard Rosenberg, *op. cit.* An excellent less technical general discussion of the nature of culture by Professor Kluckhohn is also available in *Mirror for Man,* A Premier Book (New York: Fawcett World Library, 1957).
14 M. Brewster Smith, *loc. cit.*

lations that have been advanced regarding the internal organization of societies and cultures. At the same time the exploration of specific problems of interrelationship permits the derivation of hypotheses about the ways in which the parts of a social order are related to each other. Hence, there can be a constant and fruitful interplay between deductive and inductive processes.[15]

Objective II A:

Understanding of the Institutional Location and Charcteristics of Social Welfare Services in Different Types of Social Structures and Cultures.

Within the major focus expressed in Objective II is a concept of much importance: the institutional location and characteristics of social welfare services in different types of social structures and cultures (for instance, provision of social welfare services by the guilds in medieval England). In exploring this relationship the student would appear to need an understanding of the structural context of the social welfare service.[16]

Even more important is an understanding of the various types of economic-political-social systems (*e.g.,* feudal-manorial, capitalistic-democratic, socialistic-democratic, fascistic, communistic) in terms of the significance of these "contexts" for social welfare services. This necessitates, of course, considerable knowledge of the economic and political as well as sociological components of these patterns of social organization.

[15] An interesting analysis of the ways in which societies are integrated appears in Hans Gerth and C. Wright Mills, *Character and Social Structure* (New York: Harcourt, Brace and Company, 1953), Chapter XII. It would also seem important not to ignore the writings of Marxists on this subject. One of the basic sociological tenets of Marxism is that of the complex relationship, direct and very indirect, between the various sectors of a society, particularly between the economic base and the "superstructure." There can be no question but that this constituted an important contribution to social science, even though one may agree that Marx did an inadequate detailing of the interaction between the different institutions and that he made the relationship unduly although not entirely unilateral.

[16] Dora Peyser has done an interesting study on the nature of assistance and its form under different conditions and auspices. Dora Peyser, *The Strong and the Weak* (Sidney: Currawong Publishing Co. Pty. Ltd., 1951). Among the sociological notions useful in understanding the different types of structural contexts might be paired concepts such as communal-associational societies, sacred and secular value systems, Gemeinschaft-like and Gessellschaft-like relationships, and, of course, rural-urban communities.

The student should comprehend the significance of underdevelopment for a country's system of social welfare services. Finally, he would greatly benefit from an understanding of the impact of cultural traditions, religious systems, and so forth on the provision of social welfare services; [17] for example, the fact that in some cultures the social welfare amateur is held in high esteem while the professional in this type of activity is looked upon with suspicion if not with active distaste.

From the point of view of learning experiences it would seem appropriate for this sub-objective to be emphasized at the same time that the subject of historical changes in the social welfare services is being considered. Also, an appropriately focused discussion of welfare policies and services in different countries might attain this sub-objective, at least partially.

SIGNIFICANCE OF OBJECTIVE II

The primary contribution of Objective II to the prospective social worker is in the kind of perspective it helps to provide. By being able to relate social welfare policies and services to the social cultural setting he is likely to acquire a greater understanding of the rationale (sound or unsound) for such policies and services. This, in turn, should provide him with a more informed basis for policy decisions, a greater understanding of the underlying meaning of the programs he himself may be employed in, and a valuable fund of knowledge and insight on which to draw in support of social action activities. Hence, he should be able to place his own work in the broader scheme of things and to see it from the outside in as well as from the inside out. The attainment of this objective should also be of assistance in preparing students for employment in other countries.

Objective III:

Understanding of Changes in the Social Welfare Institution

We have made two key assumptions in respect to understanding the historical development of the social welfare institution. The

17 Sir Raphael Cilento, "The World Moves Towards Professional Standards in Social Work," in *Social Work as Human Relations* (New York: Columbia University Press, 1949).

first is that the historical approach can be greatly enriched by the concepts and methodological procedures of other social sciences. We also believe that the reverse is true; that the historical approach can add much to the work of these other disciplines. The second assumption is that the key concept in understanding historical development is sociocultural change.[18]

In the two previous objectives the emphasis was on structure and structural interrelationships. It is equally important to consider the social welfare institution from the point of view of process. Unfortunately, in recent years the social sciences have done relatively little in analyzing the dynamics of large-scale sociocultural change.

Lloyd Ohlin ties in the developments in the social sciences and in social work with the implications for social action.

Even more important, however, in my judgment, the collaboration between sociologists and social workers will provide an opportunity and a challenge to develop adequate theories of social change. The areas of greatest theoretical advance in sociology in recent years have, like social work, reflected an essentially conservative ideology. Theoretical interest has focused on system maintenance rather than system change. The most frequently employed model in sociology has been that of a system in equilibrium which engages in various adaptive and accomodative responses when disturbed in order to return to a state of equilibrium. The terms "homeostasis" and "homeostatic mechanism" which have been borrowed from biology are in common use. In contrast with these theoretical interests in system maintenance, I view the growing collaboration between sociologists and social workers as a beginning step toward the development of systematic theory and practical methods for achieving social change.[19]

[18] An argument for analytical separation of social and cultural change (in contrast to our combining them) is advanced by Alvin Boskoff, among others. The same article in which this argument is presented, provides a good overview of the present state of social change analysis in sociology. Alvin Boskoff, "Social Change: Major Problems, Theoretical and Research Foci." in *Modern Sociological Theory*, ed. Becker and Boskoff (New York: The Dryden Press, 1957).

[19] Lloyd E. Ohlin, "The Development of Social Action Theories in Social Work," *Education for Social Work, Proceedings* of Sixth Annual Program Meeting, Council on Social Work Education, Detroit, Michigan (New York: CSWE, 1958), 78.

For an interesting critique of the application of the concept of homeostasis to the function of society see Jules Henry, "Homeostasis, Society, and Evolution," *The Scientific Monthly*, LXXXI (December, 1955).

It is interesting that, in the course materials analyzed in this project, there was frequent mention of social problems resulting from social change. The absence of change was not postulated, however, as resulting in social problems.

In examining the historical data involving the social welfare institution, there are certain basic questions that the student ought to seek answers for. These are: (1) what is it that changes; (2) how does it change; (3) what is the direction of change; (4) what is the tempo of change; (5) what changes in other units are correlated with changes in the unit under study; (6) what are the causes of the change? [20]

The first question is a reminder to define just what changes we are inquiring into (*e.g.*, changes in the social welfare institution). The second question concerns the types and mechanisms of change (*e.g.*, diffusion, innovation, "drift," induced). The third question involves an estimate of the consequences of the changes (*e.g.*, will hasten the advent of state capitalism, will move us further along the road to "left wing collectivism").

The fourth question is significant particularly in respect to variations in the tempo of change between two or more units (*e.g.*, Ogburn's concept of "cultural lag," the notion of active and reactive institutions). The fifth question alerts us to relating changes outside the social welfare institution to changes within it (*e.g.*, the relation of the 1834 poor law in England to the rising power of the bourgeoisie.

The sixth question is the most complex and difficult, hence we will now devote some additional attention to it. There are probably many who question the use of the term "cause," at least in this context. Nevertheless, despite long standing philosophical and scientific objections, the concept of cause merits retention. We share the position taken by the late Max Planck.

> The law of causality is neither true nor false. It is rather a heuristic principle, a signpost—and in my opinion, our most valuable signpost—to help us find our bearings in a bewildering maze of occurrences, and to show us the direction in which scientific research must advance in order to achieve fertile results. The law of causality, which immedi-

20 These questions have been taken from Gerth and Mills, *Character and Social Structure, op. cit.,* 377–380.

ately impresses the awakening soul of the child and plants the untiring question *"Why"* into his mouth, remains a lifelong companion of the scientist and confronts him incessantly with new problems.[21]

If one sees social organization in terms of structure, function and process (*i.e.,* organizing), then structure and change are not analytic opposites. Rather, they are but different foci. This suggests, as Professor Lockwood puts it, "that in principle the concepts with which we try to analyze the dynamics of social systems ought to be equally applicable to the problems of stability and instability, continuance and change of social structures." However, as he goes on to say, although this is true in principle it "does not necessarily hold true of a particular conceptual scheme . . ." [22]

There are two important relevant implications in what has been said. First, a full understanding of the change process requires an understanding of structure and function as well, and vice versa. Second, one must make sure, though, that the particular framework he uses for the analysis of change does in fact include the necessary variables for such an analysis.[23] The significance of these implications is that, if one needs to understand systems of sociocultural organization in order to understand changes in these systems, then the number of relevant variables are indeed great. It would appear necessary if one seeks explanation, rather than just endless description, to give a differential weighting to the variables. This suggests, in turn, the necessity for theoretical formulations to guide selection and weighting of the variables in a given analysis.

Objective III A:

Understanding the Sociocultural Determinants of Changes in the Social Welfare Institution.

In looking at the historical development of the social welfare institution one might first ask to what extent do large scale theories

21 Max Planck, "The Concept of Causality in Physics," in *Readings in the Philosophy of Science,* ed. Philip P. Wiener (New York: Charles Scribners' Sons, 1953), 87.
22 David Lockwood, "Some Remarks on the Social System," *British Journal of Sociology,* VII (June, 1956), 135.
23 Some social scientists (Professor Lockwood is of this persuasion) believe that the analytic system of Talcott Parsons is inadequate for the analysis of change because it tends to ignore or underemphasize non-normative variables such as economic interests, distribution of power, military means, etc. In the writer's judgment these critics are correct.

of change enrich our understanding of this process of change? For example, does the secularization of assistance become more understandable and meaningful if put within the framework of the dynamics of different general types of cultural systems? [24] Moving from inclusive sociocultural theories of change to more particularized approaches (even if done in the grand manner) our question remains the same: do these theories and concepts illumine understanding of the development of the social welfare institution? For example, does a social class (including the idea of a class struggle) analysis provide *one* useful perspective on the 1834 poor law as well as on the transition from feudalism to capitalism? How does such a perspective compare with an interpretation that sees the political institution as having the dominant impact in contemporary civilization? In examining the development of certain social welfare legislation would it not be useful to think of law as part of the political process representing various (sometimes conflicting) interests?

We might also ask, how do the characteristics (including structure) of organizations influence the direction and content of social policy. For example, what impact is the bureaucratization of social welfare services likely to have on policy? To what extent do merit system procedures at high administration levels make for a slowing down of social change?

Can we understand the emergence of the contemporary social welfare institution without understanding *the nature of the impact* of resources, science, technology, and industrialization on society, its culture, and its members? And is not our present interest in problems of "later maturity" a reflection, in large part, of demographic factors?

Another question that often arises in the examination of historical developments is the significance of the outstanding individual

[24] An example of this type of approach is the work of Pitirim Sorokin, *Social and Cultural Dynamics* (Revised and abridged in one volume; Boston: Porter Sargent, 1957). Another mode of analysis which makes use of system sociocultural integration from the point of view of change is the evolutionary approach. Here the systems of sociocultural integration are seen in terms of levels. For a contemporary analysis of this type, which, however, posits multilinear evolution rather than universal evolution or unilinear evolution, see Julian H. Steward, *Theory of Culture Change* (Urbana, Illinois: University of Illinois Press, 1955).

in the process of change. What was the causal importance of the Webbs, Jane Addams, Florence Kelley, Mary Richmond, and Harry Hopkins? Also, what types of leadership can be identified and what are their functions in promoting change?

Understanding the Determinants of Changes
in Social Welfare Ideologies

Ideologies, as well as patterns of social relationships, change over time.[25] Why do they change, and what is the relationship between such changes and changes in the economic, political and social organization of society? Also, what is the relationship between changes in one realm of ideas and those in another? Questions such as these are of great importance for any student of the historical process. Why, for example, was the "character flaw" theory of economic dependency modified? Can the individualism of Freud and the individualism of the laissez-faire economists be attributed entirely to autonomous internal developments in psychiatry and economics respectively? Or was there a connection between the individualism in these different realms? What is the significance for social welfare research of Bertrand Russell's facetious but penetrating observation that "animals studied by Americans rush about frantically, with an incredible hustle and pep, and at last achieve the desired result by chance. Animals observed by Germans sit still and think and at last evolve the solution out of their inner consciousness." [26] Finally, how influential are religious beliefs likely to be in social change? And what is the relationship of religious ideologies to the sociocultural matrix?

The theoretical questions that provide a framework for the analysis of changes in social welfare ideologies include:

1. What are the sociocultural determinants in the development and ascendancy of given ideologies?

[25] As previously indicated, we define ideology as a system of assumptions, ideas, beliefs, values, and modes of thinking characteristic of some collectivity, such as group, class, caste, profession, or other occupation, religious order, or nation. This definition differs from that used by an analyst such as Karl Mannheim.
[26] Quoted by Raymond Bauer in *The New Man in Soviet Psychology* (Cambridge: Harvard University Press, 1952), 3. This book contains an interesting discussion of the relationship between the conception of the nature of man in psychological theory and the societal milieu.

In exploring this problem one is concerned with more limited questions such as:

  a. What changes in the sociocultural matrix are associated with changes in ideology?

  b. What is the differential importance of the various components of the sociocultural matrix in influencing ideologies?

  c. To what extent are changes in ideologies a response to the internal dynamics of the ideologies?

  d. What theoretical formulations might be of assistance in analyzing the relationship between changes in the organization of society and in ideologies?

  2. What is the relationship between sociocultural and psychological determinants in the development and ascendancy of social welfare ideologies? This includes, too, the question of how much is unique and how much is socially shared in the ideology of individuals and groups?

In any such analysis the student needs to be always alert to the fact that by "discovering" the determinants of an ideology he has not, therefore, proved or disproved the validity of the ideology (except, of course, the belief that there are no determinants).

For those concerned with community organization and social action, an area of particular significance is that of the processes by which social change is induced. Some of the major processes that need to be understood are planning, innovation, diffusion, leadership, communications, cooperation, conflict, legislative processes, and organization.

We have briefly mentioned some of the determinants of changes in the organization and provision of social welfare services. We have also alluded, almost in passing, to some of the more important of the processes of change. At this point, then, it is appropriate, almost as a summing up, to point out that the two "requirements" mentioned earlier in this discussion still hold. *These were the need to do more than just describe, and the requirement to choose among determinants and theory in terms of importance and utility.* A sheer recitation of the fact that demographic, ideological, economic, political, and so forth, factors influenced the historical development of the social welfare institution is not likely to allow the student to attain the desired objectives. Facts and factors have to be organized before they illuminate. It would appear that the student should be encouraged to apply this principle as he seeks to understand the historical development of the social welfare institution. The differential weighting of factors and the selection of theoretical formulations must be tested, in the long run, in light of their explanatory usefulness. The "decisions" made by the analyst in this respect should, of course, always be tentative and subject to revision or replacement on the basis of new data adduced.[27]

Yet another point needs to be made. The student should be helped to recognize unanticipated (as well as "self-fulfilling") consequences of social action or the advocacy of certain beliefs. He should also attempt to understand the reasons for such unforeseen results.

Finally, we should make explicit our recognition of the fact that concepts and theories are not substitutes for the "content of history." Rather, their usefulness is determined precisely by the extent to which they permit the effective ordering and analysis of historical data. The development of the labor movement, the key legislative statutes, the actual conditions of populations: this is the "stuff" of history about which all social work students should be knowledgeable. No minimizing of its essentiality for understanding the historical development of the social welfare institution is intended. However, since this is the aspect of the study of social welfare history that is most fully treated at the present time in courses dealing with the content areas, we have put our emphasis elsewhere.

SIGNIFICANCE OF OBJECTIVE III

Attainment of the stated objective would, hopefully, help the student in:

1. Seeking the causes of changes in the social welfare institution. It should also assist him in identifying trends.[28]

2. Seeing social life in general, and the social welfare institution

[27] This problem will be discussed more fully in connection with the eighth objective.
[28] This point is made by Karl de Schweinitz in "Social Values and Social Action: The Intellectual Base as Illustrated in the Study of History," *The Social Service Review,* XXX (June, 1956), 123.

in particular, as a process rather than as a static structure or as the result of a series of discrete occurrences lacking continuity.

3. Separating the highly particular from the less particular attributes in past events. This promotes the possibility of scientific generalization. It also lessens the margin of error in policy determination since it cuts down, even though slightly, on the unanticipated consequences of policy decisions.

4. Recognizing that the "customary fate of new truths is to begin as heresies and end as supersitions." This recognition may help to lessen the number of both heresies and superstitions in social welfare.

The formal treatment of the relationship between social welfare ideologies and the sociocultural matrix (Objective III A1) is rather rare in present curriculum offerings. The implications of this aspect of the objective for professional practice are:

1. Richer understanding of the *sources* and *functions* of social welfare ideologies. Presumably such an understanding would be of assistance in influencing and in making policy, and it might well give added meaning to the everyday work of the practitioner who serves the client.

2. Insight into the practitioner's own ideology by enabling him to relate it to his occupancy of a particular social-historical position. Ernest Greenwood put this idea into a familiar social work context when he wrote:

> The social work profession has always recognized that effective results are predicated upon an understanding by the social worker, not only of his client, but also of himself. Until now this has been narrowly construed to mean that social workers should, if possible, undergo a period of psychotherapy. We suggest that the concept of "know thyself" be widened to include the notion that an understanding by the social worker of his position in the status system of society will improve his relationship to the client.[29]

3. Fuller understanding of the sources and function of the ideology of the user of the social worker's services. This point was also suggested in the above quotation.

[29] Ernest Greenwood, "Toward a Sociology of Social Work," *Toward a Sociology of Social Work*, Special Report Series No. 37, Research Department (Los Angeles: Welfare Council of Metropolitan Los Angeles, 1953), 25.

4. A more objective view of the sources and function of the ideology of the profession, by providing a socio-historical perspective from which to view his profession and its ideology.

5. A more realistic understanding of the problems and possibilities involved in attempting to modify conflicting ideologies (*e.g.,* those of a lay person, a board member, a member of another profession), and the ability to apply "sociology of knowledge" perspectives to his own analyses and research.

Objective IV:

$\left.\begin{array}{l}\textit{Understanding}\\ \textit{Valuing}\\ \textit{Advocating}\end{array}\right\}$ *The Service Functions of the Social Welfare Profession*

TERMINOLOGY

In this objective and its sub-divisions some terms need definition. *Service function* means the objective consequences of social welfare programs in the maintenance or enhancement of the emotional, intellectual, physical, or social aspects of the functioning of the user of service, whether this be a "patient," "client," group, or community.

By the concept of *problem* we mean something defined by an individual, group or society as a potential or actual difficulty or distress. A *need*, on the other hand, is a normal state of excitation to which all living things are subject. Hence it is not necessarily a problem but it may become so if unmet or unsatisfied. (This subject is discussed also in the project report on social welfare policy and services.)

The term *policy-making* is used to refer to that process of social decision-making which is directed toward a choice among goals and courses of actions in social enterprises.[30] In this objective the behaviors emphasized are understanding, valuing and advocating. In other words, a high regard for as well as a willingness to support the service functions of social welfare programs are called for. These behaviors, coupled with understanding, are hoped-for outcomes. In a specification of the objective, certain of the sub-sections call for more limited behaviors.

[30] This definition is quite similar to that developed by Professor Weissman in the Curriculum Study project on social welfare policy and services.

Objective IV A:

Understanding the Problems to Which the Social Welfare Programs Are Addressed.

In order to understand the service function, the student would need to understand the problems to which social welfare programs are addressed. It would be important to realize that the problems dealt with by the social welfare professions always involve people, whether as individuals or in larger or smaller groupings. This suggests the necessity for the student to always think in terms of *people* with *problems.* He should also be helped to understand *that in addition to seeing problem situations in their full individuality, he needs to be on the alert for shared and recurrent problems.* The student should become aware of the fact that it is through "generalizing" problems and their causes that institutional gaps in meeting needs and in the provision of services can be identified and remedied. He should be able not only to identify the various problems but also to know something about their causes and the varied responses to problems on the part of individuals, groups and societies.

Objective IV B:

Understanding the Varied Perceptions and Evaluations of Functions of Social Welfare Programs by Significant Publics.

Not all observers agree on what are the functions of the various social welfare programs. A social Darwinist might see interference with natural selection as the function of at least some of these programs. The conservative who has a "night watchman" conception of the role of government might view the programs as having the undermining of capitalism as one of their functions.[31] A politically oriented contemporary liberal, on the other hand, might view the preservation of capitalism as being one function of such programs. The philosophically or religiously oriented person might see the opportunity for the expression of the belief in the brotherhood of men as being a function of social welfare programs.

[31] It should be recalled that our definition of function refers to consequences, not purposes.

It would appear impossible to understand many of the strenuous controversies about welfare programs without having some grasp of the fact that the community (or society) is composed of many "publics" and that there may be considerable variations in their perceptions and evaluations of the functions of social welfare programs.

Objective IV C:

The Policy Framework of Social Welfare Programs.

1. *Understanding the Determinants of Social Welfare Policies.*

In order to understand the policy framework of social welfare programs, the student would have to understand determinants of policy, such as the sources and uses of power in the community, the types of leadership, the pressure groups involved, the strength of humanitarian impulses, the social welfare traditions, and so on.

For many students such understanding may be difficult to attain since one of the democratic folk beliefs seems to be that public policies are determined by an undifferentiated, amorphous public and that the policies adopted are necessarily in the interest of the general well-being. The other side of this coin is that concepts such as self-interest, power, and conflict are likely to be viewed as both distasteful and inappropriate. This is particularly interesting since recognition of the importance of "interest" and "self-interest" as a motivating force in human relations is shared by the political sociologist, the political theorist, and the economic historian.[32] Furthermore, many political scientists put the study of power at the central core of political science. And in social welfare the notion of power structure has become increasingly common.[33]

2. *Understanding the Relationship Between Social Welfare Policies and Policies in Other Sectors of Society.*

To understand the policy framework of social welfare programs one must be able to relate policies in this institutional sphere to

[32] Clark Kerr and Lloyd H. Fisher, "Plant Sociology: The Elite and the Aborigines," *Common Frontiers of the Social Sciences* ed. Mirra Komarovsky, *op. cit.*, 286.
[33] Professor Floyd Hunter's study was probably very influential in this respect. Floyd Hunter, *Community Power Structure* (Chapel Hill, N.C.: University of North Carolina Press, 1953).

other public policies. This interrelationship must always be kept in focus. It is also necessary to view the policies in historical perspective—to see their continuities and discontinuities. Finally, it is of crucial significance that social policies be evaluated from the vantage point of their long range and ramifying consequences as well as their more immediate and narrow results. In other words, the student should understand that it is important to gauge the impact of social welfare policies on the future direction of society.

Illustrations may be found in two concrete policy questions facing social agencies. First, should an agency institute a fee-for-service program? One of the long range considerations that might be evaluated is the effect on social attitudes and values. Would such a policy tend to reinforce the attitude that for something to be of real value one must pay for it directly? Also what would be the impact on the capacity of people to think in terms of responsibility to the community and from the community?

A second illustration involves the heavy reliance on large corporations for personnel and financial support for social welfare activities. Does the lending of executives to social welfare agencies for protracted periods without cost to the agency promote a corporate type of society? Of course, once certain of the consequences are examined, the student should be encouraged to evaluate these consequences and make his judgments accordingly.

3. *Understanding Similarities and Differences Between Social Welfare Programs in the United States and Those in Other Countries.*

One way to secure greater understanding of the function of social welfare programs is by analyzing them from a comparative perspective. This would involve consideration of the sociocultural determinants of similarities and differences in programs.

4. *Familiarity with the Organization of Social Welfare Programs.*

The student should acquire an awareness of the range of settings, variety of auspices, and types of agency structure. He should understand the advantages and disadvantages associated with the present pattern of specialized services and variegated auspices. He should be helped to face such questions as what is the place and justification for sectarian agencies in social work? Is there a useful function for both private and public agencies? [34] The student should also become aware of some of the general differences among agencies (*e.g.,* a "one profession" agency as compared with a "multi-professional" agency). Concepts from organizational sociology, such as bureaucracy, informal organization and authority, might well enhance the student's understanding of social welfare agencies. Finally, he needs to understand the relationship between the organization of agencies and the sociocultural matrix.

SIGNIFICANCE OF OBJECTIVE IV

Almost all social workers operate within an organized program of services. They will also usually work in a social welfare organization. Finally, all social workers have a part to play in the realm of social welfare policy. These facts clearly indicate the significance of this objective in the education of a social worker.

Objective IV is closely related to the social welfare policies and services content area. Hence, it is suggested that there be intimate cooperation between faculty persons responsible for the development of course materials encompassing this objective, and those responsible for teaching in the social welfare policy and services area at the graduate level.

Objective V:

Understanding and Valuing the Social Control Function of the Social Welfare Professions

TERMINOLOGY

The concept *social control* refers to all those social processes through which the individual's behavior (covert as well as overt) is oriented toward conformity with the norms of his group or of society as a whole. This implies that the entire socialization process is involved, as are those specific agencies, mechanisms, and regulations whose primary or secondary purposes are to secure adherence to group expectations.

One point of confusion which sometimes arises is the relation-

34 See, for example, Harold L. Wilensky and Charles N. Lebeaux, *op. cit.,* 247–265; Herbert Bisno, *The Philosophy of Social Work, op. cit.*

ship between social control and social change. They are by no means true opposites. This becomes apparent when we recognize that there are norms to which adherence is sought which allow for, and even prescribe, the channels through which change might be promoted or secured (*e.g.*, the First Amendment to the Constitution—the provision for amending it). Also, it is only through appropriate social change that stability and order, including adherence to norms, may be possible.

On the other hand, it is a fact that certain types of social change do come about through behaviors which are in violation of the norms. Furthermore, certain social control agencies tend to develop an anti-change orientation. Finally, as we have already had occasion to note, some theoretical systems do emphasize one of these concepts at the expense of the other.

We define a *norm* as a range of behavior which a group expects or requires of all or some of its members in a given situation and status. By a *status* we mean a position in the scheme of social relations consisting of norm-prescribed privileges and obligations.[35] Such positions are socially evaluated as well as defined. By a *role* we mean a set of expectations applied to the occupant of a particular status.[36] It may thus be thought of as a cluster of norms. By *role behavior* we mean the actual performance of the expected role by the occupant of a status.

By deviant behavior we mean behavior which is outside that range of variations allowed for within the norms governing the role and the situation. An unorthodox act or belief is not, of necessity, deviant, since the allowance for such "minority" behavior may be included within the norm itself. A pitfall to be avoided in dealing with the concept of deviation is that of equating deviant behavior and personality disorganization (or behavioral disorders). A person defined as being disordered is a deviant but a deviant is not

[35] The most extensive discussion of the various statuses known to the writer is that contained in E. T. Hiller, *op. cit.*, Part VI.

For an example of the systematic use of the concept of role as a link between the person and social structure, see Gerth and Mills, *Character and Social Structure*, *op. cit.*

[36] For a useful discussion of role, see Neal Gross, Ward S. Mason, and Alexander W. McCachern, *Explorations in Role Analysis: Studies of the School Superintendency Role* (New York: John Wiley and Sons, 1958), 67. Another valuable source is Herman D. Stein and Richard A. Cloward, eds. *Social Perspectives on Behavior* (Glencoe, Ill.: The Free Press, 1958), Section II.

necessarily disordered. Nor is there justification for treating all deviations as destructive or bad. In a real sense, social progress has been made through the "blood, sweat and tears" of deviants. On the other hand, there is nothing good or ennobling about deviation *per se*.

Objective V A:

Understanding the Normative Component in the Definition and Evaluation of Role Performance.

Communities have expectations about a considerable range of behaviors. They have expectations about such things as able bodied men being able to support themselves and their families, about families staying together, about people being able to communicate through reading, writing and speaking, and about the rights of people to be protected from harm to person or property. The student should understand that such expectations vary in respect to the permitted range of behaviors, the source of authority, the methods employed in securing conformity, the extent to which they are required rather than just desired, and the consequences of deviation to person and society. He should also understand that the specific content of these norms varies with time, place and circumstances—and so with the idea of normality. He should recognize that the concept of normality rests on certain philosophical assumptions and that a variety of sometimes conflicting sociocultural, psychological and biological criteria are employed in its determination.

The student would also need to grasp the concept of deviation (and abnormality) and its dimensions.[37] What behavior is deviant, and when; what are the criteria of abnormality? A second dimension of the same topic is the forms and causation of socially disapproved deviation, particularly those rooted in the sociocultural milieu. A third aspect is the societal response to the deviant. Two important points in this connection are (1) that continuing forms of the major disapproved deviations invoke institutionalized agencies of control, and (2) that being a deviant is a status and that there are "deviant roles" associated with such statuses.

[37] The concern here would be primarily for socially disapproved forms of deviation.

Objective V B:

Understanding the Implementation of the Social Control Function of the Social Welfare Institution.

The student should understand that the relationship of the control agency to the society is very complex.[38] For example, the agency as a creature of the community (or a part of it) has to be responsive, up to a point, to the surrounding mores and folkways. Even so, the agency (or at least the professional personnel within it) may operate in accordance with another set of norms (professional norms) which may be at variance, at least in part, with those of the community.

The social control function of social work may be readily perceived by the student when he thinks in terms of the correctional field, but he may have more difficulty in seeing it in relation to public assistance functions. Yet, as Professor Treudley points out, social independence (with some very important exceptions) is the guiding norm in our culture; hence, dependency, outside the exempted spheres, is viewed as a type of deviation that needs to be socially controlled.[39]

Even more difficult to understand, perhaps, is the fact that the social control element is operative in voluntary family service agencies. These agencies are supported by the community not only because members of the community want to help people in distress but because family disturbances (*i.e.,* deviant role behavior) are considered potentially harmful to the social well-being. Hence the community supports services which have as one of their functions the reduction of the disturbance (deviation) in the interest of effective social functioning. This is not, of course, the only function of such an agency.

The nurse, physician or social worker serving the sick are also performing a social control function. After all, society has a high stake in the sick person since, as Talcott Parsons points out,

[38] A stimulating and unusually thorough discussion of this relationship appears in Edwin H. Lemert, *op. cit.*

[39] Mary Treudley, "An Analysis of the Dependency Role in American Culture," *Social Casework*, XXXIII (May, 1952). An article by the late Willard Waller analyzing the "organizational" and "humanitarian" mores is still relevant to this point. "Social Problems and the Mores," *American Sociological Review*, I (December, 1936).

". . . too low a general level of health, too high an incidence of illness, is dysfunctional. This is in the first instance because illness incapacitates for effective performance of social roles." [40] Hence the function of the professions involved is to prevent or to reduce this type of deviation.

The student should understand that the performance of the social control function by the social worker is indeed a complicated business. He should realize that there are a variety of normative considerations involved in any given situation, and that they are sometimes in conflict. For example, although economic dependency is a disapproved form of deviation the "stealing of assistance" would be seen as an even more serious violation of norms. Hence, the former might be tolerated if it lessens the likelihood of the latter taking place.

1. *Understanding the Processes and Methods by Which Social Control Is Achieved.*

Each of the social welfare professions has its methods,[41] through the use of which the social control (as well as the service) function of the profession is accomplished. The student should be helped to see the relationship of the methods employed to the ideologies of the respective professions, including their value systems, ethical tenets, theories of causation, and so forth. An illustration of this is the differences in approach to the users of services by physicians and social workers. One reason for the differences in method, as well as attitude, is that in the case of the physical illness it is usually not thought that the "will" is impaired.[42] In many of the types of problems handled by social workers (*e.g.*, economic dependency) there is thought to be an impairment of the "will" of the user of the service. Since the physician is not as afraid as the social worker of adding to the will impairment of his patient, he consciously employs direct advice and "mystery" as well as prestige of his status to get the patient to act in accordance with his professional judgment. The social worker, on the other hand, is more concerned

40 Parsons, *op. cit.*, 430.
41 The question of whether the methods employed by certain of the professions are unique to them is not of paramount consequence to this aspect of the discussion.
42 The writer personally much prefers such concepts as motivation and drive to such as will.

with strengthening the capacity of the client to act in certain ways; hence he is less willing to employ techniques which might increase dependency. (This is not the only reason, of course, for the differences between the approach of the physician and social worker.)

The student should also realize that the methods employed depend not only on professional claims to competence, but also on the societal definition of causation. For example, a criminal who would otherwise be turned over to prison personnel is sent to the hospital if his deviant behavior is judged to be due to legal insanity. Another prisoner, who according to the medical profession might also be helped back to a state of non-deviation by their methods, may be sent to a prison instead on the basis of different theory both of causation and treatment.

The student would also benefit from comparing the methods used by social work to those of occupational groups other than the social welfare professions. For example, both the policeman and social worker have social control functions. However, they often differ in terms of their conceptions of how the social control function is best accomplished.[43] One of the sources of tension between them is that the policeman (and a significantly large segment of the "public") does not recognize the social control function of social work. This results at least in part from lack of understanding of the methods employed by the social worker. On the other hand, the social worker has often failed to recognize his own social control function.

Once the student understands the nature of the social control functions of the social welfare professions (particularly social work) he should then consider it in relation to the service function of the professions. He should be aware of the need for both and sensitized to the possibility of conflicts between them. On the one hand, the student should recognize that values are included in the use of social work methods just as they are in psychiatry; on the other hand, he should understand that, although social work cannot be value free and has a social control function, this does not

[43] An important point of difference between police and social workers would probably be their attitudes toward the use of force, and particularly illegal violence, as a major technique of social control. A case study of a municipal police force in respect to the illegal use of violence was reported by William A. Westley in "Violence and the Police," *The American Journal of Sociology*, LIX, 1 (July, 1953).

justify the social worker in using value imposition, manipulation, and the authority of status in a "free wheeling" manner, nor in subordinating the service function of the profession to that of the social control function.

Finally, the student should understand that recognition of social work's social control function does not lessen his responsibility to work actively for constructive social change. Securing conformity to undesirable or unrealistic norms is not the way social work will make its maximum social contribution. *As a matter of fact, paradoxical as it may seem, conformity to certain norms is likely to breed deviations. Thus, the student should understand, value, and advocate social work's responsibility to work for desirable changes in the social structure and culture (including changes in expectations and social evaluations).*

SIGNIFICANCE OF OBJECTIVE V

Attainment of this objective would increase the likelihood that future social workers would perform their social control function with a discipline made possible by understanding and constantly relate this to their other functions. In addition, it should help them to identify points of similarity and difference between their social control activities and those of other professions and occupational groups. Finally, an understanding of the general social control function of social work would make social work in a setting such as corrections seem less of a departure from the main stream of social work practice.

Objective VI:

Understanding the Social Welfare Professions as Professions.

The student should be able to place the social welfare professions within the more general framework of the occupational structure of the United States and to analyze them in relation to the nature of professions as such. He should also understand the similarities and differences among the social welfare professions in respect to (a) organization of services; (b) professional organization; (c) images and evaluations by various publics and the society as a whole; (d) ideologies; (e) methods; and (f) characteristics of users of service.

An important distinction the student should understand is between professions that are largely entrepreneurial (self-employed
fee-for-service) and those in which the professional practitioner is
usually an employe. He should grasp the implications for professional practice and ideology of a sizable proportion of practitioners
being employed by profit-making enterprises. This might be con-
trasted with professions in which practitioners usually work in
non-profit settings.

It would also seem essential for the student to understand the
implications of the bureaucratization of the professions and the
professionalization of many aspects of business. This might well
lead to examination of the long time distinctions between a profession and a business, to see if they are still valid.

The student would also appear to need a firm grasp of the realities of professional life, including the self-interest aspects of
professional organization and ideology. The thesis of an automatic
harmony of interests between a profession and the common good
should be carefully scrutinized. The student should be aided in
exploring the advantages and disadvantages of a closer relationship between the professions (particularly the employe professions)
and the labor movement. Also, the student should recognize that
the structure, characteristics, ideology and function of the professions are *themselves* conditioned by the social structure of which
they are a part. Furthermore, the student should be sensitized to
examining the policies and practices of professions in light of their
impact on constructive social change and the building of a better
society for all. In this respect the political behavior of professions
and professionals is a subject of marked pertinence.

Two other important components of professional life include
the recruitment and selection of personnel for the profession and
the socialization of the neophyte into the profession.

SIGNIFICANCE OF OBJECTIVE VI

It is hoped that through the attainment of this objective the student would acquire: (1) an introductory understanding of the social welfare professions on which to build his more advanced study;
(2) a breadth of understanding that would increase the likelihood
that he would view himself as a professional from a relatively ob-

jective perspective; and (3) a basis on which to evaluate professional policies.

Objective VII:

Understanding of ⎫
Valuing of ⎪
Advocating of ⎬ *The Ideology of Social Work*
Identifying with ⎭

As Muriel Pumphrey asserted in the report on the value and ethics project, it seems axiomatic that, if social work is a heavily value-laden profession, its values must be communicated to new recruits and the student social worker must learn the social work interpretation and application of value principles to specific human situations. The need for the specific teaching of social work values was also a finding of this project.[44]

There are several reasons why the student should start his understanding of social work ideology at an early stage in his professional education. One is that the ideology he will be learning may well be in conflict at important points with that of his family and friends. Also, acquisition or modification of values and other beliefs is normally a slow process. Third, since social work ideology is in disagreement in many crucial respects with that of the dominant power and influence groups in our society (including policy makers), it must be well understood and deeply ingrained if the social worker is to be able to defend and promote it in the face of very considerable counterpressure.[45] The conscious development of a behavior such as advocating is particularly important in view of social work's need for strong representation in matters of policy, ideology, and interprofessional relations.[46] Added to this is the

[44] See Chapter IV of this report. For support of this contention, see Norman Polansky, *et al.*, "Social Workers in Society: Results of a Sampling Study," *op. cit.*; and Herbert Bisno, *The Philosophy of Social Work, op. cit.*

[45] The study by Morris Rosenberg indicated that in respect to some of the most important values, and social-political attitudes and beliefs, students going into social work and those going into business, law and engineering were at opposite poles. This finding is particularly important since so many of the American policy makers are businessmen and lawyers. Morris Rosenberg, *op. cit.*, Chapter III, V, VII and VIII.

[46] For examples of this "need," see Floyd Hunter, *op. cit.*, Chapter IX; and Alvin Zander, Arthur E. Cohen, and Ezra Stotland, *Role Relations in the Mental Health Professions* (Ann Arbor, Michigan: Institute for Social Research, University of Michigan, 1957).

fact that contemporary social workers are not inclined, as a group, to "do battle" in these realms.[47] The reasons for this probably include the following: temperamental factors, the fact that most social workers are women, orientation and interests, education, and the limited prestige of the profession.[48]

Learning Experience

The learning of social work ideology presents several problems. In the first place there are some important ideological differences within social work.[49] In the second place care has to be taken to avoid a type of teaching that results in blind acceptance rather than reflective consideration. The following quotation from a workshop report is to the point:

> It was agreed that there are certain key values which social workers and potential social workers should have but, at the same time, concern was expressed over the danger of indoctrinating a core set of values which would serve as an orthodoxy to be believed in, rather than reflected upon. It was agreed that even the most fundamental assumptions of social work should be continually subject to examination and re-thinking. As one participant put it, "every time we build in a value, there should be a mechanism to question this value." [50]

The problem also arises of how the professional ideology is learned. What teaching methods should be employed? To what

[47] The findings of Professor Rosenberg's study suggest that social work students may be disproportionately drawn from compliant rather than aggressive or detached personality types. Morris Rosenberg, *op. cit.*, Chapter IV. The aforementioned study indicates that the impact of the large number of women in social work may be partly responsible for the above finding. For additional light on the compliant tendencies of social workers, see Alvin Zander, *et al.*, *op. cit.* (particularly Chapter 7).

[48] For data indicating an orientation away from political-economic matters among social workers, see Anne Roe, *op. cit.*, 98–99. An interesting comparative study showing the disproportionately limited political role of women is Maurice Duvenger, *The Political Role of Women* (Paris: UNESCO, 1955).

The educational program of social work is not noted for preparing the student for the rough and tough world of conflict and dispute that is so much tied in with policy-making. On the other hand, lawyers who are the "high priests" of American politics are so groomed. For the representation of lawyers in politics see Donald Matthews, *op. cit.*, 3–31. For the place of dispute in the training of lawyers, see Wagner Thielens, Jr., "Some Comparisons of Entrants to Medical and Law Schools," *op. cit.*, 149.

[49] Bisno, *The Philosophy of Social Work, op. cit.*

[50] Council on Social Work Education, *The Teaching of Social Philosophy and Social Responsibility in the Undergraduate Program*, Workshop Report, Annual Program Meeting 1956 (New York: CSWE, 1956).

extent is ideology learned through classroom instruction and to what extent in other learning experiences? How should the learning experiences be structured? [51] The teacher must give thought to developing learning experiences conducive to acquisition of such behaviors as valuing, advocating, and identifying with.

SIGNIFICANCE OF OBJECTIVE VII

Social work is not just a congeries of methods, activities and structures. Rather, as a profession it "stands for something." It has both ends-in-view and long range goals. It has standards of practice. When the social work practitioner acts, he should do so in terms of conscious goals. To paraphrase a well-known statement, methods without purpose are blind. When the social work practitioner makes an ethical choice he should know that he is doing so and why. When the social worker verbalizes his professional beliefs he should do so with a conviction based on understanding. When professional beliefs he has reflected upon are challenged, he should respond persuasively and courageously. The attainment of this objective will contribute the kinds of professional understanding and capacities described above.

Objective VIII:

Understanding the Place of Social Work in Institutional Contexts Other Than Social Welfare.

Social work services are provided in a variety of institutional contexts. The student will have acquired, in attaining the other objectives, an understanding of the social welfare institution. In order to accomplish the present objective, the student should gain understanding of the significance of legal, industrial, trade union, religious and similar settings for the practice of social work.[52] This means that he should acquire an understanding of the significance

---

[51] For a critical evaluation of the effectiveness of present social science courses in teaching values, see Philip Jacob, *Changing Values in College* (New York: Harper and Brothers, 1957).

[52] The writer found the following references helpful: the report of the Curriculum Study project on corrections; Bertha C. Reynolds, *Social Work and Social Living* (New York: Citadel Press, 1951); and Mary Palevsky, *Counseling Services for Industrial Workers* (New York: Family Welfare Association of America, 1945).

of *settings in general* for social work practice. For example, what problems face the social worker in a host agency? in a multi-disciplinary agency? in an agency in which top administrative authority rests in the hands of persons whose primary identifications are with institutional areas other than social welfare? How does the social worker deal with ideological conflicts under such circumstances? How does he retain his professional identification and standards and still perform his assigned tasks?

The student should be able to relate his general understanding of the significance of different institutional contexts to analysis of the major similarities and differences in the practice of social work in several specific institutional settings.

SIGNIFICANCE OF OBJECTIVE VIII

The student may at some time practice social work in a context other than social welfare. Attainment of this objective will help to give him a first understanding of the possibilities, problems, and requirements of such practice.

Objective IX:

Understanding ⎫ *The Application of Principles of Scientific*
Valuing ⎬ *Analysis to the Study of the Social Welfare*
Performing ⎭ *Institution*

The main burden of this objective is that the student should understand and value the use of the scientific method in the study of the social welfare institution, and further, should develop some degree of capacity to do this type of analysis.

Objective IX A:

Understanding There Are Different Levels of Analysis
to which Phenomena Can Be Subjected.

One of the ideas the student should be brought face to face with is that there are different levels of analysis to which phenomena can be fruitfully subjected. There are two linked propositions relevant to this point with which the student should become familiar. One is that collectivities as well as individuals are "real."[53] A strong philosophical case can be argued in support of this principle, but the most significant justification, from the point of view of scientific inquiry, rests on essentially pragmatic grounds; that is, certain types of large collectivities seem to have "real" consequences.[54] "Thus, the same Lewinian logic which compels the social psychologist to accept groups as 'real' insofar as they have 'real' effects also compels him to take social structure as equally 'real'."[55]

The second proposition is that study at the level of large collectives (*e.g.,* institution, society, culture) is important, potentially fruitful, and scientifically necessary as well as justifiable.[56] Robert Merton has recently indicated concern at the relative underemphasis on the larger collectivities. It is perhaps significant that his comment was made at a symposium dealing with a problem in which social work had had much interest, that is, juvenile delinquency: "But useful as it is, the tendency to focus on the immediate milieu (the patterns of interpersonal relations in which individuals are directly involved) has led to the relative neglect of the larger social structure."[57] The student should also understand the relevance of theories, generalizations and concepts and data from the basic disciplines to the analysis of the social welfare institution.

[53] This brings up the well-worn nominalist-realist controversy. The nominalist position has been influential in American sociology. For an effective reply by a social scientist to the nominalist position, see Charles Warriner, "Groups Are Real," *American Sociological Review,* XXI (October, 1956).

[54] For a closely reasoned argument against the "proof" that all emergents (the idea that when physical systems reach a certain complexity they acquire properties of an essentially new kind) must necessarily be epiphenomenal, see P. E. Meehl and Wilfred Sellars, "The Concept of Emergence," *The Foundations of Science and The Concepts of Psychology and Psychoanalysis,* Minnesota Studies in the Philosophy of Science (Vol. I) ed. Herbert Feisl and Michael Scriven (Minneapolis: University of Minnesota Press, 1956).

[55] Theodore M. Newcomb, "Sociology and Psychology," *For A Science of Social Man, op. cit.,* 243.

[56] *Ibid.,* 246–247. For an even stronger statement on the necessity for analysis at the cultural-societal level, see Frank H. Hankins, "A Forty-Year Perspective," *Sociology and Social Research,* XL (July–August, 1956), 395.

[57] Helen L. Witmer and Ruth Kotinsky (eds.), *New Perspectives for Research on Juvenile Delinquency* (Washington: Dept. of Health, Education, and Welfare, Children's Bureau Publication No. 356, 1956 [U.S. Government Printing Office]), 25–26. For a brief but interesting discussion of reductionism and the uses of the macroscopic approach, see Mirra Komarovsky's introduction to *Common Frontiers of the Social Sciences, op. cit.,* 14–17.

Objective IX B:

Understanding the Differing Degrees of Reliability of Knowledge about the Social Welfare Institution.

The student should have an understanding of the differing degrees of reliability and definitiveness of knowledge about the social welfare institution. He should know the difference between tentative statements still to be proved, such as hypotheses, and assumed knowledge, such as premises. For example, statements about the nature of change found in social work literature are sometimes treated as basic assumptions, even though they are, and should be treated as, hypothetical. The student should recognize that even among hypotheses some are more adequate than others, that some generalizations have more data to back them than others and that even verification is often a matter of degree. One can point out that the "proof requirements" for a venture in which thousands might be killed if something went wrong are often considerably higher than in the case where no lives are at stake. Perhaps the student can never be impressed enough with the idea that the findings of science are in a fundamental sense always tentative, continuously open for reexamination and revision. He should recognize the significance of "probability" for all scientific thinking and what this has meant to the notion of absolute certainty.

A related understanding is the distinction between a value on the one hand and knowledge (whether it be assumed, hypothetical or verified) on the other. One sometimes finds confusion on this point in social work literature. For example, a statement such as "discussion, conference and consultation are practicable methods for the solution of individual and social problems" can be tested. At any rate, it has the characteristics of knowledge rather than preference.

A particularly important point for the professional student to understand in regard to the quality of knowledge is that, when one engages in a professional problem, he cannot always wait for all the answers to be in. He often has to act as if an unproved theory or hypothesis were valid. This is frequently necessary, but it is not necessary that he should have illusions about the knowledge base upon which his actions are predicated. He should realize that, although he acts *as if* something were true, this should not confuse him into thinking it is verified knowledge.

Objective IX C:

Understanding the Problems and Requirements
Posed by the Plethora of Sociocultural Variables.

As we know, there is a plethora of sociocultural variables relevant to the social welfare institution. The student needs to understand the problems posed by so large a number of variables for attempts at explanation and generalization. He also needs to know what should and can be done about such problems, or he is likely to flounder helplessly and with growing pessimism in a sea of theories, concepts and data.

The problems and requirements facing the scientific investigator in that situation might be formulated as follows:

Problem 1:	The problem of manageability
Requirement:	The requirement of a selection among variables
Question:	What is the basis for the inclusion and exclusion of variables and how adequate are the criteria?
Danger:	The danger of excessive or inappropriate selectivity
Problem 2:	The problem of meaningfulness and usefulness
Requirement:	The requirement of an organization of the variables into a coherent analytical framework
Question:	What is the basis of the organizing system and how adequate is the system?
Danger:	The danger of a "closed system" that is self-fulfilling and impervious to new findings
Problem 3:	The problem of significance
Requirement:	The requirement of a differential weighting of the variables as to significance
Question:	What is the basis for weighting and how adequate are the criteria?
Danger:	The danger of distortion by oversimplification.

There may be some difference of opinion about the requirement under Problem 3. Yet it would appear to be clear that, for example, analyzing changes in the social welfare institution (Objective III) requires a differential weighting of the dynamic importance of variables, if any explanation or generalization is to be attempted. Undoubtedly the legitimate fear of a single factor dogma has interfered with the meeting of this requirement in actual analyses. Examples of what the writer considers to be "surrender in the face of complexity" are statements that *go no further* than saying there are multiple causes; or the use of the term "situation" as an allegedly explanatory concept, when it is actually employed simply as a label for an unanalyzed discrete configuration of factors isolated in time and space.

Objective IX D:

Understanding the Possibilities for Generalizations Pertaining to the Social Welfare Institution

The student should have an understanding of the possibilities for generalizations pertaining to the social welfare institution. This requires that, while he should recognize the importance of generalizations for purposes of data selection, designing of research, explanation, and prediction, he should also be aware of the difficulties and limitations in generalizing. As Morris Cohen put it so well:

> The efforts of human intellect may be viewed as a tension between two poles—one to do justice to the fullness of the concrete case before us, the other to grasp an underlying abstract universal principle that controls more than the one case before us.[58]

In order to get an understanding of generalizations and some experience with them the student should examine critically various generalizations. This "doing" might be accompanied by another type of performing: that is, the actual derivation of hypothetical generalizations. The history of social welfare is potentially rich ground for hypotheses, but it has scarcely been mined as yet.

[58] Morris R. Cohen, *Reason and Nature* (New York: Harcourt, Brace and Company, 1931), 368.

Objective IX E:

Understanding the Function and Utility of Theory
in the Analysis of the Social Welfare Institution.

The student needs to acquire a firm understanding of the scientific necessity for, and utility of, theory: it provides direction for research and it serves as an interpretive framework that gives meaning to the results of research. As part of his understanding of the nature of science and its methods, the student needs to comprehend the fact that science, although it is empirical, is more than just the gathering of data. "It is the collection and ordering of facts in terms of a conceptual scheme." [59]

Objective IX F:

Understanding and Valuing Science as a Basic Force
in the Contemporary World.

The student should understand that science is one of the basic forces in contemporary life. He should understand and value the scientific enterprise. This entails a grasp of the role of the scientist in society. In addition, though, he should be aware of the serious problems encountered by science, particularly social science, and some of the contemporary criticisms directed toward social science.

An important source of confusion and difficulties in effective collaboration between social workers and social scientists is the lack of clarity as to their respective roles and functions. The student should combine an understanding of the reasons for these problems with a sympathetic appreciation of the different functions of social worker and social scientist. Finally, the student should understand, value, and aggressively support freedom of inquiry in all areas, and specifically for the scientific analysis of the social welfare institution. He should also recognize that, while the scientific study of social phenomena may result in the scientist's becoming to some extent a "psychological alien," this may have positive consequences. In fact, it may be necessary if the social scientist is to avoid being a "court historian."

[59] Bernard Barber, *Science and the Social Order* (Glencoe, Ill.: The Free Press, 1952), 20.

Learning Experiences

Most of the content of this objective can be learned best in conjunction with the substantive content of the other objectives.

SIGNIFICANCE OF OBJECTIVE IX

Accomplishment of this objective would do the following:

Help to prepare the student to examine critically content taken in more advanced stages of his training.
Help to prepare the student for the social worker's function of being a consumer of research findings.
Help to interest the student in contributing later to the knowledge base of social work and to develop the capacities requisite for this function.
Enhance the possibility of effective collaboration with social scientists.
Help to create an intellectual orientation in support of the conception of social work as a science-based profession.
Help to develop a sense of the importance of "generalizing" from the particular instance. This, in turn, is important if the social worker is to see policy implications in his day to day work.

Objective X:

Understanding
Advocating
Valuing ⎱ *Social Work as a Vocational Alternative*
Identification with

The student should understand the career aspects of social work. He should be encouraged to develop a high regard for the profession and its social contribution and to "spread the word." The student whose interests and capabilities fit him for social work should be helped to identify with it sufficiently to consider it as a career. This means that he should not only understand the nature and contributions of social work, but also be familiar with the qualifications for practice and the vocational opportunities in social work.

Chart of Objectives for the Sociocultural Basis of Social Work

CONTENT ASPECTS — BEHAVIORS

Content Aspects	Familiarity With	Understanding	Valuing	Advocating	Identification With	Performance
I. Social Welfare as the Primary Institutional Context of Social Work.	X					
II. The Interrelationship between the Social Welfare Institution and the Social Structure and Culture.	X					
A. The Institutional Location and Characteristics of Social Welfare Services in Different Types of Social Structures and Cultures.	X					
III. Changes in the Social Welfare Institution.	X					
A. The Sociocultural Determinants of Changes in the Social Welfare Institution.	X					
1. The Determinants of Changes in the Social Welfare Ideology.	X					
IV. The Service Function of the Social Welfare Professions.	X	X	X			
A. The Problems to which the Social Welfare Programs Are Addressed.	X					
B. The Varied Perceptions and Evaluations of the Social Welfare Programs by Significant Publics.	X					
C. The Policy Framework of Social Welfare Programs.	X					
1. The Determinants of Social Welfare Policies.	X					
2. The Relationship between Social Welfare Policies and Policies in Other Sectors of Society.	X					
3. Similarities and Differences between Social Welfare Programs in the United States and Those in Other Countries.	X					
4. The Organization of Social Welfare Programs.	X					

Chart of Objectives for the Sociocultural Basis of Social Work (Continued)

CONTENT ASPECTS   BEHAVIORS

	Familiarity With	Understanding	Valuing	Advocating	Identification With	Performance
V. The Social Control Function of the Social Welfare Professions.	x	x				
A. The Normative Component in the Definition and Evaluation of Role Performance.	x					
B. The Implementation of the Social Control Function of the Social Welfare Institution.	x					
1. The Processes and Methods by which Social Control Is Achieved.	x					
VI. The Social Welfare Professions as Professions.	x					
VII. The Ideology of Social Work.	x	x	x	x		
VIII. The Place of Social Work in Institutional Contexts Other than Social Welfare.	x					
IX. The Application of the Principles of Scientific Analysis to the Study of the Social Welfare Institution.	x	x				x
A. There Are Different Levels of Analysis to which Phenomena Can Be Fruitfully Subjected.	x					
B. The Differing Degrees of Reliability of Knowledge about the Social Welfare Institution.	x					
C. The Problems and Requirements Posed by the Plethora of Sociocultural Variables.	x					
D. Possibilities for Generalizations Pertaining to the Social Welfare Institution.	x					
E. Function and Utility of Theory in the Analysis of the Social Welfare Institution.	x					
F. Science as a Basic Force in the Contemporary World.	x	x				
X. Social Work as a Vocational Alternative.	x	x	x	x		

SIGNIFICANCE OF OBJECTIVE X

This objective, if attained, would increase the number of students considering social work as a vocational alternative, and give them a basis for deciding whether it would be a suitable career.

SELECTED BIBLIOGRAPHY ESPECIALLY RELEVANT FOR THE SOCIOCULTURAL BASIS OF SOCIAL WORK

ON SOCIAL INSTITUTIONS:

Chapin, F. Stuart. *Contemporary American Institutions.* New York: Harper and Brothers, 1935.

Chinoy, Ely. *Sociological Perspective:* Short Studies in Sociology. Garden City, New York: Doubleday and Company, Inc., 1954.

Hertzler, J. O. *Social Institutions.* Lincoln, Nebraska: University of Nebraska Press, 1946.

Hiller, E. T. *Social Relations and Structures.* New York: Harper and Brothers, 1947.

MacIver, Robert M. and Charles H. Page. *Society: An Introductory Analysis.* New York: Rinehart and Company, 1949.

Parsons, Talcott. *The Social System.* Glencoe, Ill.: The Free Press, 1951.

Sumner, William G. *Folkways.* New York: Ginn and Company, 1907.

Znaniecki, Florian. "Social Organization and Institutions" in *Twentieth Century Sociology,* Georgil D. Gurvitch and Wilbert E. Moore (eds.). New York: The Philosophical Library, 1945.

ON SOCIAL STRATIFICATION:

Barber, Bernard. *Social Stratification.* New York: Harcourt, Brace and Company, 1957.

Bendix, Reinhard and Seymour M. Lipset (eds.). *Class, Status and Power.* Glencoe, Ill.: The Free Press, 1953.

Coser, Lewis A. and Bernard Rosenberg (eds.). *Sociological Theory.* New York: The Macmillan Company, 1957, Chap. 11.

Hiller, E. T. *Social Relations and Structures.* New York: Harper and Brothers, 1947, Chaps. 36–37.

Hinkle, Roscoe C., Jr. and Alvin Boskoff. "Social Stratification in Perspective" in *Modern Sociological Theory,* Howard Becker and Alvin Boskoff (eds.). New York: The Dryden Press, 1957.

Keller, Suzanne. "Sociology of Social Stratification, 1945–55" in *Sociology in the United States of America,* Hans L. Zetterberg (ed.). Paris: UNESCO, 1956.

Marshall, H. *Citizenship and Social Class.* Cambridge: Cambridge University Press, 1950.

Mayer, Kurt B. *Class and Society,* Short Studies in Sociology. Garden City, New York: Doubleday and Company, Inc., 1955.

Stein, Herman D. and Richard A. Cloward (eds.). *Social Perspectives on Behavior,* Part IV. Glencoe, Ill.: The Free Press, 1958.

ON TYPES OF COMMUNITIES AND SOCIETIES:

Becker, Howard. "Current Sacred-Secular Theory and Its Development" in *Modern Sociological Theory,* Howard Becker and Alvin Boskoff (eds.). New York: The Dryden Press, 1957.

Lee, Rose Hum. *The City.* Chicago: J. B. Lippincott Company, 1955.

Loomis, C. P. and J. A. Beegle. *Rural Social Systems.* New York: Prentice-Hall, Inc., 1950.

Wilson, Logan and William L. Kolb. *Sociological Analysis.* New York: Harcourt, Brace and Company, 1949, pp. 344–391, 513–521 and 552–557.

ON ECONOMIC-POLITICAL SOCIAL SYSTEMS:

Bendix, Reinhard. *Work and Authority in Industry.* New York: John Wiley, 1956.

Brady, Robert A. *Business as a System of Power.* New York: Columbia University Press, 1943.

de Schweinitz, Karl. *England's Road to Social Security.* Philadelphia: University of Pennsylvania Press, 1943.

Egbert, Donald Drew and Stow Persons (eds.). *Socialism and American Life.* Vol. I. Princeton, New Jersey: Princeton University Press, 1952.

Elbow, Matthew H. *French Corporative Theory,* 1789–1948. New York: Columbia University Press, 1953.

Galbraith, John Kenneth. *American Capitalism: The Concept of Countervailing Power.* Boston: Houghton Mifflin Company, 1952.

Girvetz, Harry K. *From Wealth to Welfare.* Stanford, California: Stanford University Press, 1950.

Heilbronner, Robert L. *The Worldly Philosophers.* New York: Simon and Schuster, 1953.

Laidler, Harry W. *Socio-Economic Movements.* New York: Thomas Y. Crowell Company, 1944.

Laski, Harold J. *The American Democracy.* New York: The Viking Press, 1948.

Loucks, William N. and J. Weldon Hoot. *Comparative Economic Systems.* New York: Harper and Brothers, 1957.

Mannheim, Karl. *Freedom, Power and Democratic Planning.* New York: Oxford University Press, 1950.

Metz, Harold W. and Charles A. H. Thomson. *Authoritarianism and the Individual.* Washington, D.C.: The Brookings Institution, 1950.

Pirenne, Henri. *Economic and Social History of Medieval Europe,* A Harvest Book. New York: Harcourt, Brace and Company, 1937.

Schumpter, Joseph A. *Capitalism, Socialism and Democracy,* 3rd ed. New York: Harper and Brothers, 1950.

Strachey, John. *Contemporary Capitalism.* New York: Random House, 1956.

ON SOCIAL SCIENCE AND HISTORY:

Cornforth, Maurice. *Historical Materialism.* New York: International Publishers, 1954, Chaps. 4–5.

de Roover, Raymond. "The Commercial Revolution of the Thirteenth Century" in *Enterprise and Secular Change,* Frederic C. Lane and Jelle C. Riemersma (eds.). Homewood, Ill.: Richard D. Irwin, Inc., 1953.

de Schweinitz, Karl. *England's Road to Social Security.* Philadelphia: University of Pennsylvania Press, 1943, Chaps. I–IV.

Durant, Will. *The Reformation.* New York: Simon and Schuster, 1957.

Durkheim, Emile. *The Division of Labor in Society.* Glencoe, Ill.: The Free Press, 1933.

Freedman, Donald, *et al. Principles of Sociology,* rev. ed. New York: Henry Holt and Company, 1956, Chaps. 5–6.

Gottschalk, Louis. "The Historian's Use of Generalization" in *The State of the Social Sciences,* Leonard D. White (ed.). Chicago: University of Chicago Press, 1956.

Hall, Jerome. *Theft, Law and Society,* 2nd ed. Indianapolis: The Bobbs-Merrill Company, Inc., 1952, Chaps. I–IV.

Komarovsky, Mirra (ed.). *Common Frontiers of the Social Sciences.* Introduction and Part I. Glencoe, Ill.: The Free Press, 1957.

Lipset, Seymour M. "A Sociologist Looks at History," *The Pacific Sociological Review,* I (Spring, 1958).

Malinowski, Bronislaw. *The Dynamics of Culture Change,* Phyllis M. Kaberry (ed.). New Haven: Yale University Press, 1945, Chaps. IV–V.

Marx, Karl. *A Contribution to the Critique of Political Economy.* New

York: International Publishing Library Company, 1904, pp. 11–12.

Marx, Karl and Friedrich Engels. *The German Ideology*. New York: International Publishers, 1947.

Robertson, H. M. *Aspects of the Rise of Economic Individualism: A Criticism of Max Weber and His School*. Cambridge: Cambridge University Press, 1933.

Tawney, R. H. *Religion and the Rise of Capitalism*. New York: Harcourt, Brace and Company, 1926.

Weber, Max. *The Protestant Ethic and the Spirit of Capitalism*, tr. by Talcott Parsons. London: George Allen and Unwin, 1930.

Yinger, J. Milton. *Religion, Society and the Individual*. New York: The Macmillan Company, 1957.

ON LAW AND SOCIAL CHANGE:

Dicey, A. V. *Law and Public Opinion in England*, 2nd ed. London: Macmillan and Company, Ltd., 1914.

Friedmann, W. *Law and Social Change in Contemporary Britain*. London: Stevens and Sons, Ltd., 1951.

Hale, Robert L. *Freedom Through Law*. New York: Columbia University Press, 1952.

Hall, Jerome. *Theft, Law and Society*, 2nd ed. Indianapolis: The Bobbs-Merrill Company, Inc., 1952.

Hoebel, E. Adamson. *The Law of Primitive Man*. Cambridge: Harvard University Press, 1954.

Mannheim, Hermann. *Criminal Justice and Social Reconstruction*. Toronto: Oxford University Press, 1946.

Rosenblum, Victor G. *Law as a Political Instrument*, Short Studies in Political Science. Garden City, New York: Doubleday and Company, 1955.

ON THE SIGNIFICANCE OF ORGANIZATIONAL STRUCTURE
TO SOCIAL CHANGE AND SOCIAL POLICY:

Bendix, Reinhard. "Bureaucracy and the Problem of Power" in *Reader in Bureaucracy*, Robert K. Merton *et al.* (eds.). Glencoe, Ill.: The Free Press, 1952.

Berle, Adolf A., Jr. *The 20th Century Capitalist Revolution*. New York: Harcourt, Brace and Company, Inc., 1954.

—— and Gardiner C. Means. *The Modern Corporation and Private Property*. New York: The Macmillan Company, 1932.

Blau, Peter M. *Bureaucracy in Modern Society*. New York: Random House, 1956.

Boulding, Kenneth E. *The Organizational Revolution.* New York: Harper and Brothers, 1953.

Burnham, James. *The Managerial Revolution.* New York: The John Day Co., Inc., 1941.

Gerth, Hans H. and C. Wright Mills. "A Marx for the Managers" in *Reader in Bureaucracy,* Robert K. Merton, *et al.* (eds.). Glencoe, Ill.: The Free Press, 1952.

——— and C. Wright Mills (eds.). *From Max Weber's Essays in Sociology.* New York: Oxford University Press, 1946, Chap. VII.

Lipset, Seymour M. "Bureaucracy and Social Change" in *Reader in Bureaucracy,* Robert K. Merton, *et al.* (eds.). Glencoe, Ill.: The Free Press, 1952.

Michels, Robert. *First Lectures in Political Sociology,* Alfred de Grazia (tr.). Minneapolis: University of Minnesota Press, 1949.

———. *Political Parties. A Sociological Study of the Oligarchical Tendencies of Modern Democracy.* Glencoe, Ill.: The Free Press, 1949.

Mills, C. Wright. *White Collar.* New York: Oxford University Press, 1951.

Selznick, Philip. "The Iron Law of Bureaucracy: Michels' Challenge to the Left," *Modern Review* (January, 1950).

Sweezy, Paul M. *The Present as History,* Chap. 3. New York: Monthly Review Press, 1953.

ON SIGNIFICANCE OF RESOURCES, TECHNOLOGY AND SCIENCE, AND INDUSTRIALIZATION FOR SOCIAL CHANGE:

Allen, Francis R., *et al. Technology and Social Change.* New York: Appleton-Century Crofts, Inc., 1957.

Barber, Bernard. *Science and the Social Order.* Glencoe, Ill.: The Free Press, 1952.

Beard, Charles A. *The Economic Basis of Politics and Related Writings.* New York: Vintage Books, 1957.

Bernal, J. D. *Science in History.* London: Watts and Co., 1954.

Brown, Harrison. *The Challenge of Man's Future.* New York: The Viking Press, 1954.

Cadwallader, Mervyn. "Three Classes of Social Change," *The Pacific Sociological Review,* I (Spring, 1958).

Cottrell, W. Frederick. *Energy and Society.* New York: McGraw-Hill Book Company, 1955.

Davis, Kingsley. *Human Society.* New York: The Macmillan Company, 1949, Chap. XVI.

De Gre, Gerard. *Science as a Social Institution,* Short Studies in Sociology. Garden City, New York: Doubleday and Company, 1955, Chaps. 1, 2.

Hield, Wayne. "The Study of Change in Social Service," *British Journal of Sociology,* V (March, 1954).

Lipset, Seymour M., *et al. Union Democracy,* Glencoe, Ill.: The Free Press, 1956, p. 17.

Lockwood, David. "Some Remarks on the Social System," *British Journal of Sociology,* VII (June, 1956).

Mills, C. Wright. "The Professional Ideology of Social Pathologists," *American Journal of Sociology,* XLIX (September, 1945).

Moore, Barrington, Jr. "Sociological Theory and Contemporary Politics," *American Journal of Sociology,* LXI (September, 1955).

Nisbet, Robert A. *The Quest for Community.* Toronto: Oxford University Press, 1953.

Popper, Karl D. *The Open Society and Its Enemies.* London: Routledge and Kegan Paul, Ltd., 1945.

Wilensky, Harold L. and Charles N. Lebeaux. *Industrial Society and Social Welfare.* New York: Russell Sage Foundation, 1958.

ON THE PLACE OF THE INDIVIDUAL IN THE HISTORICAL PROCESS:

Gerth, Hans and C. Wright Mills. *Character and Social Structure.* New York: Harcourt, Brace and Company, Inc., 1953.

Gouldner, Alvin W. (ed.). *Studies in Leadership.* New York: Harper and Brothers, 1950.

Hook, Sidney. *The Hero in History.* Boston: Beacon Press, 1955.

Michels, Robert. *First Lectures in Political Sociology.* Alfred de Grazia (tr.). Minneapolis: University of Minnesota Press, 1949, Chap. VI.

Plekhanov, George. *The Role of the Individual in History.* New York: International Publishers, 1946.

ON THE ROLE OF RELIGION IN SOCIAL CHANGE:

Childs, Marquis W. and Douglass Cater. *Ethics in a Business Society.* New York: Mentor Books, 1954.

Cowherd, Raymond G. *The Politics of English Dissent.* New York: New York University Press, 1956.

Laski, Harold J. *The American Democracy.* New York: The Viking Press, 1945, Chap. VIII.

Robertson, H. M. *Aspects of the Rise of Economic Individualism: A Criticism of Max Weber and His School.* Cambridge: Cambridge University Press, 1933.

Tawney, R. H. *Religion and the Rise of Capitalism.* New York: Harcourt, Brace and Company, 1926.

Weber, Max. *The Protestant Ethic and the Spirit of Capitalism.* London: George Allen and Unwin, Ltd., 1930.

White, Andrew D. *A History of the Warfare of Science with Theology in Christendom.* Reissued New York: George Braziller, 1955.

Yinger, J. Milton. *Religion in the Struggle for Power.* Durham, N.C.: Duke University Press, 1941.

———. *Religion, Society and the Individual.* New York: The Macmillan Company, 1957, Chaps. 7–11 and Sections 5–7.

ON SOCIOLOGY OF KNOWLEDGE:

Adler, Franz. "The Range of the Sociology of Knowledge" in *Modern Sociological Theory,* Howard Becker and Alvin Boskoff (eds.). New York: The Dryden Press, 1957.

Barber, Bernard. "Sociology of Knowledge and Science 1945–55" in *Sociology in the United States of America,* Hans L. Zetterberg (ed.). Paris: UNESCO, 1956.

Bendix, Reinhard. *Work and Authority in Industry.* New York: John Wiley and Sons, Inc., 1956.

De Gre, Gerard. *Society and Ideology.* New York: Columbia University Bookstore, 1943.

Gerth, Hans and C. Wright Mills. *Character ad Social Structure,* New York: Harcourt, Brace and Company, 1953, 61–65.

Mannheim, Karl. *Ideology and Utopia.* London: Routledge and Kegan Paul, Ltd., 1936.

Merton, Robert K. *Social Theory and Social Structure.* Glencoe: Ill. The Free Press, 1949, Chaps. VIII–IX.

Popper, Karl R. *The Open Society and its Enemies.* Vols. I and II. London: Routledge and Kegan Paul, Ltd., 1945, Chap. 23.

Smith, M. Brewster, Jerome S. Bruner and Robert W. White. *Opinions and Personality.* New York: John Wiley and Sons, Inc., 1956.

Sprott, W. J. H. *Science and Social Action.* Glencoe, Ill.: The Free Press, 1954, Chap. VIII.

Weisskopf, Walter A. *The Psychology of Economics.* Chicago: University of Chicago Press, 1955.

ON PLANNING:

Barnett, H. G. *Innovation: The Basis of Cultural Change.* New York: McGraw-Hill Book Co., 1953.

Finer, Herman. *The Road to Reaction.* Boston: Little Brown and Company, 1945.

Hayek, Frederick A. *The Road to Serfdom.* Chicago: University of Chicago Press, 1944.

Lynd, Robert S. "Foreword" in Robert A. Brady, *Business as a System of Power.* New York: Columbia University Press, 1943.

Mannheim, Karl. *Freedom, Power and Democratic Planning.* New York: Oxford University Press, Inc., 1950.

————. *Man and Society in an Age of Reconstruction.* London: Routledge and Kegan Paul, Ltd., 1940.

Mead, Margaret (ed.). *Cultural Patterns and Technical Change.* Paris: UNESCO, 1953.

Meyerson, Martin and Edward C. Banfield. *Politics, Planning and the Public Interest.* Glencoe, Ill.: The Free Press, 1955.

Rogow, A. A. *The Labour Government and British Industry—1945–1951.* Ithaca, N.Y.: Cornell University Press, 1955.

Von Mises, Ludwig. *Planning for Freedom.* South Holland, Ill.: Libertarian Press, 1952.

ON SOCIAL CONFLICT:

Cantril, Hadley (ed.). *Tensions that Cause War.* Urbana, Ill.: University of Illinois Press, 1951.

Coser, Lewis A. *The Functions of Social Conflict.* Glencoe, Ill.: The Free Press, 1956.

Lewin, Kurt. *Resolving Social Conflicts.* New York: Harper and Brothers, 1948.

UNESCO. *The Nature of Conflict.* Paris: UNESCO, 1957.

ON ORGANIZATIONAL ASPECTS OF INDUCED SOCIAL CHANGE:

Brinton, Crane. *The Anatomy of Revolution,* rev. ed. Englewood Cliffs, N.J.: Prentice-Hall, Inc., 1952.

Cantril, Hadley. *The Psychology of Social Movements in the United States.* New York: John Wiley and Sons, Inc., 1941.

Edward, Lyford. *The Natural History of Revolution.* Chicago: University of Chicago Press, 1927.

Firth, Raymond. "Function" in *Current Anthropology,* William L. Thomas, Jr. (ed.) Chicago: University of Chicago Press, 1956.

Heberle, Rudolf. *Social Movements: An Introduction to Political Sociology.* New York: Appleton-Century-Crofts, Inc., 1951.

Hoffer, Eric. *The True Believer.* New York: Harper and Brothers, 1951.

Key, V. O., Jr. *Politics, Parties, and Pressure Groups,* 2nd ed. New York: Thomas Y. Crowell Company, 1947.

King, C. Wendall. *Social Movements in the United States,* Studies in Sociology. New York: Random House, 1956.

Merton, Robert K. *Social Theory and Social Structure.* Glencoe, Ill.: The Free Press, 1949, Chap. I.

Taylor, Carl. *The Farmers Movement 1620–1920.* New York: American Book Company, 1953.

Turner, Ralph H. and Lewis M. Killian. *Collective Behavior.* Englewood Cliffs, New Jersey: Prentice-Hall, Inc., 1957.

ON DETERMINANTS OF POLICY:

Bell, Daniel. "Interpretations of American Politics" in *The New American Right,* Daniel Bell (ed.). New York: Criterion Books, 1955.

Bendix, Reinhard and Seymour M. Lipset (eds.). *Class, Status and Power.* Glencoe, Ill.: The Free Press, 1953.

Brady, Robert A. *Business as a System of Power.* New York: Columbia University Press, 1943.

Finer, S. E. "The Political Power of Private Capital," *The Sociological Review* (English), III (December, 1955).

Hunter, Floyd. *Community Power Structure.* Chapel Hill: University of North Carolina Press, 1953.

Kelley, Stanley, Jr. *Professional Public Relations and Political Power.* Baltimore: The Johns Hopkins Press, 1956.

Key, V. O., Jr. *Politics, Parties, and Pressure Groups,* 2nd ed. New York: Thomas Y. Crowell Company, 1947.

Lynd, Robert S. Review of *The Power Elite. The Nation,* May 12, 1956.

Matthews, Donald R. *The Social Background of Political Decision Makers,* Short Studies in Political Science. Garden City, New York: Doubleday and Company, Inc., 1954.

Mills, C. Wright. *The New Men of Power.* New York: Harcourt, Brace and Company, 1948.

——. *The Power Elite.* New York: Oxford University Press, 1956.

——. *White Collar.* New York: Oxford University Press, 1951, Chap. 6.

Riesman, David, Nathan Glazer and Revel Denney. *The Lonely Crowd,* Doubleday Anchor Book. Garden City, New York: Doubleday and Company, Inc., 1953.

Sapin, Burton M. and Richard C. Snyder. *The Role of the Military in American Foreign Policy,* Short Studies in Political Science. Garden City, New York: Doubleday and Company, 1954.

Wilensky, Harold L. and Charles N. Lebeaux. *Industrial Society and Social Welfare*. New York: Russell Sage Foundation, 1958.

ON INTERPENETRATION OF INSTITUTIONS:

Beck, Hubert Park. *Men Who Control Our Universities*. New York: Kings Crown Press, 1947.

Berle, Adolph A., Jr. *The Twentieth Century Capitalist Revolution*. New York: Harcourt, Brace and Company, Inc., 1954.

Clark, J. M. "America's Changing Capitalism: The Interplay of Politics and Economics," *Freedom and Control in Modern Society*, Monroe Berser, Theodore Abel and Charles H. Pase (eds.). New York: D. Van Nostrand Co., Inc., 1954.

Hunter, Floyd. *Community Power Structure*. Chapel Hill, N.C.: University of North Carolina Press, 1953.

Lynd, Robert S. "Foreword," Robert A. Brady, *Business as a System of Power*. New York: Columbia University Press, 1943.

Wilson, Logan and William L. Kolb. *Sociological Analysis*. New York: Harcourt, Brace and Company, 1949, pp. 552–557.

ON ORGANIZATIONAL ANALYSIS:

Burling, Temple, Edith M. Lentz and Robert N. Wilson. *The Give and Take in Hospitals*. New York: G. P. Putnam's Sons, 1956.

Francis, Roy and Robert C. Stone. *Service and Procedure in Bureaucracy*. Minneapolis: University of Minnesota Press, 1956.

Merton, Robert K., *et al.* (eds.). *Reader in Bureaucracy*. Glencoe, Ill.: The Free Press, 1952.

Stein, Herman D. and Richard A. Cloward (eds.). *Social Perspectives on Behavior*. Glencoe, Ill.: The Free Press, 1958, Part IV.

Wilensky, Harold L. and Charles N. Lebeaux. *Industrial Society and Social Welfare*. New York: Russell Sage Foundation, 1958, pp. 233–247.

ON DEVELOPMENT AND USE OF THE CONCEPT OF SOCIAL CONTROL:

Gurvitch, Georgil D. "Social Control," *Twentieth Century Sociology*, Georgil D. Gurvitch and Wilbert E. Moore (eds.). New York: The Philosophical Library, 1945.

La Piere, Richard T. *A Theory of Social Control*. New York: McGraw-Hill Book Company, 1954.

Mannheim, Karl. *Man and Society in an Age of Reconstruction*. London: Routledge and Kegan Paul, Ltd., 1940, Part V.

ON NORMS AND DEVIATIONS:

Davis, Kingsley. *Human Society*. New York: The Macmillan Company, 1949, Chap. 3.

Hoebel, E. Adamson. *The Law of Primitive Man*. Cambridge, Mass.: Harvard University Press, 1954.

a. *Nature of Normality and Deviation:*

Clinard, Marshall B. *Sociology of Deviant Behavior*. New York: Rinehart and Company, Inc., 1957, Chap. 1.

Davis, Kingsley. *Human Society*. New York: The Macmillan Company, 1949.

——. "Mental Hygiene and the Class Structure," *Mental Health and Mental Disorder,* Arnold M. Rose (ed.). New York: W. W. Norton and Company, Inc., 1955.

Fromm, Erich. *The Sane Society*. New York: Rinehart and Company, 1955, Chap. 1.

Halliday, James I. *Psychosocial Medicine: A Study of the Sick Society*. New York: W. W. Norton and Company, Inc., 1948.

Lemert, Edwin H. *Social Pathology*. New York: McGraw-Hill Book Company, 1951, Chaps. 1–3.

Opler, Marvin K. *Culture, Psychiatry and Human Values*. Springfield, Ill.: Charles C. Thomas, 1956.

Sutherland, Edwin H. *White Collar Crime*. New York: The Dryden Press, 1949.

Weinberg, S. Kirson. *Society and Personality Disorders*. New York: Prentice-Hall, Inc., 1952, Chap. 5.

b. *Social Conflict and Control:*

Clausen, John A. *Sociology and the Field of Mental Health*. New York: Russell Sage Foundation, 1956.

Clinard, Marshall B. *Sociology of Deviant Behavior*. New York: Rinehart and Company, 1957, Chap. VI.

Cohen, Albert. *Delinquent Boys: The Culture of the Gang*. Glencoe, Ill.: The Free Press, 1955.

Eaton, Joseph W. and Robert J. Weil. *Culture and Mental Disorders*. Glencoe, Ill.: The Free Press, 1955.

Frumkin, Robert M. "Economic Security and Major Mental Disorders," *Alpha Kappa Deltan* (Winter, 1955).

Gibbs, Jack P. and Walter T. Martin. "Status Integration and Suicide," *Americal Sociological Review,* XXIII (April, 1958).

Goldhammer, Herbert and Andrew W. Marshall. *Psychosis and Civilization*. Glencoe, Ill.: The Free Press, 1951.

Gowman, Alan G. *The War Blind in American Social Structure*. New York: American Foundation for the Blind, 1957, Chap. V.

Hollingshead, August B. and Fredrick C. Redlich. *Social Class and Mental Illness*. New York: John Wiley and Sons, Inc., 1958.

Honigmann, John J. *Culture and Personality*. New York: Harper and Brothers, 1954.

Kerr, Madeline. *Personality and Conflict in Jamaica*. Liverpool: The University Press, 1952.

Kluckhohn, Clyde and Henry A. Murray (eds.). *Personality in Nature, Society and Culture*. New York: Alfred A. Knopf, 1948.

Merton, Robert K. *Social Theory and Social Structure*. Glencoe, Ill.: The Free Press, 1949, Chap. IV.

Parsons, Talcott. *The Social System*. Glencoe, Ill.: The Free Press, 1951, Chap. X.

Rose, Arnold M. (ed.). *Mental Health and Mental Disorder*. New York: W. W. Norton and Company, 1955.

Sprott, W. J. H. *Science and Social Action*. Glencoe, Ill.: The Free Press, 1954.

Stein, Herman D. and Richard A. Cloward (eds.). *Social Perspectives on Behavior*. Glencoe, Ill.: The Free Press, 1958, Sect. V.

Sutherland, Edwin H. *Principles of Criminology*, rev. by Donald A. Cressey. Chicago: J. B. Lippincott Company, 1955, Chap. 4.

Treudley, Mary. "An Analysis of the Dependency Role in American Culture," *Social Casework*, XXXIII (May, 1952).

Wilson, Logan and William L. Kolb. *Sociological Analysis*. New York: Harcourt, Brace and Company, 1949, Chap. 8.

Witmer, Helen L. and Ruth Kotinsky (eds.). *New Perspectives for Research*, Department of Health, Education, and Welfare, Children's Bureau Publication No. 356. Washington, D.C.: Government Printing Office, 1955.

c. *Value Questions and Conformity:*

Bisno, Herbert. *The Philosophy of Social Work*. Washington, D.C.: Public Affairs Press, 1952, pp. 10–12.

de Grazia, Sebastian. *Errors of Psychotherapy*. Garden City, New York: Doubleday and Company, 1952.

Ginsberg, Sol. W. "The Impact of the Social Worker's Cultural Structure on Social Therapy," *Social Casework*, XXXII (October, 1951).

Green, Arnold. "Social Values and Psychotherapy," *Journal of Personality,* XIV (March, 1946).

McFadden, Lois Apman. *Social Caseworkers and Client Self Determination,* submitted in partial fulfillment of the degree of Master of Social Service in the Graduate School of Syracuse University, June, 1958.

Merton, Robert K. *Social Theory and Social Structure.* Glencoe, Ill.: The Free Press, 1949, Chap. IV.

Sprott, W. J. H. *Science and Social Action.* Glencoe, Ill.: The Free Press, 1954, Chap. VI.

Stein, Herman D. and Richard A. Cloward (eds.). *Social Perspectives on Behavior.* Glencoe, Ill.: The Free Press, 1958, pp. 476–480.

ON CHARACTERISTICS OF PROFESSIONS:

Adams, Stuart. "Trends in Occupational Origins of Physicians," *American Sociological Review,* XVIII (August, 1953).

American Psychological Association. *Psychology and Its Relations with Other Professions.* Washington, D.C.: American Psychological Association, 1954.

Becker, Howard S. and James W. Carper. "The Development of Identification with an Occupation," *American Journal of Sociology,* LXI (January, 1956).

——— and Blanche Geer. "The Fate of Idealism in Medical Schools," *American Sociological Review,* XXIII (February, 1958).

Bisno, Herbert. "How Social Will Social Work Be?" *Social Work* (April, 1956).

———. "On Being a Professional," Address delivered at the semiannual meeting of the Oregon Psychological Association, January 12, 1957. (Mimeographed.)

Blaustein, Albert P., Charles O. Porter and Charles T. Duncan. *The American Lawyer.* Chicago: University of Chicago Press, 1954.

Caplow, Theodore. *The Sociology of Work.* Minneapolis: University of Minnesota Press, 1954.

Cockerill, Eleanor. "The Interdependence of the Professions in Helping People," *Social Casework,* XXXIV (November, 1953).

Community Studies, Inc. *A Study of the Registered Nurse in a Metropolitan Community.* Kansas City, Missouri: Community Studies, Inc., 1955–1957, Parts I–VI.

Eaton, Joseph W. "Whence and Whither Social Work: A Sociological Analysis," *Social Work,* I (January, 1956).

Garceau, Oliver. *The Political Life of the American Medical Association.* Cambridge, Mass.: Harvard University Press, 1941.

Greenwood, Ernest. "Attributes of a Profession," *Social Work,* II (July, 1957).

Gross, Edward. *Work and Society.* New York: The Thomas Y. Crowell Company, 1958.

Hunter, Floyd. *Community Power Structure.* Chapel Hill: University of North Carolina Press, 1953, Chap. 9.

Huntington, Mary Jean. "Sociology of Professions," *Sociology in the United States of America,* Hans L. Zetterberg (ed.). Paris: UNESCO, 1956.

Kelley, Stanley, Jr. *Professional Public Relations and Political Power.* Baltimore: The Johns Hopkins Press, 1956.

Krout, Maurice H. (ed.). *Psychology, Psychiatry and the Public Interest.* Minneapolis: University of Minnesota Press, 1956.

Laski, Harold. *The American Democracy.* New York: The Viking Press, 1948.

Lewis, Roy and Angus Maude. *Professional People in England.* Cambridge, Mass.: Harvard Press, 1953.

McCormack, Thelma Herman. "The Druggists' Dilemma: Problems of a Marginal Occupation," *American Journal of Sociology,* LXI (January, 1956).

MacRae, Duncan, Jr. "Occupations and the Congressional Vote—1940–1950," *American Sociological Review,* XX (June, 1955).

Mills, C. Wright. *White Collar.* New York: Oxford University Press, 1951, Chap. 6.

Parsons, Talcott. *The Social System.* Glencoe, Ill.: The Free Press, 1951, Chap. X.

——. "The Professions and the Social Structure," *Essays in Sociological Theory, Pure and Applied.*

Reissman, Leonard. "Life Careers, Power, and the Professions," *American Sociological Review,* XXI (April, 1956).

Wardell, Walter I. "Social Integration, Bureaucratization, and the Professions," *Social Forces* (May, 1955).

—— and Arthur L. Wood. "The Extra-Professional Role of the Lawyer," *American Journal of Sociology,* LXI (January, 1956).

Watson, Robert I. *Psychology as a Profession.* Doubleday Papers in Psychology. Garden City, New York: Doubleday and Company, Inc., 1954.

Webb, Sidney. *The Teacher in Politics.* Fabian Tracts, No. 187. London: Fabian Society, 1918.

Wilensky, Harold L. and Charles N. Lebeaux. *Industrial Society and Social Welfare.* New York: Russell Sage Foundation, 1958, Chap. XI.

Wood, Arthur L. "Informal Relations in the Practice of Criminal Law," *American Journal of Sociology,* LXII (July, 1956).

Young, Donald. "Sociology and the Practicing Professions," *American Sociological Review,* XX (December, 1955).

ON GENERALIZATION VS. THE PARTICULAR CASE:

Gottschalk, Louis. "The Historian's Use of Generalization" in *The State of the Social Sciences,* Leonard D. White (ed.). Chicago: University of Chicago Press, 1956.

Komarovsky, Mirra (ed.). *Common Frontiers of the Social Sciences,* 18–22. Glencoe, Ill.: The Free Press, 1957.

Moore, Barrington, Jr. "Sociological Theory and Contemporary Politics," *American Journal of Sociology,* LXI (September, 1955).

ON THE NATURE AND IMPACT OF SCIENCE, ITS ORGANIZATION, AND THE ROLE OF THE SCIENTIST:

Bendix, Reinhard. *Social Science and the Distrust of Reason.* Berkeley: University of California Press, 1951.

Bernal, J. D. *Science in History.* London: Watts and Company, 1954.

Davis, Kingsley. *Human Society.* New York: The Macmillan Company, 1949, Chaps. 1, 16.

De Gre, Gerard. *Science as a Social Institution.* Short Studies in Sociology. Garden City, New York: Doubleday and Company, Inc., 1955.

Easton, David. *The Political System.* New York: Alfred A. Knopf, 1953, Chaps. I, IX.

Lee, A. M. (ed.). *Readings in Sociology.* New York: Barnes and Noble, Inc., 1951, Section One.

Merton, Robert K. *Social Theory and Social Structure.* Glencoe, Ill.: The Free Press, 1949, Part IV.

Simpson, George. *Man in Society,* Doubleday Short Studies in Sociology. Garden City, New York: Doubleday and Company, Inc., 1954.

Waddington, C. D. *The Scientific Attitude,* rev. ed. West Drayton, Middlesex: Penguin Books, 1948.

ON THE RELATIONSHIP BETWEEN SOCIAL WORK AND SOCIAL SCIENCE:

Boehm, Werner W. "Social Work and the Social Sciences: A Theoretical Note," *Journal of Psychiatric Social Work,* XXI (September, 1951).

Coyle, Grace L. *Social Science in the Professional Education of Social Workers.* New York: Council on Social Work Education, 1958.

Gouldner, Alvin. "Explorations in Applied Social Science," *Social Problems,* 3 (January, 1956).

Greenwood, Ernest. "Social Science and Social Work: A Theory of Their Relationship," *The Social Service Review,* XXIX (March, 1955).

Hamilton, Gordon. "The Role of Social Casework in Social Policy," *Social Casework,* XXXIII (October, 1952).

Pollak, Otto, *et al. Social Science and Psychotherapy for Children.* New York: Russell Sage Foundation, 1952.

ON THE IMPORTANCE OF FREEDOM OF INQUIRY FOR SCIENCE:

Bisno, Herbert. *The Philosophy of Social Work.* Washington, D.C.: Public Affairs Press, 1952, pp. 91–96 and 104–105.

Gellhorn, Walter. *Security, Loyalty, and Science.* Ithaca, New York: Cornell University Press, 1950.

ON THE RELATION OF "MARGINALITY"
TO INTELLECTUAL CREATIVITY AND ORIGINALITY:

Davis, Kingsley. *Human Society.* New York: The Macmillan Company, 1949, pp. 10–15.

Veblen, Thorstein. "The Intellectual Pre-eminence of Jews in Modern Europe" in *The Portable Veblen,* Max Lerner (ed.). New York: The Viking Press, 1948.

CHAPTER IX

Desirable Objectives for Content Area E—The Group Basis of Social Work

This area of content has as its primary focus the understanding of groups basic to social work practice. The underlying assumption is that all social workers deal with groups as part of their professional activity and responsibility.[1] The framework for this content area is provided by its focus and by the interlocking of the major concepts which comprise the content aspect of the objectives. It draws upon aspects of the social sciences, social work and other professions that bear upon the study of the group.

Objective I:

Understanding the Perspectives and Theoretical Orientations from Which Groups May Be Studied

The student should have an understanding of the various perspectives and theoretical orientations from which different disciplines and different schools of thought approach the study of group phenomena. He should also know something about the historical development of group theory, as well as being knowledgeable about the range and rationale for variations in the use of the concept of group. Similarly, this suggests that he should be aware of the various typologies of groups and the criteria underlying such typologies. And, of course, of central concern for the student is an understanding of the concern of professional social work with groups.

[1] See Grace L. Coyle, "A Study of Group Process," in Margaret E. Hartford and Grace L. Coyle, *Social Process in the Community and the Group* (New York: Council on Social Work Education, 1958), 65, 67–68.

SIGNIFICANCE OF OBJECTIVE I

The attainment of this objective would contribute to the development of theoretical sophistication in the selection and use of materials on the group from other disciplines. It would also help to provide the student with a sense of the relevance of such materials for social work. Additionally, it would promote the development of a broad perspective within which social work's concern with groups could be compared with that of other disciplines. This, in turn, would be likely to enhance later multi-discipline cooperation. Finally, it could reasonably be expected that the student would recognize the important role groups play in all aspects of social work.

Objective II:

*Understanding the Structure and Function of Groups
Basic to Social Work*

The student should be aware of those groups particularly relevant to social work and he should have an understanding of their structure and function. Among the more important are the family, recreational groups, professional associations, political-economic interest groups, organizations of users of service, the social worker-client dyad, agency "board," treatment groups, work groups and committees. And he should understand why these groups occupy an important place in social work practice.

Objective II A:

*Understanding the Relationship between Groups
Basic to Social Work Practice and the Sociocultural Milieu*

To understand the relationship of the relevant groups to the sociocultural milieu is important and requires both the historical and the comparative point of view. However it may be accomplished, the crucial thing is that the student perceive the relationship of such groups as family, client self help groups to the larger pattern of social organization and to the culture. And this understanding should encompass deviant as well as conforming groups. In addition, the student should be encouraged to examine the relationship of different types of pertinent groupings to social persistence and social change.

Objective II B:

*Understanding of Groups Basic to Social Work
as Systems of Social Interaction and as Sub-Cultures*

The student should acquire an understanding of groups basic to social work as systems of social interaction and as sub-cultures. This includes both the external and internal systems of groups.[2] Among the relevant environments of groups are the society, the community, other groups and the organizational setting. This means that the student must not only understand these environments but must be knowledgeable about the reciprocal relationships between the groups and their environments. For example, he should have a grasp of intergroup relations.

In order to understand the internal system of a group the student should have a general comprehension of the significance of: the structuring and distribution of authority, power and prestige; communication; roles and role networks; norms and ideologies; dynamics of interpersonal relations; associative and disassociative processes; activities; social control mechanism; methods of problem-solving; group goals and movement; membership characteristics; group climate; and so forth.

Also, the student should perceive the relationships between formal and informal structures; between goals, structure and process; and between the external and internal systems. Finally, he should be able to recognize and understand similarities and differences among groups.

SIGNIFICANCE OF OBJECTIVE II

Through accomplishment of this objective the student should have acquired a basis for his more advanced courses as well as for his professional work with, and participation in, groups. This is an essential "basis" for all the methods and settings involved in professional practice.

---

[2] An interesting and useful discussion of the meaning of the "external system" of a group appears in George C. Homans, *The Human Group* (New York: Harcourt, Brace and Company, 1950), Ch. 4.

Objective III:

Understanding of the Group Member as a Person

All groups are composed of group members who must be seen as individual persons. The student needs to understand this fact and its implications: that there are reciprocal relationships between the individual and the group and that there is individuality in the performance of group roles. The student should have an understanding of the importance for the group of the individual group member's competence in interpersonal relations—as this is expressed through role performance. And he should have a grasp of the conditions, biological, psychological, group and sociocultural, responsible for the development of interpersonal competence.[3] Of these, special attention should be devoted to the group basis of such competence. Furthermore, the student should be aware of the fact that the individual member's role performance has a reciprocal impact upon the group.

SIGNIFICANCE OF OBJECTIVE III

Since all social workers operate in relation to groups they must, of necessity, also work with individuals in groups. The attainment of this objective would help to prepare the student for this facet of social work. (Much of the understanding of the individual as such is basically to be attained by objectives of content area F.)

Objective IV:

Understanding ⎫
and ⎬ *Application of Principles of Scientific Analysis*
Performing ⎭ *to Study of Groups Basic to Social Work*

This objective, in its essence, is shared by all the content areas. Since it was discussed in the previous chapter, it will not be elaborated on at this point.

---

[3] The concept of interpersonal competence has been most fully developed by Nelson N. Foote and Leonard S. Cottrell, Jr. See particularly Ch. II–III in Nelson N. Foote and Leonard S. Cottrell, Jr., *Identity and Interpersonal Competence* (Chicago: University of Chicago Press, 1955). Also see Gertrude Wilson and Gladys Ryland, *Social Group Work Practice* (Boston: Houghton Mifflin Company, 1949), 101–115.

Objective V:

Familiarity with Group Aspects of Social Work Practice

The student should have knowledge of the variety and significance of groups basic to social work and of the ways groups are actually involved in social work practice. This means that he should be familiar with the group aspects of social work with individuals, in community organization, and in supervision and administration. He should also be aware of the social worker as a participant in instrumental groups (*e.g.*, committees, case conferences, etc.) and

Chart of Objectives for the Group Basis of Social Work

CONTENT ASPECTS   BEHAVIORS

Content Aspects	Familiarity With	Understanding	Valuing	Advocating	Identification With	Performance
I. The Perspectives and Theoretical Orientations from which Groups May Be Studied.	x					
II. The Structure and Function of Groups Basic to Social Work.	x					
A. The Relationship between Those Groups Basic to Social Work and the Sociocultural Milieu.	x					
B. Groups Basic to Social Work, as Systems of Social Interaction and as Sub-Cultures.	x					
III. The Group Member as a Person.	x					
IV. The Application of Principles of Scientific Analysis to the Study of Groups Basic to Social Work.	x			x		
V. The Group Aspects of Social Work Practice.	x					

in professional associations. Finally, he should have knowledge of the role of the social worker in working with groups that are the users of service.

SIGNIFICANCE OF OBJECTIVE V

The accomplishment of this objective would help the student to put his understanding of groups within the social work frame of reference. It may be expected to assist the student in his advanced study as well as sensitizing him, in his later role as a social worker, to the group aspects of practice.

SELECTED BIBLIOGRAPHY ESPECIALLY RELEVANT FOR THE GROUP BASIS OF SOCIAL WORK

ON GROUP THEORY—SOCIOLOGICAL AND PSYCHOLOGICAL ORIENTATIONS:

Cartwright, Dorwin and A. F. Zander. *Group Dynamics*. Evanston, Ill.: Row Peterson and Company, 1953, particularly Part I.

Coser, Lewis A. and Bernard Rosenberg (eds.). *Sociological Theory*. New York: The Macmillan Company, 1957, Chaps. 8–9.

Hare, A. Paul, *et al.* (eds.). *Small Groups*. New York: Alfred A. Knopf, 1955, Part I.

Wilson, Logan. "The Sociology of Groups" in *Twentieth Century Sociology*. Georgil D. Gurvitch and Wilbert E. Moore (eds.). New York: The Philosophical Library, 1945.

ON APPLICATION IN BASIC DISCIPLINES AND PROFESSIONS:

American Sociological Review, XIX (December, 1954). Entire issue is devoted to small groups.

Bales, Robert F., Paul A. Hare and Edgar F. Borgatta. "Structure and Dynamics of Small Groups: A Review of Four Variables" in *Review of Sociology*, Joseph B. Gittler (ed.). John Wiley and Sons, Inc., 1957.

Benne, Kenneth D. and Bozidar Muntyan. *Human Relations in Curriculum Change*. New York: The Dryden Press, 1951.

Eister, Allan W. "Basic Continuities in the Study of Small Groups" in *Modern Sociological Theory*, Howard Becker and Alvin Boskoff (eds.). New York: The Dryden Press, 1957.

Hickman, C. Addison and Manford H. Kuhn. *Individuals, Groups and Economic Behavior*. New York: The Dryden Press, 1956.

Somers, Mary Louise. "Four Small Group Theories." Unpublished doctoral dissertation. Western Reserve University, School of Applied Social Sciences, 1957.

Waldo, Dwight. *Political Science in the United States of America*. Paris: UNESCO, 1956, pp. 25–26, 76.

Welfare Council of Metropolitan Los Angeles. *Group Dynamics: Implications for Social Work,* Special Report, Series No. 24, Research Department. Los Angeles, Cal.: Welfare Council of Metropolitan Los Angeles, 1950.

Wilson, Gertrude and Gladys Ryland. *Social Group Work Practice.* Boston: Houghton Mifflin Company, 1949, particularly Chap. 2.

Znaniecki, Florian. "Social Groups in the Modern World" in *Freedom and Control in Modern Society*. Monroe Berser, Theodore Abel and Charles H. Pase (eds.). New York: D. Van Nostrand Company, Inc., 1954.

ON THE FAMILY AS A SMALL GROUP:

Clark, Helen I. *Social Legislation*. New York: Appleton-Century-Crofts, 1946.

Clinard, Marshall B. *Sociology of Deviant Behavior*. New York: Rinehart and Company, Inc., 1957, Chap. 14.

Davis, Kingsley. *Human Society*. New York: The Macmillan Company, 1949, Chap. 15.

Foote, Nelson N. and Leonard S. Cottrell, Jr. *Identity and Interpersonal Competence*. Chicago: University of Chicago Press, 1955.

Hartford, Margaret E. "A Study of Social Process" in *Social Process in the Community and the Group,* by Margaret E. Hartford and Grace L. Coyle. New York: Council on Social Work Education, 1958, pp. 33–40.

Hill, Reuben and Richard L. Simpson. "Marriage and Family Sociology, 1945–55" in *Sociology in the United States of America,* Hans. L. Zetterberg (ed.). Paris: UNESCO, 1956.

Hogan, John D. and Francis A. J. Ianni. *American Social Legislation*. New York: Harper and Brothers, 1956, Part III.

Marriage and Family Living. "International Issue on the Family," Sections I, XVI (November, 1954).

Parsons, Talcott and Robert F. Bales. *Family, Socialization and Interaction Process*. Glencoe, Ill.: The Free Press, 1955.

Stein, Herman D. and Richard A. Cloward (eds.). *Social Perspectives on Behavior*. Glencoe, Ill.: The Free Press, 1958, Part IV.

Strodtbeck, Fred L. "The Family as a Three-Person Group" in *Small*

Groups, A. D. Hare, *et al.* (eds.). New York: Harper and Brothers, 1956, Part III.

Wilensky, Harold L. and Charles N. Lebeaux. *Industrial Society and Social Welfare.* New York: Russell Sage Foundation, 1958, pp. 67–83.

Winch, Robert F. "Marriage and The Family" in *Review of Sociology,* Joseph B. Gittler (ed.). New York: John Wiley and Sons, Inc., 1957.

ON PARTICULAR TYPES OF GROUPS:

a. *General Political Economic Interest Groups:*

Key, V. O., Jr. *Politics, Parties, and Pressure Groups,* 2nd ed. New York: Thomas Y. Crowell Company, 1947.

Waldo, Dwight. *Political Sciences in the United States of America.* Paris: UNESCO, 1956, Chap. X.

b. *The Therapist–Client as a Group Dyad:*

Bernstein, Arnold. *On the Nature of Psychotherapy,* Doubleday Papers in Psychology. Garden City, N.Y.: Doubleday and Company, Inc., 1954.

c. *"Client Organizations":*

Seymour, Helen. *When Clients Organize.* Chicago: American Public Welfare Association, 1937.

d. *Work Groups:*

Gross, Edward. *Work and Society.* New York: Thomas Y. Crowell Company, 1958, Chaps. 6, 9, 15.

e. *The "Group Approach to Social Reintegration":*

Clinard, Marshall B. *Sociology of Deviant Behavior.* New York: Rinehart and Company, Inc., 1957, Chap. 19.

ON THE RELATIONSHIP OF GROUPS TO THE SOCIOCULTURAL MILIEU:

Coyle, Grace L. *Group Experience and Democratic Values.* New York: The Woman's Press, 1947, Chap. 1.

Nisbet, Robert A. *The Quest for Community.* Toronto: Oxford University Press, 1953.

Rose, Arnold M. *Theory and Method in the Social Sciences.* Minneapolis: University of Minnesota Press, 1954, Chaps. 3–4.

Wilson, Logan and William L. Kolb. *Sociological Analysis.* New York: Harcourt, Brace and Company, 1949, Chap. 11.

Wright, Charles R. and Herbert H. Hyman. "Voluntary Association Membership," *American Sociological Review,* XXIII (June, 1958).

ON THE DYNAMIC AND CONSERVING FUNCTIONS OF GROUPS:

American Sociological Review, XIX (December, 1954), Various articles.

Benne, Kenneth D. and Bozidar Muntyan. *Human Relations in Curriculum Change.* New York: The Dryden Press, Inc., 1951.

Cartwright, Dorwin and A. F. Zander. *Group Dynamics.* Evanston, Ill.: Row Peterson and Company, 1953, particularly Part III.

LaPiere, Richard T. *A Theory of Social Control.* New York: McGraw-Hill Book Company, 1954.

Murray, Clyde E., Marx G. Bowens and Russell Hogrete. *Group Work in Community Life.* New York: Association Press, 1954.

ON THE SOCIETY AND COMMUNITY:

Hartford, Margaret E. "A Study of Social Process" in *Social Process in the Community and the Group* by Margaret E. Hartford and Grace L. Coyle. New York: Council on Social Work Education, 1958.

Humher, Rose. *The City: Urbanism and Urbanization in Major World Regions.* Chicago: J. B. Lippincott Company, 1955.

Kluckhohn, Clyde. "Toward a Comparison of Value-Emphasis in Different Cultures" in *The State of the Social Sciences,* Leonard D. White (ed.). Chicago: University of Chicago Press, 1956.

Laski, Harold J. *The American Democracy.* New York: The Viking Press, 1948.

Loomis, C. P. and J. A. Beegle. *Rural Social Systems.* New York: Prentice-Hall, Inc., 1950.

Mercer, Blaine. *The American Community.* New York: Random House, 1956.

Murray, Clyde E., Marx G. Bowens and Russell Hogrete (eds.). *Group Work in Community Life.* New York: Association Press, 1954.

Stein, Herman D. and Richard A. Cloward (eds.). *Social Perspectives on Behavior,* Section III, Glencoe, Ill.: The Free Press, 1958.

Thelen, Herbert A. *Dynamics of Groups at Work.* Chicago: University of Chicago Press, 1954, Chap. 12.

Warren, Roland L. *Studying Your Community.* New York: Russell Sage Foundation, 1955.

Williams, Robin. *American Society: A Sociological Interpretation.* New York: Alfred A. Knopf, 1951.

Wirth, Louis. *Community Life and Social Policy,* Elizabeth Wirth Marvick and Albert J. Reiss, Jr. (eds.). Chicago: University of Chicago Press, 1956.

ON ORGANIZATIONAL ENVIRONMENT OF GROUPS:

Klein, Alan F. *Society—Democracy—and the Group*. New York: Woman's Press and William Morrow and Company, 1953, Chaps. I, II, V.

Northen, Helen. "The Place of Agency Structure, Philosophy and Policy in Supporting Group Programs of Social Action" in *Group Work: Foundations and Frontiers*, Harleigh B. Trecker (ed.). New York: Whiteside, Inc. and William Morrow and Company, 1955.

ON THE GROUP MEMBER AS A PERSON:

Harding, D. W. *Social Psychology and Individual Values*. London: Hutchinson's University Library, 1953, particularly Chap. V.

Haythorn, William. "The Influence of Individual Members on the Characteristics of Small Groups" in *Small Groups*, A. P. Hare, *et al.* (eds.). New York: Alfred A. Knopf, 1955.

Newcomb, Theodore M. *Social Psychology*. New York: The Dryden Press, 1950, particularly Chap. 14.

Osborn, Hazel. "Some Factors of Resistance Which Affect Group Participation"; Gordon W. Allport. "The Psychology of Participation"; Horace G. Miller, "The Psychic Trauma of Becoming Part of a Group"—in *Readings in Group Work*, Dorothea F. Sullivan (ed.). New York: Association Press, 1952.

ON GROUP ASPECTS OF SOCIAL WORK PRACTICE:

Bernstein, Arnold. *On the Nature of Psychotherapy*. Doubleday Papers in Psychology. Garden City, New York: Doubleday and Company, Inc., 1954.

Blackey, Eileen A. *Group Leadership in Staff Training*. Washington, D.C.: U. S. Department of Health, Education, and Welfare, 1957.

Coyle, Grace L. "A Study of Group Process" in *Social Process in the Community and the Group* by Margaret E. Hartford and Grace L. Coyle. New York: Council on Social Work Education, 1958.

Newstetter, Wilber I. "The Social Intergroup Work Process" in *Proceedings of the National Conference of Social Work*. New York: Columbia University Press, 1947.

Pollak, Otto, *et al. Social Science and Psychotherapy for Children*. New York: Russell Sage Foundation, 1952, Chap. 2.

Wilson, Gertrude and Gladys Ryland. *Social Group Work Practice*. Boston: Houghton Mifflin Company, 1949, Chaps. 1, 3.

CHAPTER X

Desirable Objectives for Content Area F—Social Work and the Social Functioning of Individuals

The significance of the objectives of this content area will be discussed after all of them have been considered.

Objective I:

Understanding of the Person as Role Performer.

The goal of social work was stated in *The Nature of Social Work* as the enhancement of social functioning wherever the need for such enhancement is either socially or individually perceived. Social functioning in this sense designates those activities considered essential for performance of the several roles which each individual, by virtue of his membership in social groups, is called upon to carry out. This conception of the goal of social work places role performance in a central position.

In this content area the focus is on that aspect of the person most significant for social work—the person as a role performer. The understanding of the person in this capacity is, then, the first objective of this content area.

Objective II:

Understanding Interpersonal Competence as a Condition for Effective Role Performance.

Objective II A:

Understanding the Components of Interpersonal Competence

The concept of interpersonal competence appears to be very useful for understanding role performance and, thereby, social functioning. In the analysis of Foote and Cottrell interpersonal competence is viewed as having six major components: [1] health, intelligence, empathy, autonomy, judgment and creativity. By *health* is meant the fullest development, within organic limits, of the organism's ability to exercise all of its physiological functions. This view of health is, of course, much broader than that which defines it simply in terms of the absence of disease. Although *intelligence,* the second component, has the usual characteristics attributed to it, it is thought of as an ability subject to "planned development." Thus, according to this usage, both health and intelligence are psychosocial in their development (more accurately, but also more awkwardly, biopsychosocial).[2] The third of the components, *empathy,* encompasses such abilities as those involved in being able to interpret the attitudes and perceptions of others and in being able to view situations from the perspective of others. Such abilities are, of course, closely associated with the capacity to take roles effectively and with versatility.[3] By *autonomy,* the fourth of the components, is meant a stable and a clear identity associated with considerable self-direction and self-control. It is "genuine self-government construed as an ability if not as a state of affairs." [4] The fifth of the components, *judgment,* is reflected in the capacity to choose reflectively among alternative courses of action with a recognition and weighing of the consequences. Finally, we have, as the sixth and last component, *creativity.* Though difficult to define and measure (as are some of the other components), it may be generally thought of as the ability to meet new situations in a non-habituated and non-stereotyped manner: that is, to reorganize one's behavior appropriately or to seek out new ways of problem-solving and of viewing phenomena.

[1] Foote and Cottrell, *op. cit.* Their treatment of the concept is illuminating. This objective draws heavily on their discussion of interpersonal competence, including their formulation of the characteristics of its components.

[2] This conception of all of the components as abilities subject to planning is a basic tenet in the Foote-Cottrell thesis.

[3] The possible influence of the lack of adequate abilities of this type on the development of various behavior disorders is explored in a stimulating manner by Norman Cameron, *The Psychology of Behavior Disorders* (Boston: Houghton Mifflin Company, 1947).

[4] Foote and Cottrell, *op. cit.,* 55.

Objective II B:

*Understanding the Conditions for Development of
the Components of Interpersonal Competence.*

The student should understand the importance of interpersonal
competence as a condition for effective role performance. He
should understand the conditions which appear to be important
for development of the various components of interpersonal competence. Illustrative of the kinds of understanding involved are
the following conditions influencing health.

The student should understand the prenatal origins of behavior, including recognition of the fact that intra-uterine life is
not the same for all fetuses. He should be sensitive to the existence
and significance of these differences. Parental health and attitudes,
and the quality of the relationship between the parents as well as
between the parents and child, also need to be given recognition as
extremely important determinants. The student should also realize
that in addition to interpersonal stimulation people need periods
of privacy, and that this may be even more important in one
period of life (*e.g.,* adolescence) than another. The extent and
quality of parental and peer group expectation as well as the kind
of learned responses to stress are all vital influences on the development of health. And so is the financial wherewithal to secure desirable health services (preventative as well as remedial); to have a
sound diet; and to escape from a continuous sense of deprivation
and inadequacy. Legal restrictions conveying built-in evaluations
of inferiority and undesirability would obviously work against the
achievement of health.

The above are just a few illustrations of the conditions influencing one component of interpersonal competence. As another illustration let us look at the component of autonomy. The student
should understand that an adequate sense of self would tend to be
more likely to develop when a child is permitted to respond as an
individual rather than as a faint "carbon copy" of the parent;
when he knows that he can accept the love and affection offered
him without fearing that it will be used as "emotional blackmail"
to keep him in fetters; when there is an adequate "model" for the

child as he seeks his identifications and engages in the gradual process of role learning; when he has an opportunity to develop healthy sexual attitudes and relationships.

The student should also realize that the ability to act as an autonomous person is not suddenly acquired at one point to be fixed forever more. The importance of peer group responses in the development of the adolescent's self-image must be reckoned with. And for a child with anatomical or physiological disabilities, positive peer group as well as familial relationship may help to keep the disabilities from being defeating handicaps. The student should realize that in each stage of the life cycle there are conditions influencing the person's sense of autonomy. The unemployed male suffers a loss of position in the family, in addition to his money worries; the person of 65 finds a farewell dinner and an engraved pocket watch a poor substitute for a job and a sense of doing something of importance, and of being a someone of importance; these are circumstances which tend to impair a person's self-image and, consequently, his ability to act as an autonomous individual.

In seeking out the antecedent conditions for development of the components of competence the student should be concerned with a wide range of influences including biological, interpersonal, economic, political, social, educational and recreational.[5] He should realize, though, that much of our knowledge about such conditions is incomplete or tentative. Further, he should be encouraged to evaluate the conception of interpersonal competence in respect to both its usefulness and its completeness.

Objective III:

Understanding the Requirements for and Problems in the Performance of Critical Roles by Users of Service.

The student should have a grasp of the requirements for and problems in the performance of critical roles by users of service. This necessitates understanding that specific role performances require a particular configuration of components. These configurations in-

---

[5] Foote and Cottrell advance a stimulating list of hypotheses relating to the conditions conducive to the development of the components. *Ibid.*, Ch. III.

clude, but are not limited to, the components of interpersonal competence. For example, in addition to interpersonal competence the quality of role performance is dependent upon the nature of the role and its expectancies, the role performance of others, the reasons for the assumption of particular roles (and the possibilities for alternative role achievement), role conflicts, conflicts of interests and values, and so forth. In other words, not only abilities but the substantive content of the role and the nature of the total circumstances influence role performance.

The effective performance of crucial roles is vital both for the individual and, in the aggregate, for the society. Among these are age, sex, family, student, and occupational roles. Also important are roles in recreational groups and cellular associations (*e.g.,* citizen role, community member, member of a political-economic interest group, and so on).

In addition, then, to having an understanding of the characteristics of these specific roles (and sub-roles) and the requirements for their effective performance, the student should also be somewhat knowledgeable about the dynamics of the various types of role performance problems associated with such roles. This should be augmented by an understanding of the impact of role performance difficulties on other role performers.

Objective IV:

Familiarity with the Requirements for, and Problems in, the Performances of the Roles in the Professional Relationship.

The student should develop a familiarity with the requirements for, and problems in, the professional social work relationship— that is, the roles of user of service and the social worker. He should be aware of the variety of user-of-service roles, their characteristics and the requirements for the effective performance of such roles. There also should be a familiarity with the types of problems often associated with performing the role of the user of service. The dynamics of these problems as well as their consequences for the professional relationship comprise content with which the student should be familiar.

Equally important for the student is a familiarity with the performance of the role of the social worker. The characteristics of the various types of social worker roles; the requirements for their effective performance; the reasons for the various types of problems encountered in the performance of the social worker role: all of these aspects need to be recognized by the student.

SIGNIFICANCE OF THE OBJECTIVES

The attainment of the above objectives by the student should permit him to acquire an understanding of the individual person that places him not in a vacuum but rather in relation to those aspects of social functioning most relevant for social work practice. The student also should have been helped to relate the individual to

Chart of Objectives for Social Work and the Social Functioning of Individuals

CONTENT ASPECTS   BEHAVIORS

	Familiarity With	Understanding	Valuing	Advocating	Identification With	Performance
I. The Person as Role Performer.	x					
II. Interpersonal Competence as a Condition for Effective Role Performance.	x					
A. The Components of Interpersonal Competence.	x					
B. Conditions for the Development of the Components of Interpersonal Competence.	x					
III. The Requirements for, and Problems in, the Performance of Critical Roles by Users of Service.	x					
IV. The Requirements for, and Problems in, the Performance of the Roles in the Professional Relationship.		x				

group and institutional phenomena. Finally, the introduction to the roles of the social worker and the users of service prepares the student for more advanced study of the components of social work.

SELECTED BIBLIOGRAPHY ESPECIALLY RELEVANT FOR SOCIAL WORK AND THE SOCIAL FUNCTIONING OF INDIVIDUALS

The literature relevant to the conditions for development of the components of interpersonal competence is so vast that not even a sampling would be feasible. However, we shall cite a limited number of works that are either very recent, particularly helpful, or not widely used in social work education. It will be noted that the primary works of most major theorists are not included since it is assumed that they are both well known and well used. Also, no attempt has been made to balance the listings in terms either of types of content or schools of thought.

Adams, Donald K. *The Anatomy of Personality*, Doubleday Papers in Psychology. Garden City, New York: Doubleday and Company, Inc., 1954.

Almy, Milly. *Child Development*. New York: Henry Holt and Company, 1955.

Berle, Beatrice Bishop. *80 Puerto Rican Families in New York City: Health and Disease Studies in Context*. New York: Columbia University Press, 1958.

Cameron, Norman. *The Psychology of Behavior Disorders*. Boston: Houghton Mifflin Company, 1947.

Clausen, John A. *Sociology and the Field of Mental Health*. New York: Russell Sage Foundation, 1956.

Clinard, Marshall B. *Sociology of Deviant Behavior*. New York: Rinehart and Company, Inc., 1957.

Cooley, Charles H. *Human Nature and the Social Order*. New York: Charles Scribner's Sons, 1922.

Dollard, John and Neal E. Miller. *Personality and Psychotherapy*. New York: McGraw-Hill Book Company, 1950, Parts I–IV.

Eaton, Joseph W. and Robert J. Weil. *Culture and Mental Disorders*. Glencoe, Ill.: The Free Press, 1955.

Erikson, Erik H. *Childhood and Society.* New York: W. W. Norton and Company, Inc., 1950.

Fenlason, Anne F. *Essentials in Interviewing.* New York: Harper and Brothers, 1952.

Frank, Lawrence K. *Feelings and Emotions,* Doubleday Papers in Psychology. Garden City, New York: Doubleday and Company, Inc., 1954.

————. *Individual Development,* Doubleday Papers in Psychology. Garden City, New York: Doubleday and Company, Inc., 1955.

Fromm, Erich. *Escape from Freedom.* New York: Farrar, Straus and Young, 1941.

————. *The Sane Society.* New York: Rinehart and Company, Inc., 1955.

Fromm, Erika and Lenore Dumas Hartman. *Intelligence: A Dynamic Approach.* Doubleday Papers in Psychology. Garden City, New York: Doubleday and Company, Inc., 1955.

Gerth, Hans and C. Wright Mills. *Character and Social Structure.* New York: Harcourt, Brace and Company, Inc., 1953.

Hall, Calvin S. and Gardner Lindsey. *Theories of Personality.* New York: John Wiley and Sons, Inc., 1957.

Halliday, James L. *Psychosocial Medicine: A Study of the Sick Society.* New York: W. W. Norton and Company, Inc., 1948.

Hamilton, Gordon. *Theory and Practice of Social Casework,* 2nd ed. rev. New York: Columbia University Press, 1951.

Harding, D. W. *Social Psychology and Individual Values.* London: Hutchinson's University Library, 1953.

Haring, D. G. (ed.). *Personal Character and Cultural Milieu.* Syracuse, N.Y.: Syracuse University Press, 1949.

Heiman, Marcel (ed.). *Psychoanalysis and Social Work.* New York: International Universities Press, Inc., 1953.

Hollingshead, August B. and Fredrick C. Redlich. *Social Class and Mental Illness.* New York: John Wiley and Sons, Inc., 1958.

Hollis, Florence. *Social Casework in Practice.* New York: Family Welfare Association of America, 1939.

Honigmann, John J. *Culture and Personality.* New York: Harper and Brothers, 1954.

Kardiner, Abram. *The Individual and His Society.* New York: Columbia University Press, 1939.

————. *The Psychological Frontiers of Society.* New York: Columbia University Press, 1945.

Kardiner, Abram and Lionel Ovesey. *The Mark of Oppression.* New York: W. W. Norton and Company, Inc., 1951.

Karpf, Fay B. *The Psychology and Psychotherapy of Otto Rank.* New York: Philosophical Library, 1953.

Klein, Alan F. *Society—Democracy—and the Group.* New York: Woman's Press and William Morrow and Company, 1953.

Kluckhohn, Clyde and Henry A. Murray (eds.). *Personality in Nature, Society and Culture.* New York: Alfred A. Knopf, 1948.

Knight, Robert P. and Cyrus R. Friedman (eds.). *Psychoanalytic Psychiatry and Psychology,* Austen Riggs Center. New York: International Universities Press, 1954, Vol. I.

Landreth, Catherine. *The Psychology of Early Childhood.* New York: Alfred A. Knopf, 1958.

Leighton, Alexander H., *et al.* (eds.). *Explorations in Social Psychiatry.* New York: Basic Books, Inc., 1957.

Leuba, Clarence. *The Natural Man.* Doubleday Papers in Psychology. Garden City, New York: Doubleday and Company, Inc., 1954.

Lindesmith, Alfred R. and A. L. Strauss. *Social Psychology.* New York: The Dryden Press, 1949.

Linton, Ralph. *The Cultural Background of Personality.* New York: Appleton-Century-Crofts, 1945.

Mannheim, Karl. *Man and Society in An Age of Reconstruction.* London: Routledge and Kegan Paul Ltd., 1940.

Mead, G. H. *Mind, Self and Society.* Chicago: University of Chicago Press, 1934.

Mullahy, Patrick (ed.). *A Study of Interpersonal Relations.* New York: Hermitage House, Inc., 1949.

———— (ed.). *The Contributions of Harry Stack Sullivan.* New York: Hermitage House, Inc., 1952.

Munroe, Ruth L. *Schools of Psychoanalytic Thought.* New York: The Dryden Press, 1955.

Murphy, Gardner. *Historical Introduction to Modern Psychology,* rev. ed. New York: Harcourt, Brace and Company, 1949.

————. "The Internalization of Social Controls" in *Freedom and Control in Modern Society,* Monroe Berser, Theodore Abel and Charles H. Pase (eds.). New York: D. Van Nostrand Co., Inc., 1954.

Nelson, Benjamin (ed.). *Freud and the 20th Century.* New York: Meridian Books, Inc., 1957.

Newcomb, Theodore M. *Social Psychology.* New York: The Dryden Press, 1950, Parts II–IV.

Oeser, O. A. and S. B. Hammond (eds.). *Social Structure and Personality in a City.* New York: The Macmillan Company, 1954.

Parad, Howard J. (ed.). *Ego Psychology and Dynamic Casework.* New York: Family Service Association of America, 1958.

Perlman, Helen Harris. *Social Casework: A Problem-Solving Process.* Chicago: University of Chicago Press, 1957.

Progoff, Ira. *Jung's Psychology and Its Social Meaning,* Evergreen Edition. New York: Grove Press, 1955.

Riesman, David. *Selected Essays from Individualism Reconsidered,* Doubleday Anchor Book. Garden City, New York: Doubleday and Company, Inc., 1955.

———, Nathan Glazer and Revel Denney. *The Lonely Crowd,* Doubleday Anchor Book. Garden City, New York: Doubleday and Company, Inc., 1953.

Rose, Arnold M. (ed.). *Mental Health and Mental Disorder.* New York: W. W. Norton and Company, 1955.

Ruesch, Jurgen and Gregory Bateson. *Communication: The Social Matrix of Psychiatry.* New York: W. W. Norton and Company, Inc., 1951.

Sargent, S. Stansfeld and Marian W. Smith (eds.). *Culture and Personality.* New York: Viking Fund, 1949.

Schilder, Paul. *Psychoanalysis, Man and Society.* New York: W. W. Norton and Company, Inc., 1951.

Simmons, Leo W. and Harold G. Wolff. *Social Science in Medicine.* New York: Russell Sage Foundation, 1954.

Thompson, Clara. *Psychoanalysis: Evolution and Development.* New York: Hermitage House, Inc., 1950.

Tyler, Leona E. *Psychology of Individual Differences.* New York: Appleton-Century-Crofts, Inc., 1947.

Weinberg, S. Kirson. *Society and Personality Disorders.* New York: Prentice-Hall, Inc., 1952.

Wilson, Gertrude and Gladys Ryland. *Social Group Work Practice.* Boston: Houghton Mifflin Company, 1949.

Wilson, Logan and William L. Kolb. *Social Work Practice.* New York: Harcourt, Brace and Company, 1949, Part II.

Witmer, Helen L. and Ruth Kotinsky (eds.). *New Perspectives for Research on Juvenile Delinquency.* U.S. Department of Health, Education, and Welfare, Children's Bureau Publication No. 356. Washington, D.C.: U.S. Government Printing Office, 1956.

ON ROLE PERFORMANCE:

A few helpful references pertaining to the performance of the various roles are:

Chinoy, Ely. *Automobile Workers and the American Dream.* Garden City, New York: Doubleday and Company, Inc., 1955.

Clausen, John A. and Marian Rudko Yarrow (eds.). "The Impact of Mental Illness on the Family," *The Journal of Social Issues,* XI (1955).

Clinard, Marshall B. *Sociology of Deviant Behavior.* New York: Rinehart and Company, Inc., 1957, Chaps. 5, 14.

Cohen, Albert K. *Delinquent Boys: The Culture of the Gang.* Glencoe, Ill.: The Free Press, 1955.

Connor, Ruth, Theodore B. Johannis, Jr. and James Walter. "Intra-Familial Conceptions of the Good Father, Good Mother and Good Child," *Journal of Home Economics* (March, 1954).

Duvall, Evelyn M. *Family Development.* Chicago: J. B. Lippincott Company, 1957.

Feldman, Frances Lomas. *The Family in a Money World.* New York: Family Service Association of America, 1957.

Foote, Nelson N. and Leonard S. Cottrell, Jr. *Identity and Interpersonal Competence.* Chicago: University of Chicago Press, 1955.

Gross, Edward. *Work and Society.* New York: The Thomas Y. Crowell Company, 1958, particularly Chaps. 6, 9 and 14.

Group for the Advancement of Psychiatry. *Psychiatric Aspects of School Desegregation.* New York: Group for the Advancement of Psychiatry, 1951, pp. 58–66.

Hartford, Margaret E. "A Study of Social Process" in *Social Process in the Community and the Group* by Margaret E. Hartford and Grace L. Coyle. New York: Council on Social Work Education, 1958.

Henry, George W. *All the Sexes.* New York: Rinehart and Company, Inc., 1955.

Hiller, E. T. *Social Relations and Structures.* New York: Harper and Brothers, 1947.

Knupfer, Genevieve. "Portrait of the Underdog" in *Class, Status and Power,* Reinhard Bendix and Seymour M. Lipset (eds.). Glencoe, Ill.: The Free Press, 1953.

Merton, Robert K., *et al.* (eds.). *Reader in Bureaucracy.* Glencoe, Ill.: The Free Press, 1952.

Parsons, Talcott and Robert F. Bales. *Family, Socialization and Interaction Process.* Glencoe, Ill.: The Free Press, 1955.

Pollak, Otto, *et al. Social Science and Psychotherapy for Children*. New York: Russell Sage Foundation, 1952, Chaps. 2, 7.

Stein, Herman D. and Richard A. Cloward (eds.). *Social Perspectives on Behavior*. Glencoe, Ill.: The Free Press, 1958.

Thrasher, Frederic M. *The Gang*. Chicago: University of Chicago Press, 1927.

Waller, Willard. *The Family: A Dynamic Interpretation* (rev.), Reuben Hill. New York: The Dryden Press, 1951.

Wilensky, Harold L. and Charles N. Lebeaux. *Industrial Society and Social Welfare*. New York: Russell Sage Foundation, 1958.

ON ROLE OF USERS OF SOCIAL WORK SERVICE:

There are not very many analyses of the role of the users of the social worker's service. An exploratory type of analysis of this sort in regard to the patient has been done by

Parsons, Talcott. *The Social System*. Glencoe, Ill.: The Free Press, 1951, pp. 439–447.

Contributing to an understanding of the role of the user of service are:

Maas, Henry S. "Building Social Work Theory with Social Science Tools: The Concept of Role" in *Building Social Work Theory with Social Science Tools*. Los Angeles: Welfare Planning Council of Los Angeles, 1954.

Perlman, Helen Harris. *Social Casework: A Problem Solving Process*. Chicago: University of Chicago Press, 1957, particularly Chaps. 2, 6, 7, 12.

ON THE SOCIAL WORKER AS ROLE PERFORMER:

A few discussions of the roles of social workers and other helping professions are:

Parsons, Talcott. *The Social System*. Glencoe, Ill.: The Free Press, 1951, pp. 227–254 (for the role of the physician).

Stein, Herman D. and Richard A. Cloward (eds.) . *Social Perspectives on Behavior*. Glencoe, Ill.: The Free Press, 1958, pp. 251–262.

Trecker, Harleigh B. *Social Group Work: Principles and Practice*. New York: The Woman's Press, 1948, Chap. 3.

Wilson, Gertrude and Gladys Ryland. *Social Group Work Practice*. Boston: Houghton Mifflin Company, 1949.

CHAPTER XI

Desirable Objectives for Content Area G—Components of Professional Social Work

The framework for this content area is comprised of the major analytical components in the professional provision of social work services. It draws upon the other content areas previously discussed as well as upon knowledge from the various basic disciplines and professions.

For this content area the significance of all of the objectives will be described at one time following the discussion of the separate objectives.

Objective I:

Understanding and Valuing the Society and Community as a Component

The student should understand the significance of the society and community—that is, particular configurations of social relationships and social process, with their own culture and subcultures, organized as units—as the context for the provision of social work services. The significance is that the society (and community) is the primary source of authority and of resources. It is also the source of limitations on resources and of difficulties in the social functioning of individuals, singly and in groups. The student should recognize that the society (and community) are not, in reality, homogeneous entities and that these "publics" vary in their impact on the provision of social work services.

Objective II:

Understanding and Valuing the Social Agency as a Component

Objective II A:

Understanding and Valuing the Functions of the Social Agency

The student should understand and value the strategic place occupied by the social agency in the provision of social work services. His understanding should encompass recognition of the fact that the social agency, as an instrument of society (and the community), receives its sanction from the society (or at least a portion of it) and has a responsibility to it. This is associated, of course, with the social control function provided by the services. In other words, the social control function is one expression of the agency's responsibility to the society. However, in actuality, this may be a demonstration of responsiveness to only a portion (the significant public) of the society and community. The following comment by Bertha Reynolds gets at a fundamental fact of life that must be taken into account in an examination of the relationship of the social agency to the society.

> Our agencies are social institutions, molded by the same contending interests in our communities that produce both the relationships which bring people together and those that drive them apart. Whatever we find in our communities, we find also in social agencies.[1]

This point also has relevance to "what the social agency stands for" in the eyes of the users of its services. Some perceive the social agency as being, in a general way, a societal symbol and instrumentality. Others, viewing the social agency as standing for the interests of a segment of society (*e.g.*, the upper classes, people from the "right side of the tracks," politicians, "do-gooders,") may interpret its social control function as being aimed primarily at them and others like them. Illustrative of this category of users of service would be those union members who perceive the social agency with hostility or contempt, as representing the ideal and patronizing rich, or soft-headed, character reforming do-gooders; [2]

---

[1] Bertha C. Reynolds, *op. cit.* Another dimension of the question of what and whom the agency represents is explored by Chauncey Alexander in an unusually valuable article. Chauncey A. Alexander and Charles McCann, "The Concept of Representativeness in Community Organization," *Social Work,* I (January, 1956).

[2] For an interesting treatment of social work with union personnel see Reynolds, *op. cit.*

those delinquents who view the police as being the oppressive enemy of the people in their neighborhood; and the lower class school child who sees the school largely as a custodial institution enforcing alien standards upon him.[3]

Besides recognizing that the social agency is an instrument of society, the student needs to keep constantly in mind the social agency's service function and responsibility to the user of the services. Also, it is important for him to realize that the social agency is an employer with responsibilities and rights in relation to its employes. A vital aspect in understanding the social agency as a component in the provision of social work services is recognition of the areas of conflict among the demands imposed on the social agency by its simultaneous functions as an instrument of society, a provider of services, and an employer.

Objective II B:

Understanding the Impact of the Goals and Ideology
of the Social Agency on the Provision of Services

Another area of significance is the impact of the ideology of the social agency on the provision of services. For example, what effect do given sectarian auspices have on the provision of services? Also, if we look at those social agencies of the past whose ideology included a "character flaw" explanation of poverty, we see that the impact of these premises was clearly evident in the services they rendered. Furthermore, there is an important relationship between the sociocultural matrix and the ideology of the social agency. Certainly those agencies that were operating on the "character flaw" assumption and making distinctions between "deserving" and "undeserving" clients were reflecting the then existing organization of society and the ideology of the bourgeoisie.

Objective II C:

Familiarity With the Programs of Services
Offered by the Social Agency

The student should have a general familiarity with the programs of services offered by social agencies. He should be aware of the

[3] No implication is intended as to the truth or falsehood of these perceptions.

specific aspects of social functioning toward which the services are directed. And he needs to have an *understanding* of the rationale for the services.

Objective II D:

Familiarity with the Organization and Policy Determination Process of the Social Agency

The student should be familiar with the nature of intra-agency organization, both formal and informal. He should be aware of the process of policy making in social agencies and understand the determinants of social agency policy. This entails knowledge of the charateristics of those who make policy for agencies, and those who strongly influence such policies. Also, there should be an understanding of the place of the professional staff in the process of policy-making. One of the key questions which the student should be encouraged to think through is: What should be the role of the professional person—the specialist—in the making of policy? [4] And how meaningful is the slogan that "the social worker should be on tap not on top?"

The student should also realize that one of the key functions of policy formation in social agencies is decision-making as to the distribution of its limited resources.

The student needs familiarity with the various ways in which social agencies are organized and administered. Beyond this general awareness though, he should have an understanding of the effects of intra-agency organization and dynamics upon the actual provision of service and on the users of the services. This might be related to a recognition of the various types of agencies in which social work operates and the significance of these settings for social work practice. In addition, there needs to be a knowledge of certain characteristic types of role relationships, particularly among members of different professions, within social agencies.

[4] Much of the discussion of the role of the social worker as an expert has had a rather special focus—that is, in the community organization process. There appears to be a considerable emphasis on the professional's role as guide and enabler. To what extent is this principle valid in regard to policy making as such? And isn't that most influential of American policy makers, the businessman, an expert?

Objective II E:

Familiarity with the External Relationships of the Social Agency

The external relationships of the social agency (*i.e.,* relations with other groups and agencies in the community) and the sources of its financial support are other facets of the agency's operation worth knowing about. The student should be able to see the patterns of agency financing as being related to the character of the sociocultural matrix in which the agency is imbedded.

Objective III:

Understanding and Valuing the Social Worker as a Component

Objective III A:

Understanding and Valuing the Basic Professional Roles of the Social Worker

The student should understand and value the basic professional roles of the social worker. The first of these is as an agent of the society and community. This relationship of the social worker to the society is evident in the fact that the social worker's authority and definition of function are largely derived from the society. A correlate of these "rights" is the social worker's accountability to the society and community. This responsibility should be understood, valued, and supported by the student.

The second of the professional roles of the social worker is as the provider of a professional service. In order to comprehend what is involved in this role and to value it, the student must have knowledge of the goals of the service and the methods used in rendering them. He should also understand and have a high regard for knowledge, abilities, attitudes, self-understanding and ideological convictions (including professional ethics) that comprise the social worker's "equipment." Too, the student should have a rich appreciation for the social worker's accountability to the user of his services. This regard for the social worker's responsibility to the user of service should be so developed that the student would be willing to maintain its importance and legitimacy even in the face of adverse arguments. The third professional role of the social worker is as a member of a profession. The profession provides sanction and standards. It defines for the worker his sphere of competence, his rights and his obligations. The student should understand and appreciate the importance of this. He also needs to understand, value, and support the social worker's reciprocal responsibility to the profession.

The last of the social worker's professional roles is that of an employe. The student should understand and respect this status. He needs also to grasp the significance of the employe status for the way in which the social worker functions. (For example, the social worker is typically not oriented in the direction of making a profit, operating in a non-hierarchical setting, or functioning outside of a general policy set forth by the social agency of which he is an employe.) The student should have knowledge of, and should value as important, both the social worker's rights in relation to his employer and his responsibilities. Furthermore, he should understand, have a high regard for, and be willing to "stand up and be counted" in respect to the social worker's accountability to other employes.

The student should not assume that all of the social worker's professional roles fit together harmoniously at all times. On the contrary, there are likely to be recurrent strains and conflicts. For example, in the instance of an agency with poor standards the social worker may be torn between his role as an employe and his obligations to the user of service, the community and the profession. Or he may be under community pressure to violate a professional ethic, such as confidentiality. There even may be a conflict between the community's and the profession's definition of function.

The above are merely illustrative of the strains and conflicts potentially involved in any situation in which there is multiple accountability.[5] The student should understand the sources and types of strains and conflict. He needs to think through, as well, the alternative responses to such strains and conflicts. Additionally, the student should possess the same kind of understanding in regard to the strains and conflicts that might arise for the social worker between professional roles and values and his private roles,

[5] For a brief discussion of this problem see CSWE, *The Teaching of Social Philosophy and Social Responsibility in the Undergraduate Program, op. cit.,* 1–2.

beliefs, standards, ethics, and so forth. Here, too, thought should be given to alternative response to this type of strain or conflict.

Objective IV:

Understanding and Valuing the User of Service as a Component

The student should understand and respect the user of service, be it a person, group, community or society. He should realize that there may be varying perceptions and expectations with respect to the user of service on the part of the society (and community), the social agency, the social worker, and the person or groups who are the user of service. He should recognize the possible consequences of conflicts in perceptions or expectations for the provision of service. The student should also understand that there may be incompatibilities in the definitions of the user's need for service by the interested parties. Once again the sources and consequences of the incompatibilities ought to be comprehended by the student.

A very important area of understanding for the student is that of the reasons for the need for service. What are the sociocultural, psychological and biological sources of potential or actual threats to, or limitations on, the functioning of the user of service? Are there differences between the society (or community), the social agency, the social worker, and the user of service (if not the society or community) in their causal explanations? What are the reasons for these differences if they exist? To what extent are they due to different emphases, vested interests, lack of knowledge, and so on?

The student should also have an understanding of the resources and limitations of the user of service, encompassing a knowledge of the relevant sociocultural, psychological and biological factors that might serve as resources for the user of service and those that constitute limitations.

The student should recognize the importance of understanding just what service is actually desired. There should also be recognition of the significance of the perception of the social agency by the user (or potential user) of service and of any differences that might exist between this perception of the social agency's function and the definitions of its functions by the society (and community), the social agency and the social worker.

The student should understand, value highly, and maintain stoutly the rights and responsibilities of the users of service. He should also be familiar with the procedures by which the user (or potential user) is able to secure the rights to which he is entitled. The student should develop an appreciation of the great importance and value of such procedures and should be willing to support and promote such safeguards.

Objective V:

Understanding and Valuing the Process of Providing Service as a Component

The student should perceive the process of providing service as the dynamic interplay of social agency, social worker, and the user of service within a sociocultural milieu. He should acquire a beginning understanding of the structure and dynamics of providing service, including the processes and methods involved. Furthermore, he should have the opportunity to observe the process of providing service and to participate in a well-planned, systematic and controlled fashion, in some aspect of the provision of service.[6]

The student should understand and learn the value of the professional relationship. His knowledge of its character should include recognition of how it differs from (and in what ways it is similar to) other types of relationships.

He should also understand the factors influential in the course of, and outcome of, the process of providing service, with some knowledge of both the generic aspects of all social worker-user relationships and of the special characteristics of particular types of such relationships.

It is of great importance, too, for there to be an understanding of the resources for, and limitations on, the effective provision of service. This should include knowledge of the location of the resources and limitations, as well as their sources. The distinction between location and sources might be hypothetically illustrated in this fashion: a physical disability prevents the user of service from

---

[6] This aspect of the objective will be briefly discussed under learning experiences. However, it might be well to point out that an earlier conclusion in this report was that the undergraduate program should have as functions the preparation of students *both* for graduate school and for employment in social work.

being hired for a job that he needs in order to support himself and his family. The *location* of the limitation is, thus, in the user of service. However, his disability would not have been as severe if proper medical facilities had been available in the community in which he lived. Also, if the community's attitudes toward the physically disabled were more enlightened he would have been able to get a position. Thus, the *source* of the handicap is, in two respects, in the sociocultural milieu. The student should understand and learn to value highly the social worker's professional responsibility to utilize resources to the fullest extent and to engage in vigorous action to lessen or overcome limitations in the agency and in the sociocultural milieu.

Objective VI:

Understanding the Evaluation of the Services Provided as a Component

The student should understand the responsibility of the social agency to evaluate the effects of its services on the users of the services and on the community and society.

Objective VII:

Familiarity with the Issues and Trends in Professional Social Work

The student should acquire this familiarity in considerable measure through the attainment of all the other objectives. However, this objective should be given special attention as well, to ensure that the student does become aware of the major issues and trends in professional social work.

Objective VIII:

Familiarity with Educational and Vocational Opportunities in Social Work

This objective would appear to need no elaboration.

SIGNIFICANCE OF THE OBJECTIVES IN THIS CONTENT AREA

Besides providing for the integration of content from "the three levels of analysis" within the focus of professional social work, the

attainment of these objectives would also (1) provide basic preparation for advanced study of the methods of providing social work

Chart of Objectives for the Components of Professional Social Work

CONTENT ASPECTS   BEHAVIORAL ASPECTS

	Familiarity With	Understanding	Valuing	Advocating	Identification With	Performance
I. The Society and Community as a Component.		x	x			
II. The Social Agency as a Component.		x	x			
A. The Functions of the Social Agency.		x	x			
B. The Impact of the Goals and Ideology of the Social Agency on the Provision of Services.		x				
C. The Programs of Services Offered by the Social Agency.	x					
D. The Organization and Policy Determination Process of the Social Agency.	x					
E. The External Relationships of the Social Agency.	x					
III. The Social Worker as a Component.		x	x			
A. The Basic Professional Roles of the Social Worker.		x	x			
IV. The User of Service as a Component.		x	x			
V. The Process of Providing Service as a Component.		x	x			x
VI. The Evaluation of the Services Provided as a Component.		x				
VII. Issues and Trends in Professional Social Work.	x					
VIII. Educational and Vocational Opportunities in Social Work.	x					

services; (2) provide a basis for making a decision as to which aspect of social work he wished to concentrate on in graduate school; (3) provide a basic understanding for employment in a social agency; (4) provide an understanding of the fact that effective provision of services is dependent upon a number of interlocking component parts, all of which are crucial to the final outcome; and (5) provide the student with experience in some aspects of the actual provision of professional service.

SELECTED BIBLIOGRAPHY ESPECIALLY RELEVANT FOR "THE COMPONENTS OF PROFESSIONAL SOCIAL WORK"

For survey discussion of the TYPES AND NATURE OF COMMUNITIES, see:

Murphy, Campbell G. *Community Organization Practice.* Boston: Houghton Mifflin Company, 1954, Chaps. 8, 10, 11.
Stroup, Herbert H. *Community Welfare Organization.* New York: Harper and Brothers, 1952, Chaps. 1–4.

A very comprehensive description of PROGRAMS OF SERVICES is provided in:

Friedlander, Walter A. *Introduction to Social Welfare.* New York: Prentice-Hall, Inc., 1955.

For a concise survey of various programs in England by a number of specialists see:

Archer, Peter (ed.). *Social Welfare and The Citizen.* London: Penguin Books, 1957.

For a brief description of various STUDIES OF "DECISION-MAKING" IN POLICY QUESTIONS see:

Waldo, Dwight. *Political Science in the United States of America.* Paris: UNESCO, 1956.

There are several relevant articles in:

Dubin, Robert (ed.). *Human Relations in Administration.* New York: Prentice-Hall, Inc., 1951.

A stimulating discussion of the intellectual in the context of public bureaucracies is that by:

Merton, Robert K. *Social Theory and Social Structure*. Glencoe, Ill.: The Free Press, 1949, Chap. VI.

For a study of the relation of the "man of knowledge" to the "man of power," with a trade union context see:

Hunter, Floyd. *Community Power Structure*. Chapel Hill: University of North Carolina Press, 1953.
Wilensky, Harold L. *Intellectuals in Labor Unions*. Glencoe, Ill.: The Free Press, 1956.

In keeping with the present interest in the SOCIOLOGY OF ORGANIZATION there have been many recent sociological analyses and studies of the organization of an interactional pattern with hospitals, prisons, etc. Some of these are:

Greenblatt, Milton, Richard H. York and Esther Lucile Brown. *From Custodial to Therapeutic Patient Care in Mental Hospitals*. New York: Russell Sage Foundation, 1955.
Jones, Maxwell. *The Therapeutic Community*. New York: Basic Books, 1953.
Ohlin, Lloyd E. *Sociology and the Field of Corrections*. New York: Russell Sage Foundation, 1956, Chaps. II–IV.
Powelson, Harvey and Reinhard Bendix. "Psychiatry in Prison" in *Mental Health and Mental Disorder*, Arnold M. Rose (ed.). New York: W. W. Norton and Company, Inc., 1955.
Simmons, Leo W. and Harold G. Wolff. *Social Science in Medicine*. New York: Russell Sage Foundation, 1954, Chap. 6.
Stanton, Alfred H. and Morris S. Schwartz. *The Mental Hospital: A Study of Institutional Participation in Psychiatric Illness and Treatment*. New York: Basic Books, 1954.
Stein, Herman D. and Richard A. Cloward (eds.). *Social Perspectives on Behavior*. Glencoe, Ill.: The Free Press, 1958, Section VI.

Among the interesting studies and writings on INTERPROFESSIONAL RELATINOSHIPS are:

Blackey, Eileen. "Social Work in the Hospital: A Sociological Approach," *Social Work* I (April, 1956).
Burling, Temple, Edith M. Lentz and Robert N. Wilson. *The Give and Take in Hospitals*. New York: G. P. Putnam's Sons, 1956.

Zander, Alvin, Arthur E. Cohen and Ezra Stotland. *Role Relations in the Mental Health Professions*. Ann Arbor, Michigan: Institute for Social Research, University of Michigan, 1957.

The following contains a discussion of INTERAGENCY RELATION-SHIPS:

McMillen, Wayne. *Community Organization for Social Welfare*. Chicago: University of Chicago Press, 1945, particularly Chap. III and Part II.

For more of the specifics of interagency relationships than is usually found in texts see:

Johns, Ray and David F. DeMarche. *Community Organization and Agency Responsibility*, particularly Chaps. 12–16. New York: Association Press, 1951.

For helpful discussions of the FINANCING OF SOCIAL WELFARE PROGRAMS see:

Burns, Eveline M. "The Financing of Social Welfare" in *New Directions in Social Work*, Cora Kasius (ed.). New York: Harper and Brothers, 1954.
———. *Social Security and Public Policy*. New York: McGraw-Hill Book Company, Inc., 1956.
Haber, William and Wilbur J. Cohen (eds.). *Readings in Social Security*. New York: Prentice-Hall, Inc., 1948.
Leyendecker, Hilary. *Problems and Policy in Public Assistance*. New York: Harper and Brothers, 1955.
Murphy, Campbell G. *Community Organization Practice*. Boston: Houghton Mifflin Company, 1954, Chap. 9.
Myrdal, Alva. *Nation and Family*. London: Kegan Paul, Trench Trubner and Company, Ltd., 1945.

ON RECURRENT FACTORS IN PROVISION OF SERVICE:

Although there are an almost infinite number of elements that might affect the process of providing service, certain factors recur, including such varied things as attitudes toward money and success, transference, and (in the community organization process) tensions between public and private agencies. The possible references are also almost infinite, but as an illustration a work particularly relevant to the first of the factors mentioned above is:

Feldman, Frances Loman. *The Family in a Money World.* New York: Family Service Association of America, 1957.

An example of a useful discussion of cultural factors impinging on the social worker is:

Ginsberg, Sol W. "The Impact of the Social Worker's Cultural Structure on Social Therapy," *Casework,* XXXII (October, 1951).

The cultural values of the user of services also need to be understood by the social worker. Some helpful material is presented in:

Woods, Sister Frances Jerome. *Cultural Values of American Ethnic Groups.* New York: Harper and Brothers, 1956.

CHAPTER XII

Teaching and Organization of the Undergraduate Phase of Social Work Education

THE USE OF OBJECTIVES

These comments on the use of objectives are by way of clarifying what was and what was not intended. As already indicated, the lists of objectives do not constitute course outlines. The objectives themselves are not necessarily all inclusive. Furthermore, it well may be that some of the suggested objectives are not so important as ones that have been left out. It is our hope, however, that the main body of the suggested content and behaviors, as well as the frameworks within which the content and behaviors were cast, will serve as useful guides for the development of sound curricula for the undergraduate phase of the program of social work education.

Not all the objectives were developed in the same degree of specification. The content area, Sociocultural Basis of Social Work was elaborated upon more fully than the others because it was thought these materials might be less familiar to the reader, or at least their applicability to social work might be less evident. These considerations, plus the fact that the writer was not equally conversant with all the content (nor with all the basic disciplines), help to explain the unequal development of the objectives. No implication is intended that those objectives which received less specification or exploration are necessarily less important or should receive less attention in the curriculum.

The bibliographic references are similarly selective. There was no intention to provide comprehensive bibliographies for the potential teacher or the prospective student. It is hoped that the references will prove to be useful, particularly in respect to less familiar content. It should be noted that certain disciplines such as economics, philosophy, political science and physiology, are not so well represented among the references as they deserve to be. Also, since it was assumed that the reader would be well acquainted with social work materials, these sources were intentionally slighted in the citations.

LEARNING EXPERIENCES

Regrettably, it has not been possible to make a systematic study of learning experiences. This is, of course, a serious omission since what is learned is dependent not only on the content of the course but on the learning experiences to which the student is exposed. There is good reason to think that traditional lecture procedures need to be complemented by other learning experiences such as: having classes that are studying the group operate as groups, mock legislative committee sessions and other types of role-playing experiences; observation of social welfare, and particularly social work, personnel in practice—from policy-making situations to a casework interview; the use of novels, biographies and autobiographies, and plays to enrich and deepen the student's understanding of human experiences and behavior; various types of field experiences; and discussions of case records.[1]

Many of the above types of learning experiences, as well as others not enumerated, are already in regular use or being experimented with. Several general observations are perhaps warranted. In the admirable desire to get away from stereotyped, highly formalized types of learning experiences, such as lectures, that are unrealistically "rationalistic," there is also a danger. This is that processes such as *thinking* will become unduly subordinated to *feeling*, and that knowledge of facts and ideas will be treated as of little importance when compared with "intuitive" insights and impres-

[1] Reference to various literary works is not made in our discussion of objectives since this seemed more relevant under the heading of learning experiences. The most complete and systematic discussion as well as listing of novels and plays in relation to social science and social work concepts and purposes known to the writer is Austin L. Porterfield, *Mirror, Mirror: On Seeing Yourself in Books* (Fort Worth, Texas: Leo Potishman Foundation–Texas Christian University, 1957). For a listing of useful audiovisual aids see "Films Recommended for Use in Undergraduate Education for Social Welfare." (New York: CSWE, 1958.)

sions. Insights, impressions, and above all, feelings, are vital stuff for social workers and should not be underemphasized (as they are in so many traditional classroom courses). On the other hand, they must also be kept in proper balance so that the social worker will be a person who *thinks* as well as *feels.*

A second point of some relevance is that learning often takes place, particularly in respect to attitudes, values and the subtler abilities, as the result of a proper "climate." Thus, the teacher who claims that the conflict of ideas is good and who assures the class that differences of opinion are all to the good, but whose actual behavior creates a very different atmosphere, is not likely to stimulate students to participate in a hard-hitting examination of controversial ideas. One particularly unfortunate way of lessening critical thinking, not unknown in social work education, is to respond to criticism or challenge by examining (privately or in the classroom) the "psychological reasons" behind the student "questioning." Such a response by a teacher can have two serious consequences: first, it is likely to stultify critical thinking and second, it reinforces the intellectual confusion between the validity of an idea and the reasons for the idea being advanced or maintained. This is not to say that questions as to student motivation have no place in social work education. They do—but the place is not when the matter under discussion is the correctness of a given position.

The third observation is that, while it is important "to start where the student is," it is even more important not "to end where he was." There are academic standards which must be attained regardless of "where the student was" or how hard he tried. A student whose attainment is below a given minimum, for whatever reason, may well constitute a threat to the potential users of his services.

Now we turn to one of the most controversial of questions: Should the undergraduate social work student engage in "field work"? If the answer to this question should be *yes,* then a second question follows immediately: Of what should the field work consist? In Chapter IV were discussed some of the confusions found to surround undergraduate field work. It should be remembered that one objective in the content area, "Components of Professional Social Work," included the development of "performing ability" in respect to the provision of service. What conclusions do the findings and the stated objective lead us to? Unfortunately, without a systematic study of field work as a learning experience we are in no position to make any very definite recommendations. Our findings and "impressions" do suggest the following:

1. That certain types of field experiences (field observation and/ or field participation) are feasible as a learning experience in support of "classroom objectives" at virtually every educational level.

We are in no position to specify what kinds of field experiences the student should have at the undergraduate level. It is our "hunch" that studies of the assignments and performance of social work aides, of volunteers, of summer social work education and employment programs, would offer some helpful clues in this connection.

2. Such experiences should be organizationally related to the total curriculum, and not just to the "methods" course.

3. Field experience "supporting" social welfare content should be social welfare experiences and not just social work experiences.

4. The overwhelming emphasis at the undergraduate level should be on field experiences as learning experiences carefully designed to deepen the student's understanding of what he is learning in the classroom.

5. There should be carefully planned purpose, continuity and sequence in all field experiences. Even so-called casual observation should be thoughtfully integrated within the curriculum. And certainly, there should be continuity and sequence in the field experiences of the student as he progresses through the various stages of the total program of social work education. This means that types of field experiences appropriate to both the undergraduate and graduate levels should be worked out by faculty representatives of both levels, together with agency representatives, for the use of individual schools.

6. Some learning of "performance skills" and the use of field experience to integrate knowledge, attitudes and skills, would appear to be desirable and appropriate at the undergraduate level. However, it needs to be reiterated that at no level, and this is particularly true of the undergraduate stage, should the university or

college be expected to turn out a practitioner who is well prepared to practice social work upon graduation without further in-service training and supervision on the job, at least initially.

THE TEACHER

It is evident that the burden put on a teacher by the functions and objectives of the various content areas described herein is indeed heavy. The ideal preparation for a teacher of such material would seem to be (1) knowledge of the relevant basic disciplines; (2) particular competence in one of the basic disciplines; (3) a social work degree; and (4) aptitude for and experience in teaching at the undergraduate level. These are obviously difficult qualifications for anyone to possess. It seems to us that the formal training and specific degree is less important than being informed about and sympathetic toward social work and being really knowledgeable about the basic disciplines, particularly the social sciences. It is also very important that the person demonstrate the qualities of a good liberal arts teacher. The individual who has these qualifications would probably be a good teacher of undergraduate social work content regardless of whether he had a degree in a given social science or in social work. It appears desirable, whenever possible, for the instructor responsible for the undergraduate phase of the social work program to be a full time faculty member.

SUGGESTED ORGANIZATION FOR THE UNDERGRADUATE PHASE OF THE PROGRAM OF SOCIAL WORK EDUCATION

The organization of program will be discussed under several questions. The first is: *What and how many social work content courses should be taught at the undergraduate level?*

As already stated, the content areas delimited and described earlier are not the equivalents of courses or even course sequences. Yet the structural-functional model that we developed and the content areas themselves do have implications for organization. We suggest: *that there should be one or more courses developed for each of the content areas described.*

This does not mean that what we describe as an objective for one content area must necessarily be included in a course within that area. It might prove desirable to use materials which, to some extent at least, cut across the content areas described in a given course. However, as was pointed out in the discussion of the structural-functional model, we question the wisdom of combining the concepts from all three "levels of analysis" too quickly. This would suggest that one course including objectives from all three areas would probably run into difficulty. It would also make almost impossible demands on the instructor. In the final analysis, organization of the content areas into a particular set of courses has to be worked out and tested by individual schools. Careful experimentation by a number of them should provide a basis for determining the most satisfactory patterns of course organization.

A caution regarding the total number of social work offerings might well be in order at this point. If there is to be time enough in the total undergraduate program for the student to take the necessary advanced courses in the basic disciplines on top of a general education base, with some additional allowance for the pursuit of individual interests (not associated with vocational goals), it would appear unwise to have more than a total of 24–30 semester hours of social work content courses. Of course, it may be perfectly possible to develop an adequate program with fewer units. The above figure is intended only to suggest a maximum.

A second question is: *What courses in the other disciplines would be particularly useful as prerequisites or supporting courses for social work offerings?* [2]

This is a question that has to be answered by each school. It depends on what courses are available, what the general institutional requirements are, what the particular emphasis is in a given course, and similar variables. A procedure for answering this question might be for the faculty to analyze the content of the social work offerings and then see what work given in the other

[2] By supporting courses we mean those courses from the other disciplines which are particularly relevant to social work sequences but which are taken concurrently with or following the social work offerings.

disciplines best serves as a basis for, or in support of, these social work courses.[3] This procedure was employed by the writer *for purposes of illustration only,* using the catalog of one university. It should be noted that all that was done was somewhat to narrow the field of choice. To end with a reasonable number of units, a further selection would still have to be made, even from those courses designated as being of particular importance. Also, in the university catalog examined, a number of the designated courses would normally be taken by all students in any case, as part of the general education program. The results follow:

AN APPLICATION OF THE METHOD FOR SELECTING PREREQUISITES AND "SUPPORTING" COURSES FOR SOCIAL WORK SEQUENCES

Using the proposed social work content areas as guides, certain prerequisite and supporting content was identified. Then, this content was used as the basis for the selection, *from one university catalog,* of specific courses that appeared to be particularly useful as prerequisites for, or in support of, the proposed social work sequences. The designation * indicates that a course is of particular importance.

A. Biological and chemical sciences
  1. *Human Anatomy* *

B. Humanities
  1. *Ethics* *
  2. *History of Philosophy*
  3. *Logic*
  4. *Persistent Problems of Philosophy* *
  5. *Nineteenth Century Prose* *
  6. *Social Philosophy* *
  7. *The Scientific Method* [4]

C. Law [5]

---

[3] It is assumed that the social work content offerings at a given institution will not duplicate content adequately covered in courses in other disciplines. The determination of appropriate courses in other disciplines should be a joint enterprise involving both the social work instructor and faculty member from the other disciplines.

[4] In some schools a course is taught in *Social and Psychological Insights in Literature.* Where available, such a course would be designated as being of particular importance.

[5] The particular university used for this illustrative application had no appropriate course in Law, but a course in *The Legal Institution* would appear extremely important.

D. Mathematics
1. Basic Concepts in Mathematics and Statistics *

E. Social Sciences
1. Anthropology
a. *General Anthropology* *
b. *Peoples of the World*
c. *Cultural Dynamics* *
d. *Primitive Value Systems*

2. Economics
a. *Principles of Economics* *
b. *History of Organized Labor* *
c. *Labor Legislation*
d. *Public Finance*
e. *Economic Theory*
f. *Comparative Economic Systems* *
g. *Contemporary Economic Problems* *
h. *History of Economic Thought*

3. Geography
a. *Economic Geography*
b. *Political Geography*

4. History
a. *History of Western Civilization* *
b. *Western Institutions and Ideas* *
c. *Economic History of Europe* *
d. *Economic History of the U.S.*
e. *Victorian England*
f. *History of American Thought and Culture* *
g. *History of Science*

5. Political Science
a. *American Government* *
b. *International Relations*
c. *Public Administration* *
d. *Political Parties*
e. *American Political Theory* *
f. *European Political Theory* *
g. *Public Opinion*

6. Psychology
a. *General Psychology* *
b. *Principles and Methods of Psychological Assessment* *

    c. *Character and Personality* *
    d. *Abnormal Psychology* *
    e. *Developmental Psychology* *
    f. *Group Dynamics*

7. Sociology
    a. *General Sociology* *
    b. *World Population and Social Structure*
    c. *American Society*
    d. *Introduction to Social Research* *
    e. *Marriage and the Family*
    f. *Social Psychology* *
    g. *Social Institutions*
    h. *Criminology and Delinquency*
    i. *Social Aspects of Mental Health*
    j. *Social Change* *
    k. *Theory of Social Groups* *
    l. *Community Structure and Organization* *
    m. *Social Control*
    n. *History of Social Thought* *
    o. *Social Stratification* *
    p. *The Family as a Social Institution* *
    q. *Interviewing* *

8. Speech
    a. *Fundamentals of Speech*
    b. *Speech Defects and Disorders*

9. Health
    a. *Introduction to Public Health* *

10. Recreation
    a. *History and Theory of Recreation*

A third question is: *How should the undergraduate social work offerings be organized?*

In Chapter IV the pros and cons of various organizational patterns were explored, but so many important indigenous factors affect this question that we are not in a position to make a recommendation as to the preferred academic "home" for the social work offerings. The writer has a personal preference for a social work concentration, rather than a social work major or separate social work department, but there is not enough similarity among the schools in regard to the relevant considerations to warrant any recommendation in support of this position over other possibilities. However, it would seem highly desirable to have *some type* of *distinct* undergraduate social work curriculum such as concentration or major, since the probability is that such a curriculum would tend to promote student identification with social work as an occupational entity—and thus as a vocational choice.

The fourth question is: *What should be the length of the program of social work education?*

As we have seen, the present two-year graduate program in social work, leading to the master's degree, is virtually discontinuous with the prior undergraduate period of education. We have expressed the judgment that such discontinuity makes for an inefficient and incomplete educational experience. The gaps and unproductive duplications in the existing social work programs have been spelled out, in this and other projects of the Curriculum Study. In addition, mention has been made of the shortage of trained personnel and the unfavorable competitive position of social work with respect to recruitment.

As a backdrop for these findings we set forth the propositions that (1) there should be an interweaving of liberal arts and professional education; (2) it is not the responsibility of a university or college to turn out, for any profession or occupation, accomplished practitioners who can without further training perform with independence and competence; and (3) the social work profession must assume a large measure of responsibility for seeing to it that there are enough qualified social workers to meet society's need for them.

There has been considerable experimentation of late in professional education, some in the direction of shortening the total period of professional education, some emphasizing the incorporation of more liberal content in professional programs and/or the blending of the liberal and professional programs. The following paragraphs, abstracted from a letter to the writer from Dr. Donald H. Morrison, the Provost of Dartmouth College, makes reference to similar developments at that school.

First, I believe that in several professional fields of study there are opportunities for useful integration of pre-professional and professional curricula. We are hard at work on such programs in medicine, engineering, and business administration—fields in which our own professional schools are involved. In these areas, it seems to be possible, in varying degrees, of course, to "structure" a course so that professional courses can (a) be taught at a more advanced level, or (b) be consolidated, with a saving of time for the student.

Second, from our experience, it seems essential that the objectives of the professional program be carefully thought out and agreed to. Unless this is done, their "blending" with liberal arts courses is likely to be difficult, if in fact possible.[6]

We believe that the proposed program set forth by the Curriculum Study will improve the quality and greatly enhance the efficiency of social work education. The improved efficiency will largely result from: (1) undergraduate-graduate continuity; (2) horizontal integration; (3) clarification and strengthening of the educational objectives at all levels; (4) increased reliance on a conceptual approach; and (5) reduction in the "apprenticeship residuals" that have heretofore characterized social work education.

On this basis it might be desirable to have the first professional social work degree awarded at the conclusion of an integrated *undergraduate-graduate five-year program.* We believe that the students completing such a program would at least be as well educated, and in all probability *considerably better educated,* than the products of the present two-year Master's programs.

Two points concerning this suggestion may need elaboration and clarification. First, we are definitely *not* suggesting a one-year graduate program. Rather we are thinking in terms of an *integrated five-year program with social work content distributed over*

[6] Other illustrations of interesting developments in professional education are the shortened program in medical education at Johns Hopkins; the two-year programs for registered nurses being tried out in a considerable number of schools; the accelerated 3–2 programs of engineering education involving the Columbia University School of Engineering and 44 affiliated colleges and universities (the most recent affiliate being Bard College); the 3–2 program for the Master of Arts in Teaching at Yale University in conjunction with affiliated schools; and the Harvard Internship program for the preparation of Elementary and Secondary school teachers. It should be noted that a movement toward shortening the time necessary for attaining the Ph.D. degree, particularly in the sciences, is also under way.

at least three of the five years.[7] Second, as we envision it, those students without the undergraduate portion of the integrated over-all program who enter a graduate school of social work would either be expected to make up the content they are lacking or to take a two-year graduate program. The two-year program would probably be continued in many schools during the transitional period.

In conclusion it needs to be emphasized as strongly as possible that the suggested five-year program would be neither a diluted nor a cheapened program. On the contrary, we have every reason to believe that it would result in better qualified social workers and more of them.

A fifth question is: *How should the total five-year program of social work education be divided (if such a program were tried) as to number of years in undergraduate and in graduate school?*

It is probably true that three years of undergraduate schooling followed by two years of study in a graduate school of social work would be easier to work out administratively than would a program consisting of four undergraduate years with one year of graduate study after it. We would guess that if the idea of a five-year program is accepted there would be a good deal of sentiment for the 3–2 arrangement.

However, the 4–1 pattern seems preferable for the following reasons:

1. The liberalizing influence of the undergraduate program would permeate a larger proportion of the total program.

2. There would tend to be a greater "fraternization" of social work with other faculty members.

3. Many students would not wish, or be able, to attend a graduate school of social work after their junior year. Hence the number of students completing four years of the program (associate social workers) would probably be much greater under a 4–1 program than under a 3–2 arrangement.

4. The number of students going on to graduate school would

---

[7] In some universities, colleges, and junior (or community) colleges, a non-specialized course in social work for any or all students might be offered at the sophomore level, thus spreading social work content over a four year period.

probably be considerably less under a 3–2 program than under a 4–1 plan.

5. The recruits for employment in social work would probably be less under a 3–2 program than under a 4–1 pattern.

The last question is: *What should be the relationship of the undergraduate phase of the program of social work education to programs preparing students for allied professions?*

In this project we have been able to concentrate only on the educational problems of the social worker. Our recommendations are thus necessarily limited to social work education. However, we are inclined to think that the present situation in which a large number of fragmented professions each have their own educational programs is inefficient and probably inconsistent with sound educational philosophy. Although we are not in a position to make any specific recommendations on this point, we believe that experimentation in the direction of working out common (or at least shared) programs of professional education (beginning at the undergraduate level) are all to the good. The primary difficulties in the way of such programs are: (1) different professional ideologies; (2) a lack of common prerequisite content; (3) emphasis or perspectives sufficiently different that the level of generalization necessary to encompass the various professions would be too high to be meaningful to students of particular professions. These are real difficulties but they are not necessarily prohibitive. *Thus we conclude that it would be desirable to experiment with such joint programs.*

SUMMARY OF RECOMMENDATIONS

Major recommendations of the project can be summarized as follows:

1. The long-enduring dichotomy between liberal arts and professional education should be modified by an interweaving of liberal and professional education.

2. The goal of preparation for employment in social work as a "social work associate" and the goal of preparation for graduate study in social work are both legitimate aims of the undergraduate

phase of social work education. It is desirable and feasible for both to be achieved by one undergraduate program.

3. The undergraduate and graduate programs (and the levels within them) should be conceived of as stages within a single program of social work education.

4. Social work content in the undergraduate phase should be divided into two "layers," representing consecutive mediating stages between basic knowledge courses and the social work methods and similarly practice-focused sequences offered at the graduate level.

5. The recommended objectives are divided into four major content areas: sociocultural basis of social work, group basis of social work, social work and the social functioning of individuals, and the components of professional social work.

Comparison of the above recommendations with those from the Hollis-Taylor report listed in Chapter I shows that, despite some differences, there are clear lines of continuity between that study and this and a number of significant similarities between the two.

Recommendations of this project are presented as hypotheses for experimentation. It is to be hoped that results of any experimental programs will be carefully evaluated and compared with the outcomes of present programs. Adaptations and modifications of the project recommendations will result. Years are required to plan, establish, and evaluate new educational programs, and there is no expectation that the project proposals will remake the face of social work education. It is hoped, however, that they will provide a systematic basis for creative experimentation.

The words of Francis Bacon are as applicable to social work education as to other aspects of life:

> It would be an unsound fancy and self-contradictory to expect that things which have never yet been done can be done except by means which have never yet been tried.

Patterns and Rationale
for Pre-Professional Education for Social Work [1]

MEREB E. MOSSMAN

(Report of Research Undertaken as Consultant to the Undergraduate Project)

Colleges and universities have demonstrated their concern and responsibility for undergraduate preparation for social work in a variety of ways, some structured and a formal part of the college organization; others less formal but representative of the interest of the college or university in moving toward a clarification of its part in the task of educating persons to take the jobs open to college graduates in social work. Within the college organization, many colleges have done one or more of the following: the college catalog carries a descriptive statement of a general program for those interested in social work and in some instances detailed curricula outline the students' undergraduate programs; courses with social work content are offered; special advising is available for those interested in social work; and in some instances there is a major offered with a concentration in social work. In addition, in many instances the college catalog mentions constituent membership in the Council on Social Work Education which carries with it certain formal obligations regarding a well-defined and integrated curriculum with a social work focus as a part of the undergraduate general educative program.

Illustrative of more general ways in which colleges have shown an interest in social work have been the state conferences set up in many states cooperatively by the colleges, social agencies and social workers to discuss matters of mutual interest in education for social work. One notes both the deep concern and the confusion

[1] All colleges and universities that are constituent members of the Council on Social Work Education were invited to send catalogs, brochures and other printed material. Fifty-one institutions responded in time to be included in this study. The data provided by these institutions are shown on the chart which serves as the concluding section of this Appendix.

shown in these conferences as educators and those in professional practice have struggled with the problems of state and national need for more social workers, the nature of the undergraduate curriculum and the content of social work courses. These conferences held over the last ten years are testimony of the need for the comprehensive Curriculum Study presently being undertaken by the Council on Social Work Education.

Another way in which schools have shown an interest is through brochures which present the field of social work as a career, giving a statement of preparation necessary, costs, curriculum and job opportunities. These are used both for recruitment of students to the college and then to the major within the college in which students are prepared for social work.[2]

STRUCTURED EFFORTS

Catalog statements regarding social work give descriptive accounts of the colleges' or universities' concern with social work education, and curricular suggestions with a plan for the student are often made. These suggestions range from those which are general with a few specific courses suggested and a range of electives, to those that give detailed, specific plans for the four-year program.

One or two illustrations of each type of statement will show the generality and explicitness which may characterize the statements. The first, taken from the University of Denver is a statement on pre-professional social work taken from the catalog section in which other pre-professional statements are given.[3] This statement follows:

> The pre-professional major in social work is designed for the undergraduate student who desires to prepare for graduate professional work in the School of Social Work of the University of Denver or to qualify for those positions in social agencies for which professional

2 Illustrations: Social Work as a Career, University of New Mexico; Preparation for Social Work at Sacramento State College, November, 1956; Is Social Work the Career for You?, Valparaiso University; A Profession with a Future for You—Social Work, Western Michigan College.
3 Bulletin of University of Denver, College of Arts and Sciences, 1956–58, pp. 55–56.

education is not now required. The major is provided cooperatively by the Department of Sociology and the School of Social Work. For further information concerning the School of Social Work, consult the *Bulletin of the School of Social Work.*

CREDIT HOUR REQUIREMENT FOR MAJOR AND MINOR

The Major in pre-professional social work requires a minimum of 35 quarter hours in sociology and 5 quarter hours in economics (54–359). A minor in psychology is also required. The following courses are strongly recommended: Economics 54–102, and Political Science 35–201 or 35–101. See also general requirements for the B. A. degree, Page 27.

COURSE PREREQUISITES

The student must take Social Science 39–20.1, .2, .3 as a prerequisite to all work undertaken to fulfill major requirements. This course will also fulfill the social science sequence requirement but will not count toward the required hours for the major.

REQUIRED COURSES FOR MAJOR AND MINOR		*Quarter*
Required courses for major:		*Hours*
41–382 Development of Social Thought	5	
41–385 Introduction to Social Welfare	5	
54–359 Social Security	5	
Sociology courses toward major	25	
Total Hours Required for Major		40
Psychology Minor		20
Total Hours Required for Major and Minor		60

The second statement is from Upsala College catalog: [4]

A major in sociology consists of Sociology 110 or 201, 202 and twenty-four additional credits . . . Students who are interested in social work positions (Civil Service or with private agencies) are urged to take Sociology 307, 308 and Political Science 102.

Miami University gives a brief statement in the same general vein: [5]

[4] Upsala College Catalog, 1956–57, p. 113.
[5] Miami University, College of Arts and Science Announcement, 1957–58, p. 30.

SOCIAL WORK

Schools of social work advise that the student who plans to take professional training in this field concentrate in sociology, with additional work in psychology and other social sciences, and that he have as broad an education as possible. The program which follows meets the requirements of the Council on Social Work Education, Inc., of which Miami is a member:

First Year: Sociology 11–12, Physiology 21–22, Government 11–12, English 11–12, humanities, modern language; *Second Year:* Economics 11–12, Psychology 11–12 or 201–2, Sociology 347 or 257, a modern language, a physical science, Speech 131, 132; *Third Year:* Psychology 211, 212, 331, Sociology 301, 312, 345, 341, 342; *Fourth Year:* Psychology 362, 382, 432, 451, 452, Sociology 344, 348, 352, 351, 402, 411, 432. Sociology courses listed in the third and fourth year may be taken in reverse order. In general, Spanish is the most useful language for social workers.

Many other colleges and universities have similar statements.[6]

INSTITUTIONAL ORGANIZATION FOR DEVELOPING MAJOR SEQUENCES IN PREPARATION FOR SOCIAL WORK

Four general patterns of departmental or professional school responsibility have developed for those who are preparing for social

[6] The following give further illustrations:
Bowling Green State University, 1956–57, p. 95.
Central State College, 1956–57, p. 243.
Fresno State College, 1956–57, p. 226.
University of Maine, 1956–57, pp. 113–114.
New York University, 1956–57, p. 40.
Nebraska Wesleyan, 1956–57, p. 36.
University of New Hampshire, 1956–57, p. 81.
Utah State Agricultural College, 1956–57, p. 125.
San Francisco State College, 1956–57, p. 247.
San Diego State College, 1956–57, p. 201.
Ohio University, 1956–57, p. 103.
Ohio State University, 1956–57, p. 51.
Roosevelt University, 1956–57, p. 128.
Sacramento State College, 1956–57, p. 95.
College of St. Mary of the Springs, 1956–57, pp. 30–31.
St. Olaf, 1956–57, p. 49.
West Virginia Wesleyan, 1956–57, p. 94.
University of Indiana, 1956–57, p. 7.

work. These include those controlled by (1) the sociology department,[7] (2) a graduate school of social work, (3) a division of social science, general studies or liberal arts, and (4) an undergraduate department of social welfare. Within this general framework a variety of types of majors are offered. By far the largest number of sequences are set up within sociology departments. Out of 48 catalogs studied, 31 indicated that the sociology department had responsibility for setting up the major for students planning to go into social work.

The patterns of major offerings vary widely. Even where sequences are set up within the sociology department, there are a variety of ways in which majors are planned. For example, many schools have students take a regular sociology major and include 6–9 semester hours of courses with social work content. Sometimes introductory courses in the other social sciences are required, sometimes advised, occasionally not mentioned.

Or a sociology department may work out a range of basic introductory courses in the social sciences with a concentration in sociology and anywhere from 6–18 hours of course work which has social work content. Or there may be a major in any one of the social sciences and a required number of hours in social work courses, or a group of these courses with social work content planned as a minor. A few sociology departments have an interdepartmental concentration with selected courses in social work. Hunter College calls this a pre-social work major.

The second general pattern of control is that in which a division of social sciences or department of liberal arts or general studies controls the major for those planning on social work. Here again the majors vary in concentration from the interdepartmental major with either a broad social science or sociological concentration to a more highly specialized sequence in social work with a social welfare major. Northeast Louisiana State College and Sacramento State College would be illustrative of the first type; Fresno State College of the second. In Western Michigan State College in which an interdepartmental social science major is

---

[7] Some are sociology and anthropology. A few are sociology and social work, or sociology, anthropology and social work.

offered with a B. A. degree, there is, in addition, a minor in social work, with a certificate in social work.

The third pattern of control is that of a department or division of social welfare set up in the undergraduate college with a major, and in at least one instance a degree in social work.[8] Central State College has a department and major in social welfare. In its suggested curriculum the junior and senior years have a heavy concentration of social welfare with 34 of the 64 hours in this area.[9]

The fourth pattern of control is that in which the planning responsibility for courses with social work content is in the graduate school of social work of the university. Once again there is an enormous range in the type of work that is planned by different schools. It goes all of the way from schools that advise a major in one of the social sciences in the undergraduate college with 6–9 hours of courses with social work content offered by the graduate school of social work,[10] to a graduate school of social work which offers a highly specialized undergraduate social work major with five areas of concentration in social administration for those preparing to enter employment upon graduation from college and a degree of Bachelor of Science in Social Administration.[11] The five areas are Corrections, Public Assistance, Public Recreation, Social Investigation and Social Statistics, and Youth Leadership.

ANALYSIS OF COURSE OFFERINGS WITH SOCIAL WORK CONTENT

Before discussing the rationale for these various patterns of control and concentration, it might be well to look at the range of course offerings with social work content. We will then have the picture of preparation as it is presently structured in our undergraduate programs in colleges and universities.

A study of college catalogs reveals an amazing range of courses with social work content. It is small wonder that some students

[8] Utah State Agricultural College *Catalog,* 1956–57, p. 125.
[9] Central State College *Bulletin,* Announcements for 1956–57, p. 243.
[10] As at the University of Illinois and the University of North Carolina.
[11] The Ohio State University *Catalog,* School of Social Administration, 1956–57, pp. 51–52.

entering graduate schools of social work have complained of repetition of work taken in their junior and senior years in college—they covered the social work waterfront as undergraduates.

There is a pattern, however, that is obvious. Most colleges offer 6–12 hours of work that has social work content. These usually include a general historical course, one in methods, and one in child welfare and/or community organization. In addition, field work, or field experience in a social agency is given in many institutions.

Almost all schools have 3–6 hours that is an introduction to social welfare. Ttitles differ, but the content is historical and descriptive, and it traces social work, public and voluntary, from its English and Early American backgrounds through to the present. Out of 48 catalogs studied, 42 had a course that was either one or two semesters which followed this general description. In addition, 14 of these institutions had a one semester or quarter course in public welfare (one had two semesters), 6 had a course in social security, while 2 institutions offered a course titled social welfare. From catalog descriptions, the aim of these courses is to introduce students to the major historical developments and the philosophy and principles underlying social work. These courses are sometimes spoken of as general education courses and mention is made of the fact that students from other pre-professional groups such as teachers, ministers, nurses and lawyers are encouraged to take them.

Three other courses with social work content are given in many institutions. These are Community Organization, Child Welfare and Social Casework. Over half of the 48 institutions studied had each of these courses.

The course in Community Organization is more than a sociological analysis of the nature of the community. The titles of the courses describe the content: "Community Agencies," "Community Organization," "Community Welfare Organization," "Community Organization and Planning," "Community Resources," "Community Planning for Social Welfare." Catalog descriptions spell out the organizational planning subject matter of these courses.

For example:

> An analytical study of the social needs of the community and evaluation of existing welfare agencies, public and private. Classroom discussion to be supplemented by background reading and direct observation of social agencies.[12]
>
> Community health, recreation, informal education, and welfare resources, organization and coordination of community services to meet social needs.[13]
>
> Public and private resources for meeting welfare needs in United States communities.[14]

These courses center around the community resources needed and are available for the social services.

The course in Child Welfare is descriptive and has one of two foci. Some courses are broad in foundation and use as their base the child in American society with some reference to special services:

> Cultural factors affecting social adjustment of children with emphasis on normal youth. Specialized services to children in and outside their own homes. Current provisions for foster home care, guardianship, adoptions, and institutional care of dependent children.[15]
>
> A study of children, their physical, psychological and social behavior and the services available for their care in and out of their homes.[16]

The other focus for the course is more generally followed. This is one in which there is a historical and contemporary survey of the services for special groups of children. For example:

> Special needs of dependent, neglected, and delinquent children with emphasis upon the types of agencies which have been established to deal with child welfare problems.[17]
>
> Historical and contemporary survey of social services relating to dependent and neglected children.[18]

12 Carnegie Institute of Technology *Bulletin*, 1956–57, p. 77.
13 Fresno State College General *Catalog*, 1956–57, p. 241.
14 Miami University, College of Arts and Sciences *Catalog*, 1957–58, p. 67.
15 University of Florida *Catalog*, 1956–57, p. 587.
16 Furman University *Catalog*, 1956–57, p. 113.
17 Alabama Women's College—taken from mimeographed material.
18 Bowling Green State University *Catalog*, 1956–57, p. 230.

A study of the historical development, philosophy and methods of child care; the social movements, legislation and social agencies which have been developed to promote the welfare of children.[19]

The courses in casework are in methodology. From the point of view of content they may be divided into two groups—first, there are those with the title "casework" which focus exclusively upon one method. Second, there are those titled methods in social work which are concerned generally with casework, group work and community organization methodology. Obviously, since almost all of these courses are one semester courses, the latter type which introduces all three methods to the students is less detailed than the former.

The course descriptions for the courses in casework lead one to surmise that by and large the intent of these courses is pre-professional with main consideration that of "familiarizing the student with an approach to the individual and his social situation." "An analysis of basic principles," "a survey of techniques and skills," "a general introduction to the processes," are phrases which appear repeatedly in course descriptions. However, there seem to be clear limitations in that students use the case records of others for analysis rather than their own field experiences, and, where there is experience in the field as a part of the course, it is usually described as "observation." One university titles its course "Social Services to Individuals" and indicates that, while the methods of giving services to individuals is the content of the course, the emphasis is upon the common aspects of all service professions.

The following course descriptions seem representative of the casework courses:

The development of social casework; analysis of basic principles; problems and methods as seen in theoretical and case material.[20]

A general introductory course in the basic processes of generic social casework. Case material from specific casework fields will be used.[21]

An introductory study of the field of social casework, providing

19 *Bulletin* of Mount Saint Mary's College, 1956–57, p. 86.
20 Ohio University *Bulletin*, 1956–58, p. 279.
21 The College of Saint Rose *Catalog*, 1956–58, p. 65.

orientation in the philosophy and methods of the profession. Field work experience with a local welfare agency.[22]

Of the more general Methods in Social Work courses, two descriptions are illustrative:

Methods and administrative techniques relating to social casework, social group work, social administration, and social research. Supervised field work in recognized public and private welfare agencies to tie together academic training and practical field activities.[23]

Introduction to the skills and techniques used in social casework, social group work, and community organization.[24]

The courses that have been listed are those most frequently found in the pre-professional sequences. Where only a few courses are offered in which there is social work content, those with some variation in titles and content are generally those given.

OTHER COURSES FREQUENTLY OFFERED

Two other courses are found so frequently that they should properly be included when considering the general course offerings given in undergraduate sequences. The first is a methodological course in group work, the second is some form of field work or field observation. Let us look first at group work.

An array of titles are used in describing the courses with group work methodology: "Group Process and Leadership," "Principles of Group Work," "Group Leadership," "Introduction to Group Work," "Social Group Work," "Principles and Practices of Social Group Work."

In some colleges and universities where a sequence is offered so that students may concentrate in group work, there is a proliferation of offerings with a whole series of courses including such specialized areas as "Group Work in Camping," "Development, Organization and Administration of Group Work," "Counselling in Group Work Settings," and "Group Leadership Laboratory."

As was true of the course in casework, course descriptions emphasize an introduction to the principles and processes:

[22] Furman University *Bulletin*, 1956–57, p. 114.
[23] The University Record of the University of Florida, 1956–57, p. 587.
[24] Sacramento State College General *Catalog*, 1956–57, p. 212.

The philosophy and methods of leadership of democratic groups with emphasis on the dynamic forces within the group. Application is made to clubs, schools, camps, social agencies, and adult organizations.[25]

The appraisal of social group work as a method in social work, recreation, and informal education; principles of leadership and followership; program planning; observation and analysis of group work agencies.[26]

The other course with social work content which is offered in many colleges and universities is field work. This is a course which provides students with the opportunity to observe and participate in social work programs under the supervision of professional social workers. The catalog titles are descriptive of the intention and direction of the course: "Field Observation and Experience," "Social Service Field Work," "Field Practice," "Field Experience in Social Work," "Directed Volunteer Work I and II," and "Agency Experience."

This course is set up as a laboratory course, usually offered in the senior year, with varying amounts of credit. Credit is proportionate to the number of hours in the field on the same or similar basis for which laboratory hours in other departments are equated in relation to credit.

The general practice seems to be to offer 1–2 hours of credit per semester, though a few schools offer as much as 6–8 credits per semester, or the equivalent of about one-half a semester's work in agency experience.

Once again, course descriptions show the purposes of the courses:

Supervised field training in public and private social agencies. The student selects his particular area of interest and is responsible to an agency for a definite program of in-service training. Group meetings, individual conferences, and written progress reports are required parts of the course.[27]

An introduction to field work in social agencies. Students observe and participate in social work programs under the supervision of pro-

25 University of Maine *Bulletin,* 1956–57, p. 124.
26 Marygrove College *Catalog,* 1956, p. 50.
27 See University of Maryland application for membership in CSWE.

fessional social workers. This course is designed primarily to provide seniors planning to enroll in graduate schools of social work with opportunity to develop a more mature appreciation of and identification with professional social work.[28]

A pre-professional social work course involving field experience in agencies in Glens Falls, Albany and Schenectady with study of elementary principles of group and casework; open to limited number of qualified students.[29]

A few colleges set up the agency experience with college credit for summer work that has been approved. For example:

Designed to give to the student an understanding of social work through observation and participation. Lectures, reading and conferences will be offered during college year in cooperative neighboring social agencies or during summer by eight weeks work with other accredited social work institutions. The department will arrange for a limited number of student summer placements with well-supervised settlements, correctional institutions, and casework agencies in urban centers. It is strongly recommended that students who can qualify should acquire this experience in summer following junior year.[30]

RATIONALE FOR PATTERNS OF PRE-PROFESSIONAL EDUCATION FOR SOCIAL WORK

From the study of the college catalogs and other printed material submitted by member colleges and universities of Council on Social Work Education, some deductions can be drawn concerning the assumptions underlying undergraduate education for social work as presently practiced. Certain patterns seem to recur regularly. These patterns are of dual importance viewed from the points of recruitment to social work positions which do not require graduate professional education and as preparation to graduate schools.

On the basis of the study, several assumptions seem to underlie

[28] See Pasadena College application for membership in CSWE.
[29] See Skidmore College application for membership in CSWE.
[30] See University of New Hampshire application for membership in CSWE.

the planned programs for social work education offered at the undergraduate level. The first seems to be that there should be a planned curriculum for students interested in social work. This is planned within a four-year course and leads to a bachelor's degree. Required and suggested courses to be taken prior to graduation are frequently listed and formally stated in a detailed outline in the catalog.

The second assumption is that there should be departmental location for course offerings and departmental sponsorship in such matters as academic and vocational counselling and for such co-curricular interests as social service clubs. Traditionally, the sociology department has the responsibility for these activities. Courses with social work content are most frequently included either among sociology offerings or are sub-titled social work, but still offered in the sociology department.

Two general exceptions to this occur. A few universities have separate undergraduate departments of social work, and universities which have a graduate professional school of social work offer a variety of kinds of undergraduate offerings ranging all the way from a few courses with social work content to a highly elaborated major in social work.

In the colleges, then, there seems to have been an accepted assumption that the sociology department is the most suitable sponsor for planning and administering whatever it is that is desirable in a social work curriculum. The inevitable correlate is that numerous courses in sociology are usually required and form the best possible background for social work students. Other social sciences are almost always required, but the substantial undergirding is an outlay of sociology. If sociology serves as the developing ground for social work practitioners, it is also the recipient of a substantial number of students in sociology courses which are prerequisites for courses which have social work content. As one professor said, "If we let students into social work courses with no required sociology, they might not take the sociology." No department head is unaware of the merits of such requirements from the point of view of departmental enrollments. If, on the other hand, such prerequisites are all soundly based from a theoretical point of view, the administrative question, here raised, is irrelevant.

A third assumption is that the undergraduate curriculum is pre-professional. The term "pre-professional" is frequently used, and in the description of program a careful differentiation is often made between pre-professional and professional.

Two such statements are illustrative:

> Students who wish to prepare for social work as a profession should plan to do graduate study in a recognized school of social work. For students seeking admission to graduate schools of social work the following courses are especially recommended: . . . The leading social agencies, both governmental and private, ask increasingly for workers who are prepared for such professional school training. However, some junior professional positions, such as case aides in large agencies, are available in Chicago and throughout the country for which persons with a bachelor's degree are being sought. A major in one of the social sciences, supplemented by the courses recommended and suggested above, constitutes helpful preparation for such positions. It should be understood, however, that such preparation is pre-professional only, and even with experience in the field is not a substitute for graduate professional education.[31]
>
> Undergraduate education in social work is not regarded as a substitute for graduate training, but as the best preparation for employment in those positions for which graduate training is not required, as well as the best preparation for later undertaking graduate study in social work.[32]

There are colleges and universities, however, that do not use the term "pre-professional" either in their sequence titles or curriculum descriptions.

Such terms as "Social Service Curriculum," "Social Service Work," and "Social Work" used as the title for a curriculum lead one to believe that some schools do not define their undergraduate offerings as pre-professional, though most of them are careful to indicate that undergraduate preparation is useful for only given types of social work positions and must be followed by graduate education to gain full professional status. Sometimes they even assume there is a conflict of interests.

[31] Roosevelt University Biennial *Catalog,* 1956–57, 1957–58, p. 128.
[32] Utah State Agricultural College *Bulletin,* 1956–57, p. 125.

The following excerpts are statements made by two schools which point this up:

> The curriculum for junior and senior years will depend on whether the student wishes to prepare for graduate training or for positions not requiring graduate training. Social work courses have been offered for many years at _____ University primarily to prepare the student for the civil service examination. Recently we have been approved as an undergraduate department by the Council on Social Work Education. Our objective at the present time is to prepare students to meet the undergraduate requirements for entrance into graduate schools of social work.

A further assumption seems to be the acceptance of the appropriateness of courses with social work content in an undergraduate sequence. There is no apparent agreement on an upper limit in the number of courses or hours offered but a pattern is found with three areas generally accepted as legitimate. These are (a) a historical, descriptive introduction to social work, (b) an introduction to the methods used in social work practice, and (c) some experience in a social agency either through observation or supervised activity. From these minimums there is a proliferation in some universities which suggests almost certain duplication with work offered at a graduate level.

The assumption that upon graduation with a bachelor's degree a student can enter a variety of types of social work positions is often stated. Obviously the undergraduate curriculum has developed in response to a need for trained persons, particularly in the public services. The undergraduate schools feel the pressure to provide personnel, and on the other hand are committed to their responsibility to prepare for graduate education. The following with variation in wording may be found in many catalogs:

> Students, upon its completion, are encouraged to continue their technical preparation in graduate professional schools of social work. However, our graduates are currently holding responsible positions in the public social services, group work activities, and in other social agencies at the junior professional level for which they are qualified.[33]

[33] University of Kentucky *General Catalog*, 1956–57, Vol. 49, No. 5, p. 83.

In other words, the undergraduate schools have built their programs presumably upon a plan which has the support of the graduate professional schools. The student would, I believe, have a right to assume that the curriculum which he is taking is one which the graduate school will expect or require for admission, and will build upon as the basic curriculum from which his graduate education will be developed.

Lastly, it is worth noting that membership in the Council on Social Work Education is listed frequently, and often accompanied by a statement which indicates the importance of the principle of legitimacy through recognition by the educational membership agency from the college's or university's point of view. Acceptance of colleges and universities with programs which offer such an enormous range in social work content raises many questions with both reference to minimums and maximums for course work with social work content at the undergraduate level.

CONCLUSIONS

In conclusion, it may be justifiable to make certain observations as well as raise questions upon the basis of our analysis. The first observation relates to the departmental location of the courses with social work content. The widespread placement in sociology in the past was doubtless due to the fact that many sociologists were concerned with the applied field, and social work and sociology were not unrelated. Recent developments in sociology make this departmental affiliation of much more dubious value. There is no section in the American Sociologicial Society which would include this group although some of the regional sociological groups continue to include such interests in a minor way.

The plan whereby social work is set up somewhat separately, either with a sociology department or as a department on its own, justifies careful consideration. There is the question as to whether faculty with social work education would head such departments or division of a department. This is presently often not true. On the other hand, every college administrator can tell us that the provision for a department in any area is the assured way to get a steady and constant pressure to add to the courses which are offered. In addition, a department brings with it the urge of its faculty to offer a major. This may be a danger if social work breaks off from its parent, the social sciences. If a social work educated faculty are to plan and direct these sequences, they must also be educated in the social sciences if this is their divisional affiliation. Are such faculty available? Do graduate schools encourage this combination of training? One of the hypotheses upon which under-graduate work is based is the fact that it is the basis for graduate study. This raises many questions. Most important, is this true? Is the often repeated statement made in college catalogs that the pre-professional curriculum is basis for admission to graduate school borne out in practice? Do graduate schools require a social science background, a series of courses with social work content? Gradu-ate schools vary as much in their own undergraduate social work offerings as do universities and colleges where the social work courses are in a sociology department. This leads to the conclusion that professional schools lack common practices along with all others.

One interesting conclusion is the importance attached by schools to their membership in the CSWE. Repeatedly, in letters accom-panying the other material used for study in this report, the head of the department concerned has indicated an interest in sugges-tions, or has suggested he would like help in this area. Occasionally one feels some insecurity, uncertainty, and defensiveness. As one head said, "Our set up is the same as that outlined by the Council on Social Work Education for undergraduates." The Curriculum Study is well timed to help colleges and universities get the help for which they are asking.

Data on the Structure and Content of Undergraduate Social Work Offerings in Selected Colleges and Universities [34]

College or University	Departmental Placement	Major for students taking undergraduate social work sequence [35]	Undergraduate courses with social work content which are suggested or required [36]
1. Alabama College for Women	Division of Social Science	B.A. in Sociology (Pre-professional social work sequence)	Field of Social Service—3 Group Work—2 Introduction to Public Welfare—3 Elements of Social Casework—2 The Community—2 Social Problems of Child Welfare—3 Introduction to Field Work—2
2. Bowling Green State University	Department of Sociology	Sociology	Introduction to Social Work—2 Public Welfare—3 Child Welfare—3 Field Observation and Orientation—2
3. University of Buffalo	The Graduate School of Social Work		Introduction to Social Welfare—2 Field Observation I—2 Social Services for Children—2 Public Social Services—2 Group Work in Camping—2 Field Observation—2

[34] All colleges and universities which are members of CSWE were requested to send catalogs and materials for this study. The 50 represented in this table returned the material in time to have their offerings listed in the study.
[35] In a few instances it was not clear as to the department or departments in which a major might be taken. In these instances the space was left blank.

[36] Course titles, course descriptions, and the grouping of courses (often in sequences titled Social Work) served as the bases for decision as to whether specific courses had social work content. In some instances, it was difficult to decide whether the course had primarily social science or social work content. The numerals indicate either semester or quarter hours.

College	Department	Major	Courses
4. Brooklyn College	Department of Sociology and Anthropology (with counselling set-up as college service and agency voluntary placement as a part of counselling)	Sociology and Anthropology	Introduction to Social Welfare—3 Social Welfare and the Individual—4 (2 lecture and 4 field experience) Group Process and Leadership
5. Carnegie Institute of Technology	Department of General Studies	Social Studies	Community Agencies—9 units
6. Central State College	Social Welfare	Social Welfare	Field of Social Work—2 Juvenile Delinquency—3 Elementary Principles Group Work and Group Leadership—2 Public Welfare—2 Probation and Parole—3 Social Work and Health Problems—2 Interviewing and Recording—3 Special Problems—3.3 Psychological Aspects of Social Work—2 Methodology of Social Research—3 Field Practice—15:15
7. Columbia College	Sociology	Sociology	Introduction to Social Work Methods of Social Investigation
8. University of Denver	Department of Sociology and the School of Social Work	Sociology	Introduction to Social Welfare—5 Social Security—5
9. University of Florida	Department of Sociology and Anthropology	1. Sociology *or* 2. Group work in Sociology, Psychology and a related third field	The field of Social Work—3 Methods of Social Work—3 The Child in American Society—3 Community Organization—3

Data on the Structure and Content of Undergraduate
Social Work Offerings in Selected Colleges and Universities [34] (*Continued*)

College or University	Departmental Placement	Major for students taking undergraduate social work sequence [35]	Undergraduate courses with social work content which are suggested or required [36]
10. Fresno State College	Division of Social Science	Social Welfare (required Psychology minor)	Introduction to Social Work—2.2 Field Observation in Social Work—1–2 Fundamentals of Interviewing—3 Social Welfare—2; Advanced Field Observation in Social Welfare—1–2 Social Security Administration—2 Community Welfare Organization—3 Principles of Group Work—2
11. Furman University	Sociology	Sociology	Sociology of Childhood—3 The Citizen and His Community—3 Introduction to Public Welfare—3 Introduction to Casework—3
12. George Williams College	Social Studies		Field of Social Work (others?)
13. University of Maine	Business, Economics & Sociology	Sociology	Social Welfare—3 Child Welfare—3 Group Leadership—3 Public Welfare—3 Principles of Casework—3 Field Practice in Casework, I, II—2, 2

Institution	Major	Courses
14. Marquette University	Sociology	Introduction to Social Work—3 Social Casework—3 Child Welfare—3 Community Organization—3 Community Recreation—3
15. Marygrove College	Sociology (special sequence of social work)	The Field of Social Work—2 or 3 Introduction to Casework—2 or 3 Principles of Group Action—2 Introduction to Group Work—2 Field Experience—open
16. Miami University (Oxford, Ohio)	Sociology	Social Work—3 Social Work Processes—3 Community Welfare Organization—3
17. Mount Saint Mary's College	Sociology	Community Organization—2 Group Leadership—2 Field of Social Work—3, 3 Child Welfare—3 Methods in Social Work—3
18. University of New Mexico	Sociology	One of Social Sciences (including 12 hours of social work)	Introduction to Social Service—3,3 Field Observation and Participation—3 Community Analysis—2 Social Security—3 Interviewing for Social Work—3
19. New York University (Washington Square College of Arts and Sciences)	Sociology	Sociology (with certain courses in Social Work required)	The Sociology of Childhood—3 Community Organization and Planning—3 Development of Social Welfare—3 Present Organization of Social Welfare—4 Evolution of Social Work—2

Data on the Structure and Content of Undergraduate
Social Work Offerings in Selected Colleges and Universities [34] (Continued)

College or University	Departmental Placement	Major for students taking undergraduate social work sequence [35]	Undergraduate courses with social work content which are suggested or required [36]
20. Northern Michigan College	Sociology	Sociology, Economics, Government, History, (taking required Social Service Curriculum)	Introduction to Field of Social Work—3 Field Labs in Social Work I—1 or 2 Field Labs in Social Work II—1 or 2 Principles of Social Casework—3 Community Organization and Planning—3 The Visiting Teacher—2
21. Our Lady of Cincinnati College	Sociology and Economics	Sociology	Problems of Child Welfare—2 Introduction to Social Work—2—2 Introduction to Social Casework—2—2
22. Roosevelt College	Sociology	One of Social Sciences (a required group of courses for Social Work)	The Field of Social Work Community Organization and Planning
23. Sacramento State College	Division of Social Sciences	Social Work (as occupational curriculum)	Problems of Child Welfare—2 Introduction to Social Work—2 Methods in Social Work—2 Probation and Parole—2 Techniques of Interviewing—2 Social Work in Corrections—2 Organization and Administration of Correctional Systems—2 Principles of Public Welfare—2 Field Work—3—4

Institution	Department	Curriculum	Courses
24. San Diego State College	Sociology	Social Service (special occupational curriculum)	Field of Social Work Community Welfare Organization
25. College of St. Mary of the Springs	Sociology	Sociology	Introduction to Social Work—3 Field Work—1–3
26. St. Olaf College	Sociology	Sociology	Fields of Social Work—3 Public Welfare—3
27. Syracuse University	Sociology and Anthropology	Sociology (with sequence of social work courses)	Leisure and Social Group Work—3 The Field of Social Work—3 Public Welfare—3 Introduction to Social Casework—3
28. University of Tennessee	Sociology and School of Social Work	Sociology	Methods in Social Work—4, 4, 4 (*quarters*) Survey of Field of Social Work—3 Social Services for Children—3
29. Valparaiso	The Department of Sociology and Social Work	Social Work	Child Welfare Fields of Social Work Survey of Public Welfare Social Services to Individuals Introduction to Group Work
30. Upsala College	Sociology	Sociology	Social Security and Social Legislation—3 Field of Social Work—3
31. Western Michigan College	Sociology	Interdepartmental Social Sciences (and minor in Social Work) 19-20 hours; B.A. and certificate in social work	Fields of Social Work—2 Family and Child Adjustment—3 Introduction to Public Welfare—3 Community Welfare Organization—2 Principles of Social Casework—2 Principles of Social Group Work—2 Orientation to Field Work—3

Data on the Structure and Content of Undergraduate Social Work Offerings in Selected Colleges and Universities [34] (Continued)

College or University	Departmental Placement	Major for students taking undergraduate social work sequence [35]	Undergraduate courses with social work content which are suggested or required [36]
32. West Virginia Wesleyan	Sociology	Sociology	Community Organization—2 Field of Social Work—3 Child Welfare—3
33. College of Saint Rose	Sociology	Sociology	History of Social Work—1, 1 Social Welfare—3 The Child, 1, 1 The Community—3 Introduction to Social Casework—2 Field Work—(?)
34. Indiana University	Division of Social Service Cooperation with several departments offering undergraduate work	Social Service Major	History of American Social Welfare—3 Modern Social Welfare Organization—3 Social Welfare in Rural Community—2 Introduction to Group Work—2 Social Services to Individuals—2 or 4 Social Security (Economics)—3 Nutrition (Home Economics)—2 Public Health Organization (Education)—2
35. Mundelein College	Sociology	Sociology	Community Resources—3 Introduction to Social Work—3 Child Welfare—2 or 3

			Quarter
36. Ohio State University	School of Social Administration	Social Administration with some concentration in one of following: (a) Corrections (b) Public Assistance (c) Public Recreation (d) Social Investigation and Social Statistics (e) Youth Leadership (B.S. in Social Admin.)	Introduction to Rehabilitation — 3 Social Investigation and Social Statistics — 5 Health and Welfare Needs and Resources — 3, 3 Social Work—Its Structure and Function — 3 Prin. Probation and Parole — 4 Juvenile Delinquency and Its Treatment — 5 Veteran and His Family — 3 Social Implications in Rehabilitation — 3 Practice Leading Group Recreation — 3 Guidance and Group Aspects of Camping — 3 Principles of Group Leadership — 3 Supervisory Problems in Youth Leadership and Recreation — 3 Development, Organization and Administration of Group Work — 3 Individual and Social Agency — 3 Community Health Organization — 1–15 Legal Aspects of Social Work — 3 Case Studies in Public Assistance — 3
37. Ohio University	Sociology	Sociology	Social Security System—2 Social Work in American Community—3 Child Welfare—3 Social Group Work—2 Community Planning for Social Welfare—2 Introduction to Social Casework—3 Field Services—2
38. Russell Sage College	Sociology	Sociology	Field of Social Work—3 Principles of Social Work—3, 3

Data on the Structure and Content of Undergraduate Social Work Offerings in Selected Colleges and Universities [34] (Continued)

College or University	Departmental Placement	Major for students taking undergraduate social work sequence [35]	Undergraduate courses with social work content which are suggested or required [36]
39. San Francisco State College	Division of Social Science (Sociology)	Sociology	Introduction to Social Work—3 Community Organization—3 Methods in Social Work—3 Counselling in Group Work Settings—3 Principles and Practices of Group Work—3 Public Welfare—3 Child Welfare—3 Group Leadership Laboratory—3, 3
40. Skidmore College	Sociology	Sociology	Field of Social Work—8 Field Work—6–8
41. Utah State Agricultural College	Division of Social Work in School of Business and Social Sciences	B.S. Degree in Social Work	Mental Hygiene—3 Culture and Personality—3 Field of Social Work—3 Social Treatment of Children's Problems—3 Introduction to Casework—3 Adolescence—3 Children in Institutions—3 Social Work Seminars I, II—1, 1 Independent Readings in Social Work—Credit Arranged Social Casework I, II, III—3, 3, 3 Field Work I, II, III—2–4, 2–4, 2–8 Social Work in Rural Communities—2 Social Psychiatry I, II—2, 2 Community Organization—3 Public Welfare Seminars I, II—3, 3

Institution	Department	Department	Courses
42. Youngstown University	Sociology	Sociology	Historical Introduction to Social Welfare—3, 3; Introduction to Social Casework Methods—2h. c.; Introduction to Social Group Work Methods—2h. c.; Introduction to Community Organization Methods—2h. c.
43. University of New Hampshire	Sociology	A Social Service curriculum with major in sociology	Introduction to Social Work—3, 3; Social Service Field Work—6
44. University of Oregon	Sociology	Sociology	The Sociology of Social Work—3, 3, 3; Community Welfare Organization—3
45. Wells College	Sociology	Sociology	Principles of Social Work—3; Public Welfare—3
46. Nebraska Wesleyan	Political Science and Sociology	Political Science and Sociology	Introduction to Social Welfare—3; Projects in Social Welfare—2-3
47. New Jersey College for Women, Rutgers University	Economics and Sociology	Sociology	Introduction to Social Work—3, 3
48. University of Detroit	Sociology	Sociology	Philosophy of Social Work—2 or 3; Introduction to Social Work—2 or 3; Introduction to Social Work—2; Treatment of Juvenile Delinquency—3; Applied Criminology—3; Introduction to Casework—2 or 3; Interviewing—2 or 3; Introduction to Group Social Work—2 or 3; Volunteer Services in Community Agencies—2 or 3; Senior Tutorial Course—2

Data on the Structure and Content of Undergraduate Social Work Offerings in Selected Colleges and Universities [34] (Continued)

College or University	Departmental Placement	Major for students taking undergraduate social work sequence [35]	Undergraduate courses with social work content which are suggested or required [36]
49. Florida State University	School of Social Welfare	Social Welfare	Careers in Social Work—1, 1 Rural Social Welfare—3, 3 Field of Social Work—3 Social Work in the Schools—3 Criminology and Penology—3 Problems of Child Welfare—3 Community Organization—3 Community Leadership—3 Understanding Human Behavior—3, 3 Social Legislation—3 Introduction to Social Group Work—3 Treatment of Juvenile Delinquency—3 Social Services for Those in Mentally Ill Health—3 Dynamics of Criminal and Delinquent Behavior—3 Police Problems and Practices—3 Methods of Crime Detection—3 Governmental Welfare Services—3 Organization of Community Welfare and Health Services—3 Legal Aspects of Social Relations—3 Essentials of Interviewing—3

			Social Work for Allied Professions—3 Probation, Pardons and Parole—3 Correctional Custody—3 Field Observation—1, 1 Juvenile Delinquency Control—3 Internship in Social Work—7 Seminar in Social Work—2 The Mental Hygiene Clinic—2
50. Michigan State University	School of Social Work	B.A. Degree in Social Work	Survey of Social Work—3 Workshop in Social Work—2-5 Summer Work Projects—1-3 Child Welfare—3 Introduction to Professional Social Work—4, 4, 4 Interviewing in Social Welfare—3 Social Work in Corrections—3 History, Organization & Administration of Youth Serving Agencies—4 Public Welfare: Historic Background and Current Organization—4 Public Welfare: Social Security and Other Programs—4 Field and Agency Experience: Social Work Laboratory—1-4

FIELD EXPERIENCE QUESTIONNAIRE

For the purposes of this questionnaire field experience is used to refer to regular, assigned student observation and/or participation in the activities of a social agency or institution as a planned part of the undergraduate social work-oriented educational program of a college or university.

Please answer the following questions about field experience at your school and return this questionnaire to the Curriculum Study by May 13, 1957. Use an additional sheet if necessary. If your offerings include a planned program of field trips which you consider to be distinct from "observation" (as used above), please describe this program as fully as possible under item 3 of this questionnaire.

1. Was field experience available to students with an expressed interest in social work last year? Yes _____ No _____
2. If answer is yes, please answer the following questions:
   a. Was the field experience last year made available to all or just some of the students with an expressed interest in social work? Some _____ All _____
      How many of the students with an expressed interest in social work had field experience last year? _____
      Estimate percentage of students with an expressed interest in social work who had field experience prior to graduation. _____

   b. If field experience was available last year to only some of the students with an expressed interest in social work, what were the criteria employed in the selection of students?

      Who makes the selection of students?

   c. Was the same field experience made available last year to students with an expressed interest in a field or profession other than social Work? Yes _____ No _____

If so, what were the criteria employed in the selection of these students?

d. Course credit for the field experience last year:
No credit _____ Credit _____ (check). If credit is given, how much? _____
In quarter _____ or semester _____ hours (check)
If your school uses some method other than credit hours "to compensate" the student, please describe:

e. Time spent in the field (if not uniform, give range and approximate average)
Hours, sophomore year _____
Hours, junior year _____
Hours, senior year _____
Total number of hours _____
If field experience is provided during the summer, please explain the organization of the program.

f. Characteristics of field experience offered last year:
Describe type of agency(ies) used (*e.g.,* local public welfare agency, city recreation department, state mental hospital, sectarian community center, etc.).

Type(s) of experience offered: (check)
Observation _____, participation _____, observation and participation _____, Other _____
If "other" is checked, please describe:

If observation is one type of field experience offered, please describe the nature of the observation (*e.g.,* observing administrative and office routines, observing club meetings, observing staff meetings, observing actual worker-client interviews, etc.):

If participation in the activities of a social agency or institution is one type of field experience offered, please describe the nature of the participation (*e.g.,* do general office work, answer telephone, serve as receptionist, do research for agency, serve as club leader, check on eligibility of clients involving direct relationship with such clients, verification of eligibility data without direct contact with client, solicit for United Appeal drive, carry entire case in limited selective OAA caseload, etc.)

g. Please describe the nature and utilization of the recording required of the students, if any, of their field observation and/or participation.

h. Who was responsible last year for supervising the students' field experiences: (check)
Instructor of course with social work content (if this is checked, indicate nature of course) _____

Faculty field experience coordinator (if different from instructor in course with social work content) _____
Agency staff member (if checked, indicate if this is specified function of person for whom formal release of time is given, and position held by supervisor in agency) _____

Joint supervision by faculty member and agency staff member _____   Other _____
If other is checked, please describe:

i. Describe function(s) of supervisor(s) (e.g., orient students to agency; confer regularly with students on their performance in agency in order to (1) help students gain insight into their own motivations, strengths and limitations, (2) improve student's understanding of the client's behavior and the services of the agency, (3) improve skills of the students, (4) evaluation of students for purposes of arriving at a grade or in terms of potentialities for immediate social work employment or for graduate training; integration of classroom experience with agency observation and/or participation, etc.):

j. If there was a planned integration of field experience with class work last year, please describe how this was accomplished (e.g., regular discussion of agency problems in class discussion of case material from agency, conferences in agency to campare actual operations of agency with discussion of agency in class, application of principles of casework to actual case worked with, etc.)

k. 1) Total number of students in field experience program _____.
If you have both observation and participation programs, give
sub-totals for each: sub-total in observation _____ sub-total in
participation _____

2) How many of the students in your field experience program
last year were primarily interested in one of the occupational
areas listed below rather than in social work?

		Data not
Occupational area	*Number*	*available*
Business	_____	_____
Clinical (or Counseling) Psychology	_____	_____
Education	_____	_____
Industrial Relations	_____	_____
Journalism	_____	_____
Law	_____	_____
Medicine	_____	_____
Nursing	_____	_____
Personnel Work (business or government)	_____	_____
Police Work	_____	_____
Public Administration	_____	_____
Social Science (as a Social Scientist)	_____	_____
Other(s)		
_____	_____	_____
_____	_____	_____
_____	_____	_____

1. Please enclose with the completed questionnaire copies of any available written materials (*e.g.,* instructions, manuals) used in connection
with the field experience program.
2. Other comments on field experience

3. Planned field trips (if these are not included under discussion of field
experience program), please describe your program of planned field
trips as fully as possible.

SPECIAL QUESTIONNAIRE

1. Number of students in your basic social work course offerings last year _____
2. Estimate number of students in your basic social work course offerings last year who were:
   a. Primarily interested in a profession or occupation other than social work _____
   Of this group indicate number primarily interested in the occupational areas listed below:

Occupational area	Number	Data not available
Business	_____	_____
Clinical (or Counseling Psychology)	_____	_____
Education	_____	_____
Industrial Relations	_____	_____
Journalism	_____	_____
Law	_____	_____
Medicine	_____	_____
Nursing	_____	_____
Personnel Work	_____	_____
Police Work	_____	_____
Public Administration	_____	_____
Social Science (as Social Scientist)	_____	_____
Other		
_____	_____	_____
_____	_____	_____
_____	_____	_____

   b. Primarily interested in such courses for general liberal arts purposes rather than from the point of view of occupational goals   _____   _____
3. Estimate number of students in your basic social work course offerings last year who:

   a. Took jobs in some aspect of social work
     without securing graduate training in social
     work   _____   _____
   b. Went on to a graduate school of social work
     immediately after graduation   _____   _____
   c. Went on to take graduate training in a field
     or profession other than social work   _____   _____

4. In order to ensure our securing a comprehensive up-to-date list of colleges and universities offering undergraduate social work courses, please list the names of those institutions of higher education in your state with such offerings (regardless of whether they are members of the Council on Social Work Education or whether they have a sequence of social work courses or just a single such course, and irrespective of the division, department or major in which such offering(s) is located).

5. Other remarks. (Feel free to comment on the questionnaire or any other aspect of the Undergraduate Project of the Curriculum Study. Your remarks, of any nature, will be welcomed.)

Criteria for the Vertical Distribution of the Educational Objectives

INTRODUCTION

The identification of desirable educational objectives for the undergraduate phase of the program of social work education was the foremost purpose of this project.[1] However, in the determination of desirable objectives *for a given phase* of the program of social work education one must perforce also make decisions, implicitly or explicitly, as to where the other objectives should be located within the span of the total program. It was agreed that it would be desirable to use an explicit set of guiding principles so as to illumine the reasoning behind these decisions as to the appropriate placement of the objectives. The Study staff was unable, though, to discover a set of ready made criteria that would serve sufficiently well as a basis for the distribution of the objectives between the various stages of the program of social work education. It thus became necessary for this project to take primary responsibility for the development of such criteria.

POSTULATES

1. The educational objectives should be distributed between successive stages [2] of an articulated program of social work education.
   2. Effective articulation of the various components of the pro-

[1] As was noted previously, we are employing the term, educational objective, in accordance with the usage suggested by Ralph W. Tyler. As used by Dr. Tyler the term refers to both the kinds of behavior to be developed in the student and the areas of content in which the behavior is to be applied.
[2] As related to traditional academic divisions a "stage" may be defined as a unit within a given academic period (*e.g.*, quarter semester), or as identical with such a period, or as encompassing several such periods.

gram of social work education requires continuity, sequence, and integration.[3]

3. The program of social work education should be thought of as encompassing the following components:

   a. Study of relevant content *in* the basic disciplines.
   b. Study of related content from the other professions.
   c. Study of social work content.[4]

4. The beginning stages of the program of social work education should stress the "liberalizing" aspects. As the student progresses there should be an increasing emphasis on social work practice; however, the "liberalizing" quality should continue to permeate the entire program of social work education.[5]

CRITERIA

1. *The early stages of social work education should emphasize basic and general concepts with specialized content of a higher degree of specificity being introduced gradually through subsequent stages.*[6]
   a. Although there should be an emphasis on the relationship between social work and its sociocultural milieu throughout the program of social work education, there should be particular stress on this at the beginning and perhaps very advanced stages of the program.
      1) Although there should be an emphasis on social work as a profession functioning largely within the social welfare

---

[3] As used by Ralph W. Tyler and *adapted* by the Study staff, continuity refers to the vertical reiteration of major curriculum objectives, while sequence implies that each successive educational objective will be built upon the previous one in such a way as to involve a broadening and deepening of the materials previously considered. Integration, on the other hand, refers to the horizontal relationship of curriculum objectives, Tyler, *Basic Principles of Curriculum and Instruction* (Chicago: The University of Chicago Press, 1950), 55.
[4] The referent for the term social work in this project is the description of it provided by Boehm, "The Nature of Social Work," *Social Work*, III, 2 (April, 1958), 13.
[5] The concept of "liberalizing" is discussed in Chapter III.
[6] The term "basic" is used to refer to that which is fundamental while the term "general" is employed in contrast to specific.

*framework throughout the program of social work educa-
tion, there should be particular attention devoted to this
during the beginning stages of the program.*[7]

Comment: The subheadings are criteria in their own right as
well as being illustrative of the fact that there is a range of specificity even within the idea of "basic and general concepts."

A concrete application of the point expressed in these criteria
would be having students acquire an understanding of the function of the Aid to Dependent Children program in our society
prior to their focusing on the role of the social worker in A. D. C.
programs.

A rationale for the principles expressed in these criteria is that
once a general frame of reference is developed the specific parts
that fit within it can be viewed against this backdrop, thus acquiring added dimensions. Also, this approach would seem to be particularly compatible with the fact that, since the beginning stages
of the program of social work are likely to be organized within
liberal arts colleges, they should be characterized by an adherence
to its "liberalizing" purposes.

2. *The synthesizing of content from the basic sciences and humanities within a social work frame of reference should be preceded
by study in the disciplines from which this content is drawn.*

Comment: The implications of this criterion are twofold: First,
it means that it is usually desirable to have at least the basic content of the various disciplines learned within the frame of reference of the disciplines themselves; second, that an analytical
treatment of social work content necessitates the prior acquisition
of the necessary conceptual "tools" (and many of these are drawn
from outside of social work). For example, an understanding of
phenomena such as social institution and social classes should be
acquired by the student in a sociology class although such understanding may be deepened and put with a different framework
when employed in a social work course.

a. *The synthesizing of content from the basic disciplines within
a social work framework is desirable relatively soon after*

[7] The term "social welfare" is used to refer to a social institution, the primary activities of which center about the maintenance and enhancement of the emotional, intellectual, physical, and social aspects of human functioning.

study of at least the fundamentals of the various disciplines from which the content is drawn.

Comment: It is obvious that if the time interval between the exposure to content from the basic disciplines and its later use in a social work offering is considerable the student will be at a disadvantage in effectively applying such content. An illustrative situation is one in which a student attempts to apply knowledge from an introductory economics course three years later in a course in a graduate school of social work although there has been no utilization of the economics content nor any additional study in this field during the interim period.

3. *Content equally suitable to several of the professions is likely to be most appropriate at a relatively early stage (and perhaps again at a very advanced stage) in the program of social work education.*

Comment: Content that is equally appropriate for several professions is likely to be of a fairly high order of generality. Hence, in accordance with our prior criteria this type of rather widely applicable content should precede more specialized social work offerings. For example, it would seem reasonable that a course in interviewing serving several disciplines or professions (*e.g.*, interviewing in research, in various types of helping relationships), should precede a course in social casework. However, there are certain types of interdisciplinary seminars of a very advanced character that might best be offered at a late stage in the program of social work education.

4. *Although there should be preparation for scholarly contributions to social work throughout the program of social work education, there should be particular emphasis on this during the later stages of the program.*

Comment: Scholarly contributions are usually the products of a protracted period of preparation. The development of communication skills, an understanding of the theory and methodology of research and a disciplined interest in scientific inquiry are not suddenly achieved after a course or two in social work research. Hence, provision must be made for the gradual development of such essentials throughout the program. However, there should be more emphasis of the special requisite knowledge, skills and attitudes during the later stages of the program of social work education.

5. *The process of socialization into the social work profession should be continuous throughout the program of social work education.*

    a. *In each succeeding stage of the program the student should be further immersed in the professional subculture.*

    Comment: The socialization of a student into a profession includes, among other things, identification with the professional ideology and the internalization of a particular set of attitudes. This process of socialization requires an extended period of time, particularly when the profession lacks high prestige and when its ideology and attitudes run counter, at some important points, to those prevalent in the culture. One implication of this fact is that the teaching of the social work ideology and exposure to certain requisite attitudes should be initiated early in the program of social work education and deepened in each successive stage.

6. *Although it may sometimes be necessary in social work methods sequences and field work to employ certain still debated theoretical formulations as a basis for professional problem-solving the student should have previously acquired the beginnings of the understanding necessary for evaluating the degree of certainty to be attached to these "givens."*

Comment: The student, in his preparation for professional practice, quite justifiably learns to employ various still unproved theoretical formulations in professional problem solving. "The caution of the scientist appropriate in the laboratory, is a luxury which only persons with no responsibility for action can afford. To paraphrase Leighton, if clients were treated by scientists, the number of mistakes would probably decline, but so would the number of clients treated." [8]

However, if progress is to be made, and the dogma of the uninformed avoided, the professional (as student or practitioner) needs to be able to differentiate between the heuristic rationale

[8] Ernest Greenwood, "Social Science and Social Work: A Theory of Their Relationship," *The Social Service Review*, XXIX, 1 (March, 1955), 27.

for employing certain theoretical formulations and that justification which is based on certainty of the knowledge. For example, in a casework course, it may be necessary and helpful to use various psychoanalytic formulations as a framework for problem-solving. The student should know, though, to what extent these formulations have been verified and what alternative hypotheses might be appropriate. In order to develop the beginnings of a basis for such an evaluation, in this instance, his previous study should have included an examination of various theories of personality and the extent of their theoretical validation.

7. *Preparation in the professional methods should be preceded by an understanding of basic social work knowledge content.*

Comment: Since the social work methods courses necessarily draw heavily upon content from the foundation sequences (*e.g.,* human growth and behavior) background in each of these basic areas would seem to be a reasonable prerequisite for the study of the methods themselves. An alternative would be to include a certain amount of foundational content in the methods courses. However, this would be an extremely inefficient procedure as well as running the risk of an oversimplified or confused treatment of such content.

8. *The process whereby the student learns to practice social work "by doing" should permit the following sequential ordering of experiences:*
   a. *From lesser to greater responsibilities (e.g., degree of autonomy in decision-making, potential consequences of decisions reached, etc.)* [9]
   b. *From lesser to greater complexity*
   c. *From problems putting less severe demands on the student's disciplined "use of the self" to those making more strenuous demands*
   d. *From situations involving less testing of the students' commitment to professional values and attitudes, and identification with the professional, to those making greater demands in respect to these aspects.*

[9] For a proposed classification of occupations, and positions within occupations, based upon degrees of responsibility, capacity, and skill, see Roe, *op. cit.,* 149–152. Regardless of whether the overall classification is satisfactory there are useful suggestions for a differentiation of function according to the three aforementioned factors.

Comment: These criteria suggest the direction of the progressive involvement of the student in social work problem-solving. In so doing they also function as guides to appropriate learning experiences.

9. *It is desirable to have a continuous interplay between course work and related experiences outside the classroom throughout the entire program of social work education.*

Comment: The implications of this criterion are twofold: first, that there should be a sequential development of extra-classroom experiences, and; second, that it is undesirable to expect students to engage in the practice of social work (*e.g.,* conduct a casework interview) without having had a chance to hear or see qualified social workers perform similarly. Although there is some advantage to the learner in "on the spot observation" when this is not feasible use can be made of various audio-visual aids (*e.g.,* films, recordings). It should be recognized that, to a greater extent in social work than other professions, the neophyte is expected to employ the various professional methods without having seen or heard them employed (this is particularly true of casework).

10. *The evaluation of the students' intellectual and psycho-social potential to practice social work in an adequate manner should be a continuing process throughout the program of social work education.*[10]

   a. *The evaluation of the students' readiness to practice social work in an adequate manner is a particularly appropriate part of the educational program in the stage immediately preceding the students' seeking of employment.*

Comments: The essential point of both of these criteria is that while evaluation of the student should be continuous, it is inadvisable to tie such evaluation too closely to the point of actually entering the field. The implication is that premature evaluative judgments based on readiness to practice should be discouraged without, however, minimizing the importance of judgments being made throughout the entire program of social work education as to potential.

---

[10] "Potential" should be thought of in relation to the students' stage of development.

APPENDIX D

REPORTED FIELD EXPERIENCES— OBSERVATION AND PARTICIPATION

Observation

1. Observation of administrative and office routines.
2. Observation of staff meetings.
3. Observation of inter-agency experience.
4. Observing club meetings.
5. Sit in on intake interviews.
6. Participation in rehabilitation. Case conference.
7. Visited Good Will Industries.
8. Reading records.
9. Sit in on board meetings.
10. Accompanying worker on visits.
11. Observations of court hearings.
12. Observation by instructor accompanying students to agencies—and later discussion.
13. Attendance at State Chapter of NASW.
14. Tour of mental hospitals.
15. Related reading (reference texts)

Participation

1. Carry some responsibility in limited selected public assistance cases.
2. Trips to clinics to take adults and children.
3. Clearance of applications referred by Community Chest in regard to school lunches.
4. Field visits to other agencies.
5. General office work.
6. Answer phone.
7. Serve as club leader.
8. Solicit for United Appeal drive.
9. Verification of eligibility.
10. Agency research.
11. Did one intake interview.
12. Any assignments.
13. Progresses from role of orientation to role of regular worker
14. Accompanying worker on visits.
15. Assisting in routine in children's institutions.
16. Arranging medical care.
17. Referrals.
18. Visits to O.A.A. recipients.
19. Office procedures.
20. Reading records.
21. Preparation of case summaries.
22. Carrying entire caseload in limited selected O.A.A. cases.
23. Interviewing applicants for foster care.
24. Working as receptionists.
25. Recording and dictating.
26. Taking psychiatric social history.

APPENDIX E

VOCATIONAL INTERESTS, OTHER THAN SOCIAL WORK, OF STUDENTS
ENROLLED IN THE BASIC UNDERGRADUATE SOCIAL WORK OFFERINGS.[1]

Field of Vocational Interest	Number of Students	Number of Schools Reporting Enrollment of Students with Such Vocational Interests
Nursing	349	16
Education	272	31
Clinical (or Counseling) Psychology	105	20
Business Administration	80	17
Police Work	50	14
Personnel Work	49	16
Public Administration	35	9
Medicine	13	7
Law	12	9
Industrial Relations	10	5
Journalism	9	8
Other	148	
Specified		
Ministry	31	10
Recreation	29	3
Occupational Therapy	6	1
Medical Librarian	5	1
Speech Therapy	3	2
Dentistry	2	1
Health and Physical Education	2	2
Child Development	1	1
Criminology	1	1
Government Service	1	1
Home Economics	1	1
Physiotherapy	1	1
Non-Specified	65	

[1] From analysis of 45 *special* questionnaires which were usable returns from 102 distributed.

SELECTED BIBLIOGRAPHY

(Additional references to those cited in the selected bibliographies concluding Chapters VIII, IX, X and XI.)

Addams, Jane. *Twenty Years at Hull-House.* New York: The Macmillan Company, 1910.

Alexander, Chauncey A. and Charles McCann, "The Concept of Representativeness in Community Organization," *Social Work,* I (January, 1956).

Allport, Gordon W. "The Psychology of Participation," *Readings in Group Work,* Dorothea F. Sullivan (ed.). New York: Association Press, 1952.

American Association of Schools of Social Work. *Education for the Public Social Services:* a report of the Study Committee. Chapel Hill: University of North Carolina Press, 1942.

American Federation of Teachers, Commission on Educational Reconstruction. *Organizing the Teaching Profession; The Story of the American Federation of Teachers.* Glencoe, Ill.: The Free Press, 1955.

American Humanist Association. "A Special Issue on Education," *The Humanist,* XVII, 3 (May–June, 1957). Yellow Springs, Ohio: AHA, 1957.

Aptekar, Herbert H. *The Dynamics of Casework and Counseling.* Boston: Houghton Mifflin Company, 1955.

Bauer, Raymond A. *The New Man in Soviet Psychology.* ("Russian Research Center Studies" No. 7.) Cambridge, Mass.: Harvard University Press, 1952.

Becker, Howard and Harry Elmer Barnes. *Social Thought from Lore to Science,* 2nd ed.; with the assistance of Émile Benoît-Smullyan, *et al.* Washington, D.C.: Harren Press, 1952.

—— and Alvin Boskoff (eds.). *Modern Sociological Theory in Continuity and Change.* New York: The Dryden Press, Inc., 1957.

Bell, Daniel (ed.). *The New American Right.* New York: Criterion Books, 1955.

Bendix, Reinhard and Seymour M. Lipset (eds.). *Class, Status and Power.* Glencoe, Ill.: The Free Press, 1953.

Berelson, Bernard (ed.). *Education for Librarianship;* papers presented at the Library Conference, University of Chicago, Graduate Library

School, August 16–21, 1948. Chicago: American Library Association, 1949.

Berser, Monroe, Theodore Abel and Charles H. Pase (eds.). *Freedom and Control in Modern Society*. New York: D. Van Nostrand Co., Inc., 1954.

Bierstedt, Robert. *The Social Order*. New York: McGraw-Hill Book Co., Inc., 1957.

Blauch, Lloyd E. (ed.). *Education for the Professions*. Washington, D.C.: Department of Health, Education, and Welfare. U.S. Government Printing Office, 1953.

Boehm, Werner W. "The Nature of Social Work," *Social Work*, III (April, 1958).

Boskoff, Alvin. "Social Change: Major Problems in the Emergence of Theoretical and Research Foci," *Modern Sociological Theory* . . . , ed. by Howard Becker and Alvin Boskoff. New York: The Dryden Press, Inc., 1957.

Bremner, Robert H. *From the Depths; the Discovery of Poverty in the United States*. New York: New York University Press, Inc., 1956.

Brookover, Wilbur B. *A Sociology of Education*. New York: American Book Company, 1955.

Brown, Esther Lucile. *Nursing for the Future;* a report prepared for the National Nursing Council. New York: Russell Sage Foundation, 1948.

Brown, Josephine C. *Public Relief: 1929–1939*. New York: Henry Holt and Company, Inc., 1940.

Bruno, Frank J. *Trends in Social Work, 1874–1956;* a history based on the *Proceedings* of the National Conference of Social Work. [With chapters by Louis Towley.] 2nd ed. New York: Columbia University Press, 1957.

Carr, E. H. *The New Society*. London: Macmillan & Co., Ltd., 1951.

Carr–Saunders, A. M. and P. A. Wilson. *The Professions*. Oxford: The Clarendon Press, 1933.

Carter, Paul A. *Decline and Revival of the Social Gospel: Social and Political Liberalism in American Protestant Churches, 1920–1940*. Ithaca, N.Y.: Cornell University Press, 1954.

Cilento, Sir Raphael. "The World Moves toward Professional Standards in Social Work," *Social Work as Human Relations,* anniversary papers of the New York School of Social Work . . . New York: Columbia University Press, 1949.

Cogan, Morris L. "Toward a Definition of Profession," *Harvard Educational Review,* XXIII (Winter, 1953).

Cohen, Morris R. *Reason and Nature.* New York: Harcourt, Brace and Company, 1931.

Cohen, Nathan E. *Social Work in the American Tradition.* New York: The Dryden Press, Inc., 1958.

Cole, G. D. H. *A Short History of the British Working-Class Movement,* 1789–1947, rev. ed. London: George Allen & Unwin Ltd., 1948.

Cole, Margaret. "Education and Social Democracy," *New Fabian Essays,* R. H. S. Crossman (ed.). London: Turnstile Press, 1952.

Commission on Human Resources and Advanced Training. *America's Resources of Specialized Talent;* report prepared by Dael Wolfle. New York: Harper and Brothers, 1954.

Coser, Lewis A. and Bernard Rosenberg (eds.). *Sociological Theory.* New York: The Macmillan Company, 1957.

Council on Social Work Education. *Bibliography for Use by Instructors in the Undergraduate Sequence in Social Welfare.* New York: CSWE, 1954.

————. *"Films Recommended for Use in Undergraduate Education for Social Welfare."* New York: CSWE, 1958.

————. *Introductory Course on the Field of Social Work.* New York: CSWE, 1954.

————. *On-going Education,* Workshop Report, Annual Program Meeting, 1954. New York: CSWE, 1954.

————. *Proceedings,* Annual Program Meetings, 1953, 1954, 1955, 1956 and 1957. New York: CSWE.

————. *School-Agency Responsibility in Extending Professional Education—No. 1 The Team Approach to Staff Development in Agency and School.* Workshop Report, Annual Program Meeting, 1956. New York: CSWE, 1956.

————. *Selection of Students for Schools of Social Work.* New York: CSWE, 1955.

————. *Social Work Education,* Special Recruitment Issue, III. New York: CSWE (June, 1955).

————. *Student Assessment—Selection and Continuing Evaluation,* Workshop Report, Annual Program Meeting, 1954. New York: CSWE, 1954.

————. *Student Assessment—Selection and Continuing Evaluation,* Workshop Report, Annual Program Meeting, 1955. New York: CSWE, 1955.

————. *The Teaching of Social Philosophy and Social Responsibility in the Undergraduate Program,* Workshop Report, Annual Program Meeting, 1956. New York: CSWE, 1956.

Council on Social Work Education. *The Undergraduate Department and the Graduate School—How Can the Integration of Undergraduate and Graduate Education be More Effectively Accomplished?* Workshop Report, Annual Program Meeting, 1953. New York: CSWE, 1953.

———. *Undergraduate Education for Practice.* Workshop Report, Annual Program Meeting, 1955. New York: CSWE, 1955.

Cox, Oliver C. *Caste, Class, & Race.* Garden City, N.Y.: Doubleday & Co., Inc., 1948.

Coyle, Grace L. *Group Work with American Youth.* New York: Harper and Brothers, 1948.

Cranefield, Eleanor G. and S. Jerome Roach. *The Educational Needs of Personnel in the Field of Corrections.* New York: Council on Social Work Education, 1956.

Curti, Merle. *The Growth of American Thought,* 2nd ed. New York: Harper and Brothers, 1951.

Dahl, Robert A. and Charles E. Lindblom. *Politics, Economics, and Welfare.* New York: Harper and Brothers, 1953.

Deitrick, John E. and Robert C. Berson. *Medical Schools in the United States at Mid-Century.* New York: McGraw-Hill Book Company, Inc., 1953.

Department of Health, Education, and Welfare. "The Training Center, A Method of Staff Development," prepared by Anne Wilkens. Washington, D.C.: Bureau of Public Assistance, 1950. (mimeographed).

———. *Training Personnel for Work with Juvenile Delinquents.* Children's Bureau Publication no. 348. Washington, D.C.: U.S. Government Printing Office, 1954.

de Schweinitz, Karl. "Social Values and Social Action—The Intellectual Base as Illustrated in the Study of History," *Social Service Review,* XXX (June, 1956).

Deutsch, Albert. *The Mentally Ill in America; A History of Their Care and Treatment from Colonial Times,* 2nd ed., rev. and enl. New York: Columbia University Press, 1949.

DeVane, William Clyde. *The American University in the Twentieth Century.* Baton Rouge: Louisiana State University Press, 1957.

Dewey, John. *Liberalism and Social Action.* New York: G. P. Putnam's Sons, 1935.

Diekhoff, John S. *The Domain of the Faculty in Our Expanding Colleges.* New York: Harper and Brothers, 1956.

Durkheim, Émile. *Suicide.* Glencoe, Ill.: The Free Press, 1951.

Duverger, Maurice. *The Political Role of Women.* Paris: UNESCO, 1955.

Ebenstein, William (ed.). *Man and the State: Modern Political Ideas.* New York: Rinehart & Co., Inc., 1947.

Faulkner, Harold U. *The Quest for Social Justice, 1898–1914.* New York: The Macmillan Company, 1931.

Fauri, Fedele F. "The Shortage of Social Workers—A Challenge to Social Work Education," 1955 *Proceedings,* Third Annual Program Meeting, Council on Social Work Education. New York: CSWE, 1955.

Feder, Leah H. *Unemployment Relief in Periods of Depression; A Study of Measures Adopted in Certain American Cities, 1857 through 1922.* New York: Russell Sage Foundation, 1936.

Finch, James Kip. *Trends in Engineering Education, The Columbia Experience.* New York: Columbia University Press, 1948.

Fine, Sidney. *Laissez Faire and the General-Welfare State; A Study of Conflict in American Thought, 1865–1901.* Ann Arbor: The University of Michigan Press, 1956.

Firth, Raymond. *Human Types,* rev. ed. New York: The New American Library (A Mentor Book), 1958.

Fisher, Jacob. *The Rank and File Movement in Social Work, 1931–1936.* New York: The New York School of Social Work, 1936.

Flexner, Abraham. "Is Social Work a Profession?" *Proceedings* of the National Conference of Charities and Corrections, 1915. Chicago, Ill., 1915.

Frankel, Charles. "Professional Education as University Education," 1958 *Proceedings,* Sixth Annual Program Meeting, Council on Social Work Education. New York, CSWE, 1958.

Frazier, E. Franklin. *Race and Culture Contacts in the Modern World.* New York: Alfred A. Knopf, Inc., 1957.

Friedlander, Walter A. (ed.). *Concepts and Methods of Social Work.* Englewood Cliffs, N.J.: Prentice-Hall, Inc., 1958.

Garrett, Annette M. *Interviewing; Its Principles and Methods.* New York: Family Welfare Association of America, 1942.

Gellhorn, Walter. *Individual Freedom and Governmental Restraints.* Baton Rouge: Louisiana State University Press, 1956.

Gillin, John (ed.). *For a Science of Social Man.* New York: The Macmillan Company, 1954.

Gittler, Joseph B. (ed.). *Review of Sociology.* New York: John Wiley and Sons, Inc., 1957.

Glazer, Nathan. "Ethnic Groups in America: From National Culture to Ideology," *Freedom and Control in Modern Society,* ed. by Morroe

Berger *et al.* New York: D. Van Nostrand Company, Inc., 1954.

Goldman, Eric F. *Rendezvous with Destiny; A History of Modern American Reform.* New York: Alfred A. Knopf, Inc., 1952.

Goldmark, Josephine. *Impatient Crusader: Florence Kelley's Life Story.* Urbana, Ill.: University of Illinois Press, 1953.

Goldstein, Bernard. "Some Aspects of Unionism among Salaried Professionals in Industry," *American Sociological Review,* XX (April, 1955).

Golob, Eugene. *The "Isms".* New York: Harper and Brothers, 1954.

Gordon, Milton M. "Social Structure and Goals in Group Relations," *Freedom and Control in Modern Society,* ed. by Morroe Berger, *et al.* New York: D. Van Nostrand Company, Inc., 1954.

Greenblatt, Milton, *et al.* (eds.). *The Patient and the Mental Hospital.* Glencoe, Ill.: The Free Press, 1957.

Gregg, Pauline. *A Social and Economic History of Britain, 1760–1950.* London: George G. Harrap & Co., Ltd., 1950.

Gross, Neal C. *et al. Explorations in Role Analysis: Studies of the School Superintendency Role.* New York: John Wiley and Sons, Inc., 1958.

Gurvitch, Georgil D. and Wilbert E. Moore (eds.). *Twentieth Century Sociology.* New York: The Philosophical Library, 1945.

Haber, William *et al.* (eds.). *Manpower in the United States: Problems and Policies,* Industrial Relations Research Association Series, Publication no. 11. New York: Harper and Brothers, 1954.

Halsey, Margaret. *The Folks at Home.* New York: Simon and Schuster, Inc., 1952.

Hankins, Frank H. "A Forty-Year Perspective," *Sociology and Social Research,* XL (July–August, 1956).

Hare, A. D. *et al.* (eds.). *Small Groups.* New York: Alfred A. Knopf, 1955.

Harno, Albert J. *Legal Education in the United States:* a report prepared for the Survey of the Legal Profession. San Francisco: Bancroft-Whitney Co., 1953.

Hartford, Margaret E. and Grace L. Coyle. *Social Process in the Community and the Group.* New York: Council on Social Work Education, 1958.

Harvard University, Committee on the Objectives of a General Education in a Free Society. *General Education in a Free Society; Report of the Harvard Committee.* Cambridge, Mass.: Harvard University Press, 1945.

Hauser, Philip M. "Demography and Human Ecology in Relation to Social Work," *Social Welfare Forum,* Official Proceedings of the National Conference of Social Work, 1956. New York: Columbia University Press, 1956.

Hayek, F. A. (ed.). *Capitalism and the Historians*. Chicago: The University of Chicago Press, 1954.

Henry, Jules. "Homeostasis, Society, and Evolution; A Critique," *Scientific Monthly*, LXXXI (December, 1955).

Hinkle, Roscoe C., Jr. and Gisela J. Hinkle. *The Development of Modern Sociology*. Garden City, New York: Doubleday & Co., Inc., 1954.

Hofstadter, Richard. *The Age of Reform; From Byran to F.D.R.* New York: Alfred A. Knopf, Inc., 1955.

———. *The American Political Tradition: And The Men Who Made It*. New York: Alfred A. Knopf, Inc., 1948.

———. *Social Darwinism in American Thought, 1860–1915*. Philadelphia: University of Pennsylvania Press, 1944.

Hollis, Ernest V., and Alice L. Taylor. *Social Work Education in the United States*. New York: Columbia University Press, 1951.

Homans, George C. *The Human Group*. New York: Harcourt, Brace and Company, 1950.

Jacob, Philip E. *Changing Values in College; An Exploratory Study of the Impact of College Teaching*. New York: Harper and Brothers, 1957.

Jahoda, Marie. "Toward a Social Psychology of Mental Health," *Mental Health and Mental Disorder*, Arnold M. Rose (ed.). New York: W. W. Norton & Company, Inc., 1955.

Jameson, J. Franklin. *The American Revolution Considered as a Social Movement*. Boston: Beacon Press, Inc., 1956.

Jones, Howard Mumford. "Education and One World," *Goals for American Education*, 9th Symposium, New York, 1948, of Conference on Science, Philosophy and Religion . . . Lyman Bryson *et al.* (eds.). New York: Harper and Brothers, 1950.

———. *Education and World Tragedy*. Cambridge, Mass.: Harvard University Press, 1946.

Jones, Maxwell. *The Therapeutic Community; A New Treatment Method in Psychiatry*, with a foreword by Goodwin Watson. New York: Basic Books, Inc., 1953.

Kandel, I. L. *American Education in the Twentieth Century*. Cambridge, Mass.: Harvard University Press, 1957.

Kantor, David. "The Use of College Students as 'Case Aides' in a Social Service Department of a State Hospital: An Experiment in Undergraduate Social Work Education," *The Patient and the Mental*

Hospital, Milton Greenblatt, et al. (eds.). Glencoe, Ill.: The Free Press, 1957.

Kasius, Cora (ed.). *New Directions in Social Work.* New York: Harper and Brothers, 1954.

———— (ed.). *Principles and Techniques in Social Casework; Selected Articles, 1940–1950.* New York: Family Service Association of America, 1950.

Kerr, Clark and Lloyd H. Fisher. "Plant Sociology: The Elite and the Aborigines," *Common Frontiers of the Social Sciences,* Mirra Komarovsky (ed.). Glencoe, Ill.: The Free Press, 1957.

Kindelsperger, Kenneth W. *An Approach to the Study of the Public Social Services and its Relationship to Undergraduate Education for Social Welfare.* New York: Council on Social Work Education, 1956.

Kluckhohn, Clyde. *Mirror for Man; The Relation of Anthropology to Modern Life.* New York: Whittlesey House, 1949.

————. "The Study of Culture," *Sociological Theory.* Lewis A. Coser and Bernard Rosenberg (eds.). New York: The Macmillan Company, 1957.

————, and Henry A. Murray (eds.). *Personality in Nature, Society and Culture.* New York: Alfred A. Knopf, 1948.

Lane, Frederic C. and Jelle C. Riemersma (eds.). *Enterprise and Secular Change.* Homewood, Ill.: Richard D. Irwin, Inc., 1953.

Laughton, Charles W. *Staffing Social Services in Texas: The Problem and the Challenge.* Austin, Texas: The School of Social Work, University of Texas, 1957.

Leigh, Robert D. (ed.). *Major Problems in the Education of Librarians.* New York: Columbia University Press, 1954.

Lerner, Max (ed.). *The Portable Veblen.* New York: The Viking Press, 1948.

Levi, Albert William. *General Education in the Social Studies.* Washington, D.C.: American Council on Education, 1948.

Lindesmith, Alfred R. and Anselm L. Strauss. "Critique of Culture-Personality Writings," *American Sociological Review,* XV (October, 1950).

Lipset, Seymour M. "Political Sociology, 1945–55," *Sociology in the United States of America: A Trend Report,* Hans L. Zetterberg (ed.). Paris: UNESCO, 1956.

Lower, Katherine D. "Undergraduate Preparation Prerequisite to Admission to Graduate Schools of Social Work: From the Graduate

Point of View," *Undergraduate Education*—Selected Papers. New York: Council on Social Work Education, 1958.

Luckey, E. H. "Role of Undergraduate Medical Education in Preparation for Graduate Education," *Journal of the American Medical Association,* 163 (April 27, 1957).

Madge, John H. *The Tools of Social Science.* London, New York: Longmans, Green & Co., Inc., 1953.

Madison, Bernice. *The Public Assistance Job and the Undergraduate Social Work Curriculum.* San Francisco: The Rosenberg Foundation, 1957.

Madison, Charles A. *Critics & Crusaders: A Century of American Protest,* 2nd ed., enlarged. New York: Frederick Ungar, 1959.

Matson, Floyd W. "Social Welfare and Personal Liberty: The Problem of Casework," *Social Research,* 22 (Autumn, 1955).

McGlothlin, William J. "The Aims of Professional Education," 1958 *Proceedings,* Sixth Annual Program Meeting, Council on Social Work Education. New York: CSWE, 1958.

McPartland, Thomas S. "Formal Education and the Process of Professionalization: A Study of Student Nurses," [Part V of] *A Study of the Registered Nurse in a Metropolitan Community* by Community Studies, Inc. Kansas City, Mo.: Community Studies, Inc., 1957.

Mead, George Herbert. *Mind, Self & Society,* Charles W. Morris (ed.). Chicago: The University of Chicago Press, 1934.

Meehl, P. E. and Wilfred Sellars. "The Concept of Emergence," *The Foundations of Science and the Concepts of Psychology and Psychoanalysis.* Herbert Feigl and Michael Scriven (eds.). ("Minnesota Studies in the Philosophy of Science," Vol. I).

Merriam, Charles Edward. *The Role of Politics in Social Change.* New York: New York University Press, 1936.

Merton, Robert K. "Some Preliminaries to a Sociology of Medical Education," *The Student-Physician.* Robert K. Merton, *et al.* (eds.). Cambridge, Mass.: Harvard University Press, 1957.

———, *et al.* (eds.). *Reader in Bureaucracy.* Glencoe, Ill.: The Free Press, 1952.

———, *et al.* (eds.). *The Student-Physician: Introductory Studies in the Sociology of Medical Education.* Cambridge, Mass.: Commonwealth Fund by Harvard University Press, 1957.

Miles, Arthur P. "Undergraduate and Graduate Study in the Training of Public Welfare Personnel," *Public Welfare,* IX (February, 1951).

Miller, Horace G. "The Psychic Trauma of Becoming Part of a Group,"

Readings in Group Work, Dorothea F. Sullivan (ed.). New York: Associaion Press, 1952.

Mitchell, Broadus: *Depression Decade; From New Era through New Deal, 1929–1941.* New York: Rinehart & Co., Inc., 1947.

Monahan, Fergus T. "The Case Aide in a Military Setting," *Conference on Individualized Services; the Use of Case Aides in Casework Agencies.* New York: National Social Welfare Assembly, 1959.

Mossman, Mereb E. "Preprofessional Education for Social Work," *Virginia Public Welfare,* XXV (September, 1947).

National Conference of Social Work *Proceedings.* New York: Columbia University Press, 1947.

National Social Welfare Assembly. Conference on Individualized Services; *The Use of Case Aides in Casework Agencies.* New York: NSWA, 1959.

Newcomb, Theodore M. "Sociology and Psychology," *For a Science of Social Man.* John Gillin (ed.). New York: The Macmillan Company, 1954.

Ohlin, Lloyd E. "The Development of Social Action Theories in Social Work," 1958 *Proceedings,* Sixth Annual Program Meeting, Council on Social Work Education. New York: CSWE, 1958.

Pacey, Lorene M. (ed.). *Readings in the Development of Settlement Work.* New York: Association Press, 1950.

Palevsky, Mary. *Counseling Services for Industrial Workers.* New York: Family Welfare Association of America, 1945.

Peyser, Dora. *The Strong and the Weak.* Sydney: Currawong Publishing Company, 1951.

Pittsburgh, University of, Graduate School of Public Health. *The Functions and Education of Medical Record Personnel;* a survey report to the American Association of Medical Record Librarians, by Antonio Ciocco *et al.* Pittsburgh: University of Pittsburgh Press, 1957.

Planck, Max. "The Concept of Causality in Physics," *Readings in Philosophy of Science,* Philip P. Wiener (ed.). New York: Charles Scribner's Sons, 1953.

Polansky, Norman, William Bowen, Lucille Gordon and Conrad Nathan. "Social Workers in Society: Results of a Sampling Study," *Social Work Journal,* XXXIV (April, 1953).

Pollak, Otto. *Integrating Sociological and Psychoanalytic Concepts.* New York: Russell Sage Foundation, 1956.

Pope, Liston. *Millhands & Preachers; A Study of Gastonia* ("Yale Studies in Religious Education," XV). New Haven: Yale University Press, 1942.

Porterfield, Austin L. *Mirror, Mirror; On Seeing Yourself in Books.* Fort Worth, Texas: Leo Potisham Foundation, Texas Christian University, 1956.

President's Committee on Education Beyond the High School. *Second Report to the President.* Washington, D.C.: U.S. Government Printing Office, 1957.

Prothro, James Warren. *The Dollar Decade; Business Ideas in the 1920's.* Baton Rouge: Louisiana State University Press, 1954.

Pusey, Nathan M. "The Role of the Liberal Arts," *Higher Education in the West,* Western Interstate Commission for Higher Education, III. (April, 1957).

Randall, John Herman. *Making of the Modern Mind,* rev. ed. Boston: Houghton Mifflin Company, 1940.

Reiss, Albert J., Jr. "Occupational Mobility of Professional Workers," *American Sociological Review,* XX (December, 1955).

Reynolds, Bertha Capen. *Learning and Teaching in the Practice of Social Work.* New York: Farrar and Rinehart, Inc., 1942.

————. *Social Work and Social Living.* New York: Citadel Press, 1951.

Rich, Margaret E. *A Belief in People; A History of Family Social Work.* New York: Family Service Association of America, 1956.

Richmond, Mary Ellen. *The Long View; Papers and Addresses by Mary E. Richmond.* Joanna C. Colcord and Ruth Z. X. Man (eds.). New York: Russell Sage Foundation, 1930.

Robinson, Ruth B. "The Case Aide in a Multi-function Agency," *Conference on Individualized Services; the Use of Case Aides in Casework Agencies.* New York: National Social Welfare Assembly, 1959.

Roe, Anne. *The Psychology of Occupations.* New York: John Wiley and Sons, Inc., 1956.

Rogoff, Natalie. "The Decision to Study Medicine," *The Student-Physician,* Robert K. Merton *et al.* (eds.). Cambridge, Mass.: Harvard University Press, 1957.

Rose, Arnold M. (ed.). *Mental Health and Mental Disorder.* New York: W. W. Norton and Company, Inc., 1955.

Rosenberg, Morris *et al.* (eds.). *Occupations and Values.* Glencoe, Ill.: The Free Press, 1957.

Ross, Margery R. "Influences Affecting the Development of Undergraduate Social Work Education in Seven Michigan Colleges from 1920–1955." Unpublished Ph.D. dissertation, University of Michigan, 1957.

Russell, Ellery C. "Case Aides Free Casework Time," *Child Welfare,* XXXVII (April, 1958).

Russell, James E. (ed.). *National Policies for Education, Health and Social Services.* Garden City, N.Y.: Doubleday & Company, Inc., 1955.

Sanderson, Herbert. *Basic Concepts in Vocational Guidance.* New York: McGraw-Hill Book Company, Inc., 1954.

Schmidt, George P. *The Liberal Arts College; A Chapter in American Cultural History.* New Brunswick, N.J.: Rutgers University Press, 1957.

Schneider, Louis. *The Freudian Psychology and Veblen's Social Theory.* New York: King's Crown Press, 1948.

Seligman, Edwin R. A. *The Economic Interpretation of History,* 2nd ed., rev. New York: Columbia University Press, 1934.

Sims, Newell L. *The Problem of Social Change.* New York: Thomas Y. Crowell Company, 1939.

Smith, Elliott Dunlap. "Education and the Task of Making Social Work Professional," *Social Service Review,* XXXI (March, 1957).

Smith, M. Brewster. "Anthropology and Psychology," *For a Science of Social Man,* John Gillin (ed.). New York: The Macmillan Company, 1954.

Sorokin, Pitirim A. *Social and Cultural Dynamics,* rev. and abr. in 1 vol. Boston: Porter Sargent, 1957.

Southern Regional Education Board. *Social Work Personnel for Mental Health Programs,* Report of a Conference held under the Southern Regional Program in Mental Health Training and Research, March 21–22, 1956. Atlanta, Georgia. Atlanta, Ga.: The Board, 1956.

Stevenson, George S. *Mental Health Planning for Social Action.* New York: McGraw-Hill Book Company, Inc., 1956.

Steward, Julian H. *Theory of Culture Change.* Urbana, Ill.: University of Illinois Press, 1955.

Stroup, Herbert. "But Speak the Word Only; An Analysis of Certain Objectives in the Teaching of Social Work to Undergraduates." New York: Brooklyn College Department of Sociology and Anthropology, 1952. (mimeographed)

Sullivan, Dorothea F. (ed.). *Readings in Group Work.* New York: Association Press, 1952.

Survey of Medical Education, Subcommittee on Preprofessional Education. *Preparation for Medical Education in the Liberal Arts Col-*

lege; the Report of the Subcommittee, Aura E. Severinghaus, *et al.* (eds.). New York: McGraw-Hill Book Company, Inc., 1953.

Taylor, Harold. "The World of the American Student," *Higher Education in the West,* Western Interstate Commission for Higher Education, III (April, 1957). Also found in *Current Issues in Higher Education, Proceedings* of the Annual Conference of the National Education Association, 1956, G. K. Smith (ed.). Washington, D.C., 1956.

Teggert, Frederick J. (ed.). *The Idea of Progress; A Collection of Readings,* rev. ed., with an introduction by George H. Hildebrand. Berkeley: University of California Press, 1949.

Thielens, Wagner, Jr. "Some Comparisons of Entrants to Medical and Law School," *The Student-Physician,* Robert K. Merton, *et al.* (eds.). Cambridge, Mass.: Harvard University Press, 1957.

Thomas, William L., Jr. (ed.). *Current Anthropology.* Chicago: University of Chicago Press, 1956.

Thompson, Ronald B. "The Search for More Space," *Higher Education in the West,* Western Interstate Commission for Higher Education, III (April, 1957).

Towle, Charlotte. *The Learner in Education for the Professions: As Seen in Education for Social Work.* Chicago: The University of Chicago Press, 1954.

Townsend, Agatha. *College Freshmen Speak Out,* prepared for the Committee on School and College Relations of the Educational Records Bureau. New York: Harper and Brothers, 1956.

Trecker, Harleigh B. (ed.). *Group Work: Foundations and Frontiers.* New York: Whiteside, Inc. and William Morrow and Company, 1955.

Tyler, Ralph W. *Basic Principles of Curriculum and Instruction.* Chicago: The University of Chicago Press, 1950.

——, *et al. Analysis of the Purpose, Pattern, Scope, and Structure of the Officer Education Program of Air University,* Officer Education Research Laboratory, Maxwell Air Force Base, Alabama, May, 1955. (mimeographed)

Tylor, Edward B. "The Science of Culture," in *Sociological Analysis* by Logan Wilson and William L. Kolb. New York: Harcourt, Brace and Company, 1949.

United Nations, Department of Social Affairs. *Training for Social Work; An International Survey.* Lake Success, N.Y., 1950.

Vanderbilt, Arthur T. *Men and Measures in the Law.* New York: Alfred A. Knopf, Inc., 1949.

Veblen, Thorstein. *The Higher Learning in America; A Memorandum on the Conduct of Universities by Business Men.* New York: Sagamore Press, Inc. (The American Century Series), 1957.

Waller, Willard. "Social Problems and the Mores," *American Sociological Review,* I (December, 1936).

Wardwell, Walter J. and Arthur L. Wood. "The Extra-Professional Role of the Lawyer," *American Journal of Sociology,* LXI (January, 1956.

Ware, Anna B. "The Case Aide in a Single Function Agency," *Conference on Individualized Services; the Use of Case Aides in Casework Agencies.* New York: National Social Welfare Assembly, 1959.

Warriner, Charles K. "Groups are Real," *American Sociological Review,* XXI (October, 1956).

Watson, Frank D. *The Charity Organization Movement in the United States; A Study in American Philanthropy.* New York: The Macmillan Company, 1922.

Wecter, Dixon. *The Age of the Great Depression, 1929–1941.* New York: The Macmillan Company, 1948.

Welfare Council of Metropolitan Los Angeles. *Group Dynamics: Implications for Social Work,* Special Report Series No. 24. Los Angeles: Welfare Council, 1950.

Westley, William A. "Violence and the Policies," *American Journal of Sociology,* LIX (July, 1953).

White, Leonard D. (ed.). *The State of the Social Sciences.* Chicago: University of Chicago Press, 1956.

White, Morton G. *Social Thought in America; The Revolt Against Formalism.* Boston: Beacon Press, Inc., 1957.

Wisner, Elizabeth. "What is the Nature of the Educational Experience in the Undergraduate Department; What is Basic Preparation for Professional Education?" *The Undergraduate Department and the Graduate School, Workshop Reports, 1953 Proceedings,* First Annual Program Meeting, Council on Social Work Education. New York: CSWE, 1953.

Witmer, Helen L. *Social Work; An Analysis of a Social Institution.* New York: Farrar & Rinehart, Inc., 1942.

Wittman, Milton. *Scholarship Aid in Social Work Education.* New York: Council on Social Work Education, 1956.

Woodring, Paul. *New Directions in Teacher Education.* New York: The Fund for the Advancement of Education, 1957.

Woody, Thomas. *Liberal Education for Free Men.* Philadelphia: University of Pennsylvania Press, 1951.

Wrong, Dennis H. *Population*. New York: Random House, Inc., 1956.

Young, A. F. and E. T. Ashton. *British Social Work in the Nineteenth Century*. London: Routledge & Kegan Paul, Ltd., 1956.

Younghusband, Eileen L. *Report on the Employment and Training of Social Workers* (Carnegie United Kingdom Trust). Edinburgh: T. and A. Constable, Ltd., 1947.

————. *Social Work in Britain; A Supplementary Report on the Employment and Training of Social Workers* (Carnegie United Kingdom Trust). Edinburgh: T. and A. Constable, Ltd., 1951.

Zetterberg, Hans L. (ed.). *Sociology in the United States of America*. Paris: UNESCO, 1956.

Zietz, Dorothy. "Undergraduate Social Work Education: Redefined," *Public Welfare*, VIII (November, 1950).

Date Due